Green Woodwork

Working with wood the natural way

Mike Abbott

with a foreword by
Richard La Trobe Bateman

Guild of Master Craftsman Publications

To my grandmother, Phyllis Boddie, for teaching me the love of woodlands.

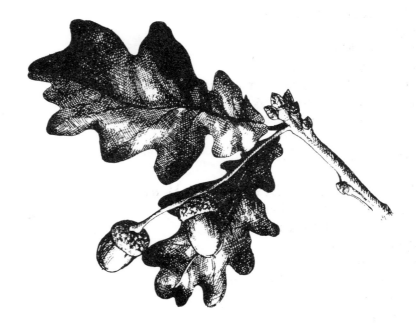

First Published in 1989 by
Guild of Master Craftsman Publications Ltd,
Castle Place, 166 High Street, Lewes, East Sussex BN7 1XU

Reprinted 1991, 1992, 1994, 1996, 1998

© Mike Abbott 1989

ISBN 0 946819 18 1

Designed by Robert and Jean Wheeler Design Associates

Photography by Linda Whitwam and Richard Ball

Illustrations by Damien Rochford

Printed and bound by Hillman Printers (Frome) Ltd, Frome,
Somerset

Contents

Acknowledgements

First I would like to thank the following organisations for providing me with premises, support and encouragement while running courses and writing this book: Windmill Hill City Farm, Bristol; British Trust for Conservation Volunteers, Avon; The Dean Heritage Centre, Gloucestershire and the Commonwork Trust, Kent. My sincere thanks also to Brian Maggs, in whose woodland I have spent so many happy days.

I wish to thank several of the American green woodworkers who have brought country crafts to the notice of the younger generation: notably John Alexander, Roy Underhill, Dave Sawyer and Drew Langsner. I have not yet seen Drew's latest book, *Green woodworking*, but I hope we do not duplicate each other too much. In Britain I owe an enormous debt to Herbert Edlin and Fred Lambert as the main threads linking the modern green woodworker with the craftsmen of the past. I am, of course, greatly indebted also to the many generations of craftsmen before me who so ingeniously worked out the techniques I now use.

I would like to thank Jack Hill not only for his writing but for his vitality and warmth when we have worked together. On my first courses I sat down with the members, carefully noting every word of Jack's country crafts book before putting it into practice. Since those days not a course has passed without my learning something new. Grateful thanks also go to the many hundreds who have stretched my knowledge on the Living Wood courses; many of you have now become friends and have helped me out on frequent occasions. Although too numerous to mention everyone by name, I must single out Dean Cooper for his invaluable assistance in my early days and Paul Girling for his recent help and frequent pots of tea.

I also owe thanks to those people at the Guild of Master Craftsmen who have patiently guided the book along: especially Alan Phillips, Elizabeth Inman, Roger Buse and Bernard Cooper. I shall always remember the working lunches that sustained my writing. The photographs are mostly the work of Linda Whitwam and Richard Ball, both of whom brought with them enthusiasm and good weather. Some of the steam-bending photographs were taken by Marianne Moser and one by Dennis Butler. I also took a few myself. Damien Rochford (a Living Wood graduate) was responsible for the concise illustrations, and he now knows better than most how to weave a stool seat. Many people passed comments on the manuscript, but I am especially grateful to Stephen de Brett, Dr John Brazier and my father for their contributions. Nonetheless, I accept full responsibility for any mistakes they missed.

My greatest thanks go to Marianne, not only for taking some of the photographs and typing some of the chapters, but also for looking after the home and organising the courses while I was writing. Thank you also to Hannah for putting up without her dad for so many evenings, weekends and holidays.

To all of you, I offer this book in thanks.

Foreword

'Because people are dead, it does not follow that they were stupid,' or so David Pye used to remind his students.

Working freshly felled timber is so rewarding at a level deep down inside oneself, that the more I do it the more dissatisfied I become with what we think of nowadays as 'normal' dry woodworking ('normal', of course, only in quite recent times, historically).

But to do it requires a mental 'jump' that many woodworkers seem to find hard. Skilled woodworking has come to be thought of as the achievement of the most geometrically regulated forms. This means as stable a material as possible, the highest degree of control and the total imposition by the maker of the forms he intends *in advance*, on the material. Not so with 'green' woodworking; the joy is to work *with* the material – and maybe let the material work on you. That 'jump' from the pursuit of a highly regulated geometry to the freer workmanship that results from using green timber was a key moment of liberation in my creative development.

The author of this book started from the same point that I did, namely *Woodland Crafts of Britain* by Herbert Edlin. In the forty years since that book was published there has been a shift in approach as Oliver Rackham puts it, '. . . the rise of interest in rural history as a practical not a purely literary field of study . . .' This book is one of the products of that shift in perspective.

Our whole technology grew out of what developed over tens of thousands of years in the woods. Countless generations in the past evolved methods of fashioning the world around them without the chemistry and the unlimited horsepower we so abuse today.

If Edlin's book described a part of our history before it went forever – as it might have seemed forty years ago – this book is a straightforward account of one worker's rediscoveries back down that road, with detailed descriptions to help others along the same or similar roads.

If it succeeds it will help its readers 'connect' with much in themselves and the natural world. In a small way, it is a book of healing.

Richard La Trobe Bateman
Somerset

Author's note

On the whole I have thoroughly enjoyed writing this book. However, two points have nagged at me throughout, so I would like to mention them and ask for your understanding.

First, I risked offending some women by using the term craftsman to mean a person carrying out a craft, be they male or female. I have likewise used 'he' in a general sense. After much consideration I was unable to find any alternative that did not seem too cumbersome. Many of my most skilled students have been women and I do not wish my use of these words to imply that green woodwork is better suited for males, because that is not so.

Second, I had a problem with units of measurement. I dislike measuring things in units anyway, but when I have to do so, my natural inclination is towards feet and inches. I do use millimetres for very small measurements, but as with any numbers they start to lose significance for me after about 20. As a result I jump around between millimetres, centimetres and metres, attempting to round them up or down unless precision is really called for. I hope you do not find this too confusing. I have more to say on the subject in Chapter 5.

I am glad that is off my chest. Now let the fun begin!

One

Introduction

'The good worker loves the board before it becomes a table, loves the tree before it yields the board, loves the forest before it gives up the tree.'
                                                                    Wendell Berry

It is now generally accepted that for the world to survive in its present state there have to be large areas of trees. They act as the lungs of the Earth and enhance our living environment, softening the landscape, giving us shelter from the wind and shade from the sun. We also need the wood that they provide for our housing, furniture, household utensils and much more. But for our dependence on trees, we would probably have destroyed even more than we already have.

This dependence was thoroughly appreciated by the woodland craftsman of old for whom the woodlands provided not only his livelihood but a large part of his tool-kit, as well as a workplace and often a place in which to live. It was in his interest to care for the woods and he is largely responsible for some of the magnificent stands of beech and oak in southern England.

I grew up in the countryside and spent most of my childhood playing in the woods, but my first serious encounter with woodland crafts was when I read *Woodland Crafts in Britain* by Herbert Edlin while studying tree surgery in 1975. It was here that I first read about the craft of 'chair-bodging' where chair-legs were made out of freshly felled logs using two wonderfully simple devices called a shaving-horse and a pole-lathe (see cover).

Since then I have studied a number of books on 'British country crafts', most of which devote a chapter or so to woodland crafts with only two or three pages on the pole-lathe and shaving-horse. Nearly all of these (with the exceptions of Fred Lambert's and Jack Hill's) treat such skills very

much as a thing of the past – something of interest to be recorded for posterity, but of little practical use for the twenty-first century. Recently a number of good American books have been written by the new generation of 'back-woodsmen', notably Drew Langsner and Roy Underhill, and by chair-makers Michael Dunbar and John D. Alexander Jnr.

All this literature has played an important part in my learning, together with a decade of working with green wood full-time: firstly training a team of youngsters in woodland skills, and more recently running my own training enterprise 'Living Wood Training' (Fig. 1.1).

The projects covered in this book form the basis of the courses I now run, and many of the photographs were taken while these were in progress (Fig. 1.2). I make no claims – either on my courses or in this book – to teach the quickest or most productive way to make any particular item. My intention is to describe methods that can be followed with a minimum of specialised equipment and a maximum of satisfaction. I certainly hope that the end products will be of use in themselves be it in the form of furniture (Fig. 1.3), kitchenware (Fig. 1.4) or tools (Fig. 1.5). But at least as important is the process of making: using not only your brain or your hands in isolation, but *all* of your body, *all* of your senses and *all* of your imagination.

The phrase that best sums up the type of work I now practise is 'green woodwork'. In one respect it means simply working with green (or un-seasoned) wood. But having learned how to

Fig 1.1   The Living Wood Workshop, 1989.   Fig. 1.2   The end of a green woodwork course.

make the most of the extraordinary properties of green wood, I have come to realise that many projects can be carried out without the need to rely on powered machinery. This liberation from the noise, the cost and the danger of such equipment gives rise to the other interpretation of 'green woodwork': it is energy-efficient, non-polluting and unbelievably fulfilling. It can be equally enjoyed by the life-served carpenter, the inquisitive novice and the primary-school pupil.

What never ceases to amaze me (and all my students) is how quickly the simple secrets of green woodwork have been all but forgotten by modern society. It is certain that while we continue to use up the finite supplies of fuel such as coal, oil and gas, machinery will generally produce things more cheaply than labour. But in Britain alone there are 8 million 'Do-It-Yourself' enthusiasts who presumably carry out their projects for a combination of saving money and enjoying their pastime. In this book I hope to show how to carry out many such projects without the need for expensive and dangerous machines, and how to obtain top quality raw materials at a

Fig. 1.4   Items for the kitchen.

fraction of the price asked by even the cheapest of timber yards.

The days when woodlands were filled with chair-bodgers (Fig. 1.6) working every hour of the day to earn a meagre living are fortunately gone for ever. However, there are a host of situations where green woodwork still holds great potential:

Fig. 1.3   A collection of chairs.

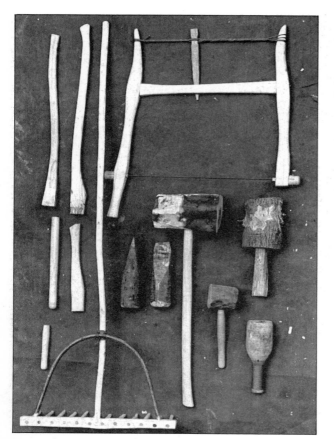

in schools, colleges and city farms, to show that wood *does* grow on trees;

in therapeutic centres for the handicapped to provide a creative outlet without the danger of powered machinery;

at craft fairs and farm parks to provide a crowd-drawing attraction;

for the elderly as a hobby to keep fit;

for people in stressful jobs as a healthy way to unwind;

for parents as a pleasant activity to share with their children;

for woodland workers to turn firewood into high value produce;

for furniture restorers to reproduce spare parts authentically;

for wood craftsmen to create unique furniture without the noise, dust and cost of powered machinery (Fig. 1.7).

Fig. 1.5   Items for the workshop.

Fig. 1.6   My daughter Hannah showing how to 'bodge'.

Fig. 1.7   Paul Girling and his chairs: one of a new generation of full-time bodgers.

When setting up a green wood workshop, the biggest problem is knowing just where to start. I have had to cast my mind back thirteen years to my first pole-lathe in an attic and the struggle I had first in finding out how to make it work, and then in getting hold of suitable tools. With the help of some of my friends who are now starting out on that same road, together with the benefit of thirteen years' experience, I hope to retrace these steps.

In Chapter 2 I shall examine what *is* wood and try to explode the myth that it has to be seasoned before it can be worked to shape. Chapter 3 will outline the most common hardwood trees in Northern Europe and the main features of their timbers. Then Chapters 4 and 5 give some ideas on obtaining suitable wood, also details of all the tools you will need for working it. Chapters 6–9 cover the practical projects required to set up

your workshop, including instructions on how to make your own pole-lathe and shaving-horse. Chapter 10 describes some delightful projects to get you used to the pole-lathe (Fig. 1.8) before launching into the serious business of chair-making in Chapters 11–15. These projects range from a very simple frame stool through to the challenges of a bow-back Windsor or a spindle-back chair, both of which include the art of steam-bending. The pinnacle of pole-lathe turning – making bowls – is covered in Chapter 16, and the book concludes with a variety of interesting projects which extend your horizons into many other green wood crafts. All these projects can be carried out without *any* powered machines and depend for their success entirely on your own energy, skill and imagination.

One of my main aims is to convey the joy to be derived from working with green wood and from using the pole-lathe in particular. You have to experience this to appreciate the relaxing rhythm and the sweet sound of the chisel removing

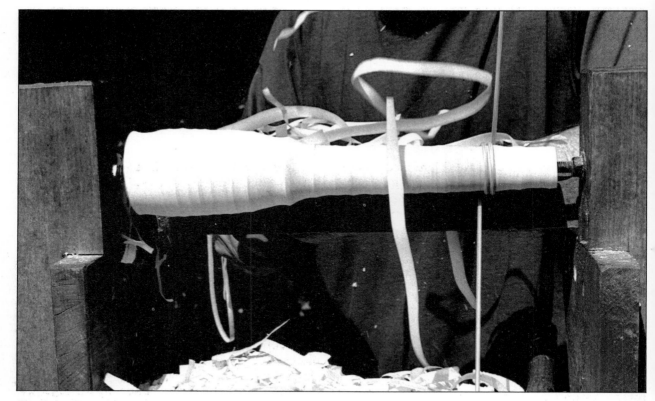

Fig. 1.8   Turning the blank for a birch spoon.

succulent ribbons of fresh wood as a chair-leg emerges from a piece of firewood. After this you will never again see woodwork through the same eyes.

I hope that through this book, you will be able to share in my enthusiasm for the subject. For me it provides one of the most absorbing, satisfying, and relaxing activities I can imagine. I wish you every success with your projects and many happy hours of green woodwork.

Two

Why Work Wood Green?

As we all know, wood comes from trees. Like animals and other plants, trees are living beings: they feed, they grow, they reproduce and sooner or later they die. Unlike animals and most other plants, however, they are commonly used by man not as food but in the construction of his home and many of the objects around him. In this sense, wood has more in common with man's other traditional raw materials such as stone, clay and iron, and modern materials such as steel, plastic, and fibre-glass. But the fact that wood has grown on a living tree means that it is unique in being our only building material which is capable of regenerating itself. At any moment, millions of tons of wood are being produced in forests around the world. Compare this with the production of other raw materials!

Imagine a steelworks run entirely on solar energy, producing all its own solar panels and making no noise; or a plastics factory that actually purified the atmosphere and required at most only a few hours' human input a year; picture a fibre-glass works supporting all kinds of wildlife where people would drive for miles to spend a day strolling around the production unit.

Because the process of wood production continues quietly, cleanly and with very little need for human intervention, we take it very much for granted. But if we lived in a world relying totally on steel, plastic and fibre-glass, where wood was unknown, imagine the public acclaim if some scientist were suddenly to invent a tree! Trees were on the Earth long before humans and are deeply embedded in the culture of every society that encounters them: sometimes as gods, sometimes as equals, sometimes as a source of people's livelihood, but in most cases they have been regarded with respect. In comparing trees with factories, I do not wish to dismiss all the other characteristics which make them so important in

the world. Having said this, I would now like to examine the workings of a typical 'wood factory' (Fig. 2.1).

The Wood Factory

To describe the precise 'workings' of a tree would be far beyond the scope of this book, so I shall attempt to simplify it by concentrating on those aspects which relate to the production of wood.

Raw Materials

As with any factory, the tree needs raw materials. The most important of these are two simple chemicals – water (H_2O) and carbon dioxide (CO_2). Water is taken in through the roots and drawn up the trunk and branches along tubes called *vessels*. Carbon dioxide is taken from the air through minute holes in the leaves.

Sugar Production

The leaves act as solar panels absorbing sunlight and using its energy to combine the water with the carbon dioxide so as to form sugars (carbohydrates). As a by-product, this process gives off oxygen which is used by the tree itself and by other plants and animals for breathing. The process is described by the chemical equation:

$$6CO_2 + 6H_2O \rightarrow C_6H_{12}O_6 + 6O_2$$
(carbon   (water)   (glucose)   (oxygen)
dioxide)

Sugar Transport

The sugars produced in the leaves are then sent down through a layer of cells known as the *bast*, just beneath the bark, to feed the rest of the tree.

Cell Production

Just inside the bast is a thin layer called the

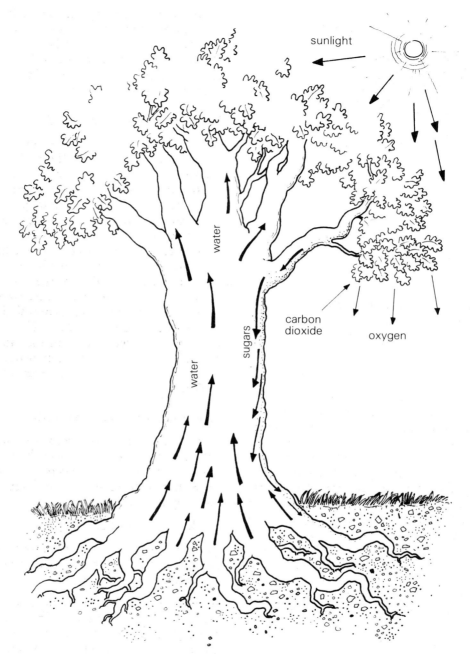

sunlight

water

water

sugars

carbon
dioxide

oxygen

Fig. 2.1   The wood factory.

cambium. In this layer, some of the sugars produced in the leaves are converted into the
starches which go to build up the wood cells.
Throughout the growing season – that is, spring
and summer – these cells are constantly dividing

to form the various types of wood cell, each with
its own special function (Fig. 2.2).
   There are three main types of cell which make
up the wood as we know it:

1   Fibres

As the name suggests, the fibres of wood are long

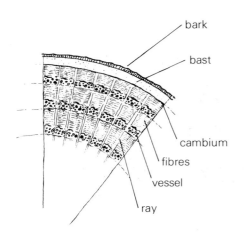

Fig. 2.2   A section of oak log.

and thin. They are packed together tightly to form a rigid structure which is nonetheless able to flex slightly in order to absorb the stresses caused by the wind.

2   Vessels

Amongst the fibres are the vessels which transport water (with dissolved minerals) up the tree to the leaves. These vessels are formed by a string of hollow cells joining together into long tubes. In some trees (e.g. the oak) the vessels produced during rapid growth in the spring are much larger than those produced in the summer; this forms a ring of vessels which emphasise the annual growth rings. Wood formed like this is known as *ring-porous*. In other woods (e.g. beech), the vessels are of an even size throughout. Wood formed like this is called *diffuse-porous*. When working with wood, this is a distinction which not only affects the appearance of the grain but can have a considerable effect on how the wood behaves.

3   Rays

At right-angles to the growth rings, the third type of cells are laid in thin vertical layers like ribbons radiating from the centre of the wood. These are the rays, their main function being to store food for the tree. In the oak these rays are particularly prominent, creating an attractive feature when the wood is quarter-sawn (i.e. sawn towards the

centre, thus exposing the rays). In other woods (e.g. sweet chestnut), rays are present but are hardly visible to the naked eye. One effect of the rays on the structure of wood is that they tend to produce a line of weakness down which it will more readily split.

Heartwood and Sapwood

As the tree grows older, so the inner cells of the trunk and branches find themselves increasingly far from the growing area beneath the bark. In most trees, the inner cells start to undergo a chemical change and cease to play a part in the tree's growth other than helping to hold it up. The wood which makes up this part of the tree is known as the heartwood, and the part where the sap still flows is called the sapwood. In some trees the difference is quite marked – as in oak and sweet chestnut – with the heartwood cells containing deposits of a chemical called tannin which makes the wood turn dark. However, in some other trees – such as ash and sycamore – there is no visible difference between heartwood and sapwood, and their timber is generally less resistant to rot.

Differences between Woods

The classification of trees and timber can be rather confusing, some words being used in a way which could be somewhat misleading. I hope the following will at least clarify if not simplify the situation.

Broadleaves and Conifers

With a few exceptions which you are unlikely to meet (e.g. ginkgo), trees fall into two categories – broadleaves and conifers.

Broadleaves: Their main feature is that they have flat 'leaf-shaped' leaves. The fruit can take a variety of forms such as the nuts of hazel, the 'helicopters' of sycamore, the berries of holly or the acorns of oak.

Conifers: This group, as its name implies, consists of trees which produce some form of woody cone – although it also includes the yew which has a berry-like fruit. Many conifers, such as pine, spruce and fir, have needle-like leaves; while in others, such as cypress, they are scale-like.

Softwoods and Hardwoods

In temperate climates, the timber of broadleaved trees tends to be harder than that of conifers. For this reason, the convention has arisen of referring to broadleaved trees as hardwoods and to conifers as softwoods. Although there are numerous exceptions, especially in tropical timbers – such as balsa, which is a soft hardwood – these terms are still generally used.

Evergreen and Deciduous

Another area of confusion creeps in when distinguishing between evergreen and deciduous trees – those which in temperate climates lose their leaves in autumn. Most conifers are evergreen and most hardwoods north of the tropics are deciduous, but there are some common trees which are notable exceptions:

a the larch, which is a deciduous conifer.

b holly, box, and evergreen oak, which are evergreen broadleaves.

Seasoning Wood

When a living tree is felled or blown down, the timber obtained from it is called green wood. Once the tree has ceased to live, its wood will steadily go through the process we call seasoning, starting to lose the water held within it. The proportion of water in the wood is called its *moisture content*, and is expressed by the following formula:

$$\text{moisture content} = \frac{\text{weight of water in the wood}}{\text{oven-dry weight of wood}} \times 100$$

This varies considerably between different species; for example, ash has a moisture content of about 50 per cent, beech 90 per cent and elm 140 per cent (signifying that green elm is more water than wood). Moisture content can also vary between trees of the same species, between heartwood and sapwood of the same tree, and according to the time of year.

Some of this water is held in the cavities of the cells and is readily lost from the wood; in fact, a sycamore log stood vertically will soon produce a pool on the ground at its base. Water retained like this is known as *free water*; when the wood has lost all its free water, it is said to be at *fibre-*

saturation point, which in most hardwoods is around 30 per cent moisture content. After this, as the wood dries out further, water is steadily lost from the actual cell walls. This water is referred to as *bound-water* and its loss causes the cells to shrink. During this phase, the cells lose much of the softness of the living tree and the wood becomes much harder. It is this second phase of drying which causes the problems of shrinking, warping and splitting which are associated with seasoning. When no more water can evaporate from the wood, it is said to have reached its equilibrium moisture content (*emc*). This *emc* will vary according to the atmospheric humidity: the drier the atmosphere, the lower the *emc*. Dry wood left in moist conditions for some time will steadily absorb some of this moisture and start to swell again. If wood were to shrink evenly in all directions, many (but not all) of the problems of seasoning could be avoided. Unfortunately this is not the case, since any piece of wood has three different rates of shrinkage (Fig. 2.3).

Looking at a section taken out of a log as shown, it shrinks most of all in its tangential plane. In some woods this shrinkage can be up to 15 per cent. It also shrinks radially, but only about half as much. The line of least shrinkage is

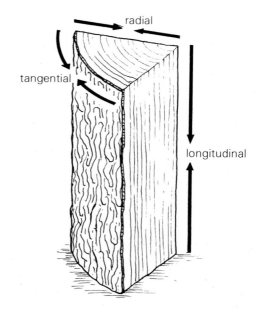

Fig. 2.3 Different rates of shrinkage.

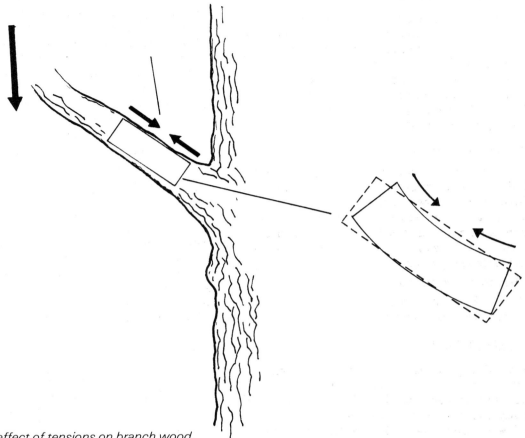

Fig. 2.4   The effect of tensions on branch wood.

longitudinally, which is normally around 0·1 per cent. There are some occasions when different rates of longitudinal shrinkage can cause the wood to warp. Wood taken from branches or from curved trunks of hardwoods will have developed tensions to restrain its uneven loading; when the wood is cut to length, these forces can deflect the wood slightly as it dries (Fig. 2.4).

This effect can also be seen occasionally even in some straight-grown trunks (e.g. ash) where the sapwood is under tension whereas the heartwood is under compression. This can cause the log to open outwards soon after it is cut (Fig. 2.5).

As wood dries in the log, the outside surfaces – and especially the end grain – dry out much more quickly than the wood in the centre. When combined with the different rates of shrinkage in each direction, it is easy to see why logs tend to crack.

If a cross-sectioned slice is cut from a freshly

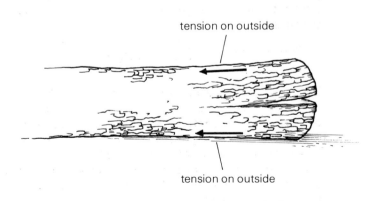

tension on outside

tension on outside

Fig. 2.5   A log splitting open.

felled log, this too will crack. Such cracking is due entirely to the different amounts of radial and tangential shrinkage. The cells are trying to shrink sideways more than they shrink in

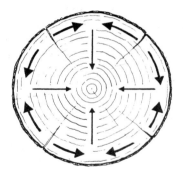

Fig. 2.6   The formation of radial cracks.

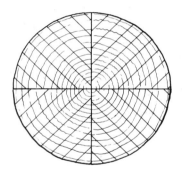

Fig. 2.8   Quarter-sawn wood.

towards the centre. The result is one or more radial cracks as shown in Fig. 2.6.

This uneven shrinkage also explains why planks sawn 'through and through' will have a tendency to 'cup' (Fig. 2.7).

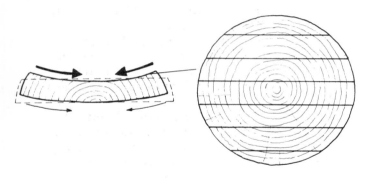

Fig. 2.7   A plank 'cupping'.

In the plank shown, the wood on the upper surface lies at more of a tangent to the growth rings than does the wood on the lower surface. This will cause the upper surface to shrink more, thus forming the 'cup' shape. The problem of cupping can be alleviated by a process known as 'quarter-sawing': sawing all the planks radially out of the log, thereby ensuring even shrinkage on both surfaces (Fig. 2.8).

However, this process is more laborious as well as rather wasteful in wood, and is therefore not commonly practised.

A more usual solution is to hold the planks tightly under pressure so as to retain their shape against the uneven forces of shrinkage. This

ensures a flat plank, but if it is subsequently cut into smaller sections some of the stresses will be released and it may change shape at this stage.

Where an accurate finish is required and surfaces have to be even, such as in cabinet-making, the only reliable method is to start off with well-seasoned planks. These should then be cut slightly larger than the required final dimensions, and allowed to undergo a secondary seasoning. Only then should the parts be assembled and finished. However, where the surfaces required are not perfectly flat and where precise dimensions are not the most important factor, a different approach can be taken.

One example of wood used in such a situation is in the making of 'treen': domestic utensils such as spoons and bowls. With such objects, there are no perfectly flat surfaces and no joints which have to fit accurately. By carving or turning the object *before* it has seasoned, a large surface area is exposed enabling the wood to dry out quickly. It is then able to shrink and to change its shape without building up uneven pressures, and is therefore *less* likely to crack. This is best carried out in one operation as quickly as possible; good examples of the method are seen in the 'natural-edged' bowls which many wood-turners are keen to make nowadays.

The green wood approach can, of course, be extended to other objects where final precise dimensions are not critical. This brings me, inevitably, to the chair-leg – an object whose main function is lightness and strength. In making a leg for a Windsor chair, for example (i.e. to be socketed into a solid plank seat), the leg is turned to shape on the lathe while the wood is still green, leaving the top of the leg oversized. It is then allowed to shrink and warp until it reaches the desired moisture content of around 8–12 per cent. When the chair is assembled, the tenon at the top of the leg can be turned down to the exact size for the hole drilled in the seat.

When I explain this process of making a chair-leg, people usually accept that it is possible but nevertheless ask me why I should bother with green wood rather than using the customary seasoned wood. In some ways, this question is like asking a potter why he makes his pots out of wet clay rather than cutting them out of bricks. As discussed above, there are many situations where wooden objects are much more efficiently made out of wood which has been sawn into planks and then thoroughly seasoned. However, in the next few pages I hope to show that in certain situations – such as making furniture parts, treen and tools – there are a host of advantages in using green wood.

1 Improved seasoning

As mentioned earlier, there are many problems involved in seasoning wood. By reducing it to smaller dimensions it is more able to shrink and warp, which in fact reduces the danger of cracking. After turning a chair-leg on a lathe from green wood, it will obviously have a round cross-section; subsequently subjected to differential rates of shrinkage, it will dry with its cross-section becoming oval (Fig. 2.9).

With a larger proportion of surface area than wood in plank form, it will therefore dry out much more quickly. I have found that green turned legs can be taken directly into a centrally

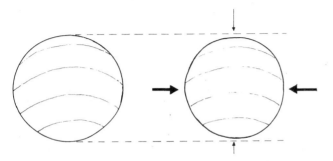

Fig. 2.9   Oval shrinkage.

heated environment and are able to dry within a month or so with no danger of splitting. I have also found that wood which is reduced to small cross-sections while it is green will shrink proportionately more than comparable wood which dries out in a larger section. The cells of wood in a chair-leg which is turned when green will be more free to change shape than if constrained by the surrounding cells within a plank. This implies that fewer stresses are built up in the green turned leg and, as a result, it will tend to be more stable in the long term and less inclined to distort later on.

In summary, although wood that is shaped while green will shrink and change shape, it will season more quickly and with less cracking, resulting in a more stable end product than wood seasoned in plank form.

2 Cheaper raw materials

Most woodworkers would agree that well seasoned quality hardwood planks are not cheap, while most woodland owners are surprised how little they can obtain for their timber. In between these two parties much time, labour and machinery is involved in converting timber. In 1988, standing timber for firewood logs cost from £10 per cubic metre (30p/cu. ft). On the other hand, kiln-dried hardwood planks may cost £30 a cubic foot or more (£1000/cu. m); a hundred times as much! Obviously, by using firewood instead of kiln-dried wood your raw materials will cost very much less.

3 Environmental advantages

As we shall see, green wood can be used in smaller dimensions than would normally be used commercially. For some projects, such as spoon making, small branchwood which would otherwise have no commercial use can be employed. But even for chair making, small round wood a few inches in diameter can be utilised if it is of sufficient quality. Certainly wood 8" (20 cm) in diameter can be used for quality furniture. Harvesting such logs will not require heavy machinery; a chain-saw may well be a help, and possibly a vehicle to get it home. Individual trees can be selected without having to create special access tracks. All this results in a much more 'light-weight' approach to timber harvesting which has a great deal in common with the system used by traditional chair-bodgers in the Chiltern Hills. This approach will utilise wood which would have comparatively low value as firewood. Greater revenue can therefore be earned by woodland managers, which in turn will result in increased efforts to put more care into our native woodlands.

By making use of our own native resource of wood, we will – albeit in a small way – lessen the demand for woods from the tropical rain forests which hopefully will help to improve the world's environment. There is also the satisfaction which arises from knowing exactly where one's raw materials come from, especially if selected personally as a tree.

4 *Greater strength*

While wood is still green, its fibres tend to be easier to separate, which makes it easier to *cleave* the wood. Cleaving is the process by which some kind of wedge is forced into a log so as to split the fibres apart along its length (Fig. 2.10).

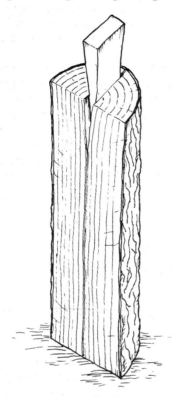

Fig. 2.10 Cleaving a log.

With most (but not all) species of temperate hardwood, this is a surprisingly easy operation provided they have a straight grain and no large knots. Again it lessens the need for powerful saws to rip the wood down its length; and when reducing logs to small dimensions, it also saves all the wood which would be wasted as sawdust. However, the main advantage of cleaving wood is the significant increase in the strength of the end product.

The strength of wood lies in its fibres. By cleaving a piece of it, you follow the grain and the fibres remain intact. All trees grow with a spiral (Fig. 2.11), which in some trees is almost negligible but in many is quite significant. This can be observed in the way some planks warp with a

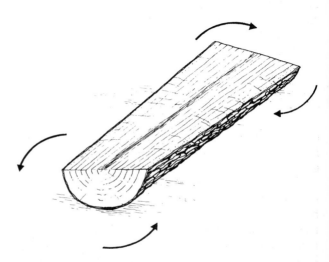

Fig. 2.11   Spiral growth in a log.

twist (or wind), and how the grain works better in one direction on one half of a plank and in the opposite direction on the other half. If such a log is converted into planks, some of the fibres will be severed.

By splitting wood along the direction of the fibres, the end product will follow the spiral and retain the maximum fibrous strength.

When wood arrives ready planked, it is much more difficult to see any irregularities in the grain. However, by cleaving it any irregularities become obvious. Knots are always a problem in woodwork, but they are easily detected in cleft wood since the grain tends to run around them

Fig. 2.12   Grain running round a knot.

(Fig. 2.12). Sometimes curved grain can be used for a specific purpose – in some tool handles, for example.

Otherwise it is easy to select straight sections of the log for quality work. The leftovers can either be utilised where strength is unimportant or, if the worst comes to the worst, these inferior sections can be used for firewood. Considering that it would probably have been sold as firewood in the first place, there really is no great loss – in fact, it is now split up nicely for the fireplace! Interestingly, it was for this factor of greater strength and reliability that all chairs made for the British Government before the First World War had to have legs made from wood which had been cleft. The same stipulation was also applied to ladder rungs and tent-pegs.

5   Easier to bend

As noted earlier, the cells of green wood have not yet undergone the hardening process involved with seasoning but are still relatively pliable, making green wood much easier to bend than seasoned wood. This property is used quite widely in the country chairs that were usually made from green wood; the best-known example is the bows in many Windsor chairs which were invariably bent, usually from yew, ash, beech or elm.

6   Softer wood

Not only are the cells of green wood more pliable, but they are softer and therefore much easier to cut with edge tools such as axes, knives and chisels. The traditional techniques of the chair-bodger and other woodland craftsmen were developed to make the most of this attribute. Fine edges on the tools are far less likely to get chipped and will hold their edge much longer. Considerably less force is needed to reduce a piece of wood to size. Because a finer edge on the tool can be used, a sweeter cut is obtained and a good finish achieved without the need for abrasives such as sandpaper.

This property of the wood being softer and easier to work means that green wood can be satisfactorily worked using very simple low-powered equipment. Here is where the other interpretation of *green* woodwork applies; it employs simple technology, using up a minimum of fossil fuels and creating a minimum of pollution.

By working with cleft green wood, it becomes a feasible proposition to completely shape it by using such equipment as shaving-horses and pole-lathes. They can easily be constructed by the amateur woodworker and, together with a small range of hand tools, can be used to make a variety of wooden products. This in turn results in many more benefits to the green woodworker:

a   *Efficient use of money and equipment:*

tools and equipment are cheaper;

power bills are much less;

tools need sharpening less often;

tools last much longer;

less money is spent on sandpaper.

b   *Safety:*

if an accident happens on the pole-lathe, it cuts out immediately. Clothes are not caught up in the machinery, neither are tools hurled across the workshop;

green woodwork is therefore ideal for beginners, children and the handicapped.

c   *Efficient use of the human body:*

using the whole body and all its senses is much more enjoyable than using just the head, hands and eyes;

slight irregularities in the wood are easily noticed and anything below standard can be rejected;

less noise enables the craftsman to hear how the work is going;

steady exercise is provided, keeping the green woodworker fit and also keeping him warm when the weather is cold;

the pole-lathe offers great sensitivity, enabling the operator to stop, start or alter speed instantaneously without the need for buttons or switches;

the shaving-horse enables the craftsman to sit down on the job, only having to put effort into gripping the workpiece as an automatic response to pulling with the drawknife.

d   *Sheer pleasure:*

it can be practised outdoors in good weather or brought indoors when it is bad;

there is no need for protective clothing, goggles or dust masks (except perhaps for steel-toe-capped boots!);

the smells of the green wood and the fresh air can be enjoyed to the full;

the green woodworker can happily listen to the song of the robin, Radio 4, or Rachmaninov;

the rhythm of the pole-lathe reaches deep into the natural rhythms of the body.

To sum up, green woodwork provides a remarkably inexpensive, fulfilling, safe and pleasant way to pass the time.

Three

Types of Tree

Some of the trees used in British wood crafts are not technically native, having been introduced here after the separation of Britain from mainland Europe by the Channel. Two such examples are sweet chestnut and sycamore, both of which are now so firmly entrenched in our tradition that I propose to treat them as natives. Although many conifers have also been introduced during the last two centuries, the use of their timber has usually been in conjunction with powered machinery. As a result, there has until recently been little development of techniques to work with softwoods in any form other than seasoned planks. The one exception to this, which no chair-maker dare ignore, is of course the yew which has been a very popular wood in the making of Windsor chairs.

I shall therefore be working mainly with common British hardwoods, the main varieties of which are briefly described below. However, there is no reason why you should not experiment with softwood, either from the log or in plank form. I am also sure that many of the techniques described in this book could equally well be applied to the native trees of other parts of the world.

Ten Trees and their Woods

When working green wood using only hand tools, you will soon find just how much its properties differ from tree to tree and, in fact, from different parts of the same tree.

Some crafts have grown up based entirely on the wood from one type of tree. Others require a particular combination of woods, while others still are able to use a wide range. For this reason, certain crafts grew up in certain areas where the right materials were readily available.

The next stage therefore is to describe some of the varieties we shall be using and point out the distinguishing features of both the wood and the tree from which it comes. First of all, I shall describe ten trees which produce timber of use to the green woodworker and are fairly common in Britain. Then I shall briefly mention a number of others which either have a limited use or are not so common. That I shall not refer to many of the ornamental trees to be found in the British Isles does not mean they cannot be used. If someone offers you some wood, try it out and see just what you can do with it. That is how woodland crafts developed in the first place!

Common Ash (*Fraxinus excelsior*)

Distinguishing features

The ash tends to be a slender tree, often growing taller than most. The bark is light grey, usually smooth when young but becoming wrinkled with

Fig. 3.1 Common ash (Fraxinus excelsior).

age. The leaves are compound (i.e. made up from a number of 'leaflets'). In winter it has distinctive black buds and is often adorned with bunches of 'keys' – spiral-shaped winged seeds – which have turned from summer green to a winter brown.

The wood (ring-porous)

The wood is generally pale cream in colour and, being ring-porous, has very distinct growth rings. When slowly grown (more than 25 rings to the inch), it tends to have a low proportion of fibres and will therefore be rather weak. Faster-grown ash is usually very strong, being especially tough; this makes it ideal for uses where it has to withstand shock, as for example in tool-handles and hockey sticks. It was always used for the felloes (rims) of cartwheels, and more recently for the framework of Morris Traveller estate cars. Ash is also widely employed in furniture, in particular in chairs as they have to absorb a lot of knocks. In addition it is highly suitable for steam-bending, a process which will be discussed later in the chair-making projects.

The common ash is widespread throughout the British Isles and northern Europe, growing best on deep soils covering limestone rocks. Although ash has no distinctive heartwood, the wood of an older tree may well develop a brown or even black stain; this is due to fungal invasion and makes it unsuitable where strength is important. However, it looks attractive and is widely used, being referred to as olive ash.

Beech (*Fagus sylvatica*)

Distinguishing features

The beech is generally regarded as an attractive tree with a crown formed from gracefully curved branches bearing slender twigs. The oval leaves are fairly small, emerging a bright green with a soft, hairy surface, turning a striking golden colour in the autumn. The buds are brown, slender and pointed. Its fruit is a small triangular nut known as mast, which is encased in a woody shell. However, in Britain it is more common for the shell to be empty, with a good 'mast' year occurring only occasionally.

The wood (diffuse-porous)

Beech wood varies from a cream colour to a

Fig. 3.2   Beech (Fagus sylvatica).

medium brown. Being diffuse-porous, it has only a subtle grain pattern with its prominent rays being more distinctive than the growth rings. Compared with ash, it has an almost clay-like consistency which makes it very easy to work on the lathe without the grain tearing out. This property, along with its hardness, probably explains its popularity for the craft of 'chair-bodging' where chair-legs are produced on simple pole-lathes. It is also used for a wide variety of purposes where a dense, even wood is needed, such as mallet heads, plane-blocks, chopping-blocks and spoons.

It grows best in warmer, temperate regions such as southern Germany and Czechoslovakia. In Britain its natural limit is the limestone hills of the Chilterns and Cotswolds, where it is the dominant tree. Beyond that range, it will grow to a large tree but the grain is not so straight, thus making it less easy to work with hand tools.

Sycamore (*Acer pseudoplatanus*)

Distinguishing features

The sycamore is a member of the maple family, its foliage sharing the typical 'maple leaf' pattern. The buds are green and rather egg-shaped. Probably its most notable features are its 'helicopter' seeds which hang in pairs, each seed being attached to a large wing which spins as it falls in the autumn.

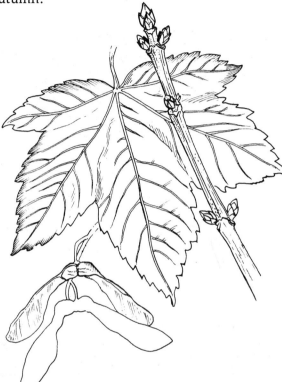

Fig. 3.3 Sycamore (Acer pseudoplatanus).

The wood (diffuse-porous)

The wood is pale cream, similar to that of the ash, but in many other respects it resembles beech. It has a fairly indistinct grain, but a delicate flecking due to its rays. It is easy to work with hand tools as well as on the lathe, and if worked while still wet tends not to crack when it dries. Having no taste, it is therefore ideal for all kitchenware such as spoons, bowls and rolling-pins. It was widely used in the dairy industry where large bowls and ladles were turned, using the pole-lathe, particularly in Wales. Occasionally a tree will grow with a rippled grain, which is highly sought after in making the backs of violins.

Sycamore grows in most parts of Britain and is often regarded by conservationists as a weed since it harbours only a small range of wildlife. Nowadays it is frequently being thinned out of amenity woodlands, thus making it readily available to the green woodworker. Its one drawback is that it is highly prone to staining, so care is needed with storage.

English Oak (*Quercus robur*)

Distinguishing features

This is one of the best known of our native trees with its distinctive leaves and acorns. There are hundreds of species of oak throughout the world, a number of which are to be found in Britain. Of these, there are two distinct forms of English oak, but since most trees are a mixture of both I shall treat them as being the same. The buds are brown and grow in small clusters on the pale green twigs. The bark is wrinkled from an early age, with deep ridges by the time the tree is old. Oaks tend to live longer than most of the other trees in this list, often developing very wide trunks.

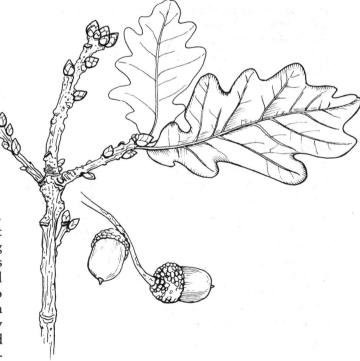

Fig. 3.4 English oak (Quercus robur).

The wood (ring-porous)

Fig. 3.5   Making oak 'swill' baskets.

Unlike the trees mentioned above, the oak has a very distinct heartwood and sapwood; the heartwood is a deep brown as opposed to the much paler sapwood. It also has a very distinctive smell, which is rather acidic due to the high concentration of tannin. This has a considerable drawback when working the wood green, as the tannin has a very corrosive effect on steel tools. At first it creates a deep purple stain, but if this is not removed it will steadily eat into the steel. However, it is this particular property which makes the heartwood so resistant to rot. Being tough as well as durable, oak was traditionally the preferred wood for fence-posts, building beams, ships' timbers and barrels. Ideal for pegs and wedges which have to be driven in hard to hold wooden joints, it is of course also very common in furniture construction, not only for its strength but also because of its attractive looks due to the distinct growth rings and prominent rays.

Oak can be found in most parts of the British Isles. In some areas it was grown as coppice (i.e. cut back to the ground at regular intervals) to produce poles for charcoal and bark for use in tanning leather. In Lancashire and the Lake District, it was coppiced widely to produce the raw material for 'swill' baskets (Fig. 3.5). To make these, oak logs are split down into smaller and smaller sections until they can be woven into robust baskets, traditionally used to carry coal or potatoes. In other areas, oaks are grown into tall 'standard' trees for the uses described above; there are still some fine examples in the Royal Forest of Dean and the New Forest.

Sweet Chestnut (*Castanae sativa*)

Distinguishing features

This tree has a large symmetrical leaf with a serrated edge. The fruit – after which the tree is named – is a large edible nut encased in a very prickly shell. This should not be confused with the horse chestnut, which produces inedible 'conkers' and is not a close relative. The bark in mature trees is heavily ridged, developing a strong spiral with age.

The wood (ring-porous)

In some ways, sweet chestnut has much in common with oak. It has a similar colour, the same acidic reaction with tools, a similar smell and is also ring-porous. Where it differs is that its rays are hardly visible, it dries out to a much lighter weight and is not as tough. Sweet chestnut is one of the most stable of the woods in this list, shrinking only slightly as it dries and therefore 'moving' very little with changes in humidity – a factor quite important in modern furniture. Its sapwood tends to turn to heartwood after only three years, with the result that quite young trees have

a high proportion of heartwood. It also cleaves easily and for this reason is the wood still grown to make cleft paling fences. One major disadvantage is that it is prone to cracks within the wood, known as 'shakes', which make it less popular for converting to planks. However, by cleaving the wood these 'shakes' can often be avoided.

Like beech, sweet chestnut grows best in the warmer climates of mainland Europe and southeast England, although it can be found growing in northern Britain. In southern England, it is still commonly coppiced at intervals of 12–15 years to produce a regular crop of the poles employed to support hops used in beer-making. Now it is used for chestnut palings, and when coppiced over a 3- or 4-year rotation for walking sticks.

English Elm or Field Elm (*Ulmus procera*)

Distinguishing features

Sadly the elm's most common feature is that it is dead! During the 1970s and 1980s, Dutch Elm disease has swept through Britain and Europe killing the vast majority of elms. In northern Britain and a few pockets of southern England

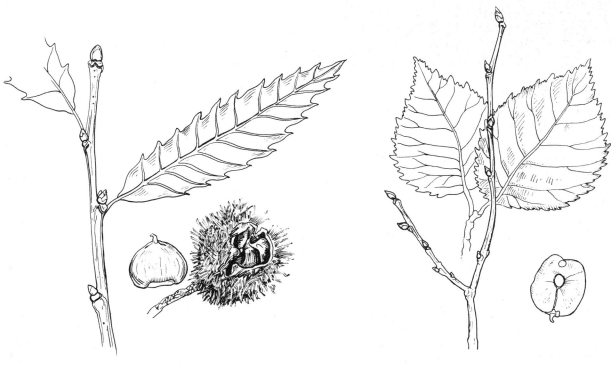

Fig. 3.6   Sweet chestnut (Castanae sativa).

Fig. 3.7   English elm, or field elm (Ulmus procera).

(notably around Brighton), they still survive. The English elm grows into a tall stout tree with small dark green, hairy leaves. In spring it bears attractive flowers which produce pale green winged seeds; however, these seeds are usually infertile and the tree spreads by suckers emerging from the roots. Consequently, it is usually found in hedgerows and rarely in woodlands.

The wood (ring-porous)

The heartwood of the English elm is deep brown with a highly irregular grain, which makes it very difficult to split – especially the wood from the trunk. This property makes it ideal for the planks used for the seats of Windsor chairs which have to take sockets for up to 20 or more chair parts. For the same reason, it was always the chosen wood for wheel-hubs. The very property which makes elm so useful also makes it difficult to convert from the log without power tools. Being virtually impossible to cleave, elm logs must normally be converted by sawing into planks. Without power, this is an extremely tedious job requiring great skill and accuracy, and invariably would have been carried out by teams of itinerant sawyers who travelled around cutting what the carpenter needed. To my knowledge, all sawyers nowadays use powered machinery – so, like the chair-makers of old, I buy my elm ready planked.

Wych Elm (*Ulmus glabra*)

Distinguishing features

The complicated family of elms has several different species with many hybrids (cross-breeds) between them. One other species is worth differentiating – the wych elm which, unlike the British elm, spreads by seed rather than suckers and is therefore found more commonly in woodlands. It tends to have a broader crown and is generally shorter. One of the main distinctions is that it has much larger leaves.

The wood (ring-porous)

Although similar in colour and general appearance to the English elm, the wood of the wych elm has a straighter and more even grain, making it possible to cleave young trunks or branches. Its bast or inner bark is very fibrous and, as I shall describe later, I have found this to be one of the

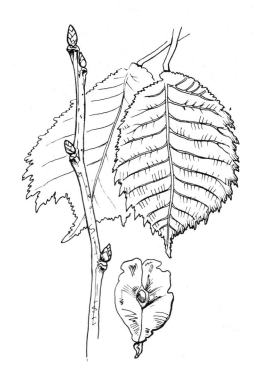

Fig. 3.8   Wych elm (Ulmus glabra).

best materials – in the absence of hickory – to weave bark chair-bottoms (see Chapter 13).

Wych elms can be found throughout Britain, although they too have been badly affected by Dutch Elm disease.

Wild Cherry (*Prunus avium*)

Distinguishing features

The wild cherry can be a tall, straight tree with an almost glossy purple bark which peels off the tree in rings. It grows rather like conifers by putting on a burst of growth approximately a yard long and then sending out a whorl of branches all at one point. This is quite useful, enabling the woodworker to harvest a number of short but clean (i.e. knot-free) sections. In spring, these trees suddenly stand out in the woodland as they become covered in white cherry blossom; this then ripens in the summer to produce dark red cherries, although they are unlike the cherries we eat as they are smaller with a large stone and only a little flesh.

The wood (diffuse-porous)

The heartwood is an attractive golden-brown, but the sapwood is generally paler. It has a strange property of turning orange if it is worked green but, if the surface is cut when dry, it reveals a pale cream colour which does not subsequently change. Although diffuse-porous, it has quite distinct growth rings, but is very easy to work and excellent on the lathe. It is closely related to the many ornamental cherries, the wood from these relatives having characteristics similar to those of their wild ancestor.

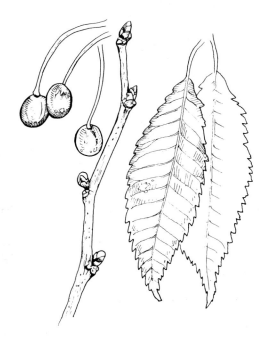

Fig. 3.9   Wild cherry (Prunus avium).

Silver Birch (*Betula pendula*)

Distinguishing features

The birch is a rather smaller and shorter-lived tree than those mentioned so far. It is easily recognised by its distinctive silver bark, small leaves and delicate – frequently pendular – twigs. Very hardy, it is often one of the first to invade an area of barren ground. Its seeds are very small and light, hanging in catkins until distributed far and wide by the wind.

The wood (diffuse-porous)

The wood of the silver birch is similar in appearance and other characteristics to that of beech and sycamore. In Britain, it rarely grows in long straight lengths and is therefore not widely used as a timber, but when suitable sections can be found they turn very well on the lathe and are admirably suited for spoons and small carvings. Most of the birch used in furniture comes from Scandinavia, where it is peeled to make plywood often referred to in the furniture industry as 'laminated birch'. There is another species known as the hairy birch (*Betula pubescens*), which has very similar properties. One of the most common uses for birch is harvesting the twigs of coppice-grown trees to be made into besom brooms, a craft still practised today.

Birch is more common on poor soils and in colder climates, being most widespread in Scotland.

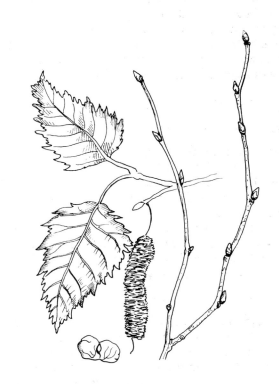

Fig. 3.10   Silver birch (Betula pendula).

Fig. 3.11 Alder (Alnus glutinosa).

Alder (*Alnus glutinosa*)

Distinguishing features

Young alders grow fast and straight, but usually slow down at about 20 feet and then spread out. They grow close to water, either by woodland streams, or ponds and ditches between fields. In early spring before the leaves emerge, they bear long yellow catkins. The fruit is a light seed hidden within a small woody cone.

The wood (diffuse-porous)

The wood of the alder is cream coloured, although it will often turn an orange-pink shade if worked while green. Like birch, it is seldom found in large dimensions, but is fairly easy to work and is good on the lathe. Its most common use was – and still is in some areas – in the making

of wooden clog soles which, like bodging, was a craft carried out in the open by specialised craftsmen. They would work the wood while green, leave it to season and then send it to workshops to be made into finished clogs.

Other Trees

Yew

This is the one coniferous softwood in my list – although, as I have said, its fruit is berry-like and its wood is hard. An evergreen with flat needles, it is native to the British Isles and grows quite commonly in woodlands, but is also frequently found in churchyards. The heartwood is a deep red-brown, with a very pale sapwood. Wood from the trunk is usually deeply fluted (i.e. having a very uneven cross-section) and with a fairly wavy grain, making it less suitable for cleaving. However, it is an ideal wood for steam-bending when bent in branch form and subsequently shaped. In this form, it was traditionally widely used (and sometimes still is) in making the bows for Windsor chairs. Another traditional use was for long-bows, but the best yew wood for this purpose came from Spain.

Lime

Lime grows wild in many of our ancient woodlands, but is also frequently planted as an ornamental tree in streets, parks and estates. The wood is cream in colour, with only a very faint grain pattern. For a hardwood, it is relatively soft and works very evenly, making it ideal for carving. Like the wych elm, its bast or inner bark is very strong and its fibres were used for making rope.

Willow

There are many distinct species of willow found in Britain, and many hybrids between them. As a timber, willow has a very open, fibrous texture, drying out to become light in weight. It can be employed for making cleft gate-hurdles and hay-rakes, but its most common use is for making cricket bats for which a variety known as the cricket-bat willow is cultivated for the purpose. Otherwise its main use is in basket-making, where it is cut back annually to produce long pliable twigs.

Poplar

Poplars are similar to willows in their great variety and in that they need wet ground in which to grow. Plantations appeared around the countryside in the 1950s in the hope of providing the raw materials for matchsticks. The wood is made up of very thin-walled cells which means that it dries to a very light weight, but is also able to absorb shock without splitting. Its main use nowadays is to make wooden pallets.

Horse Chestnut

This is another wood which is light in weight, soft in texture and neither very strong nor durable. It grows mainly as an ornamental tree and is really only of use for decorative carving or turnery.

Plane

In Britain the plane is nearly always found in towns and cities, where its ability to withstand pollution makes it ideal for streets and parks. The timber tends to be resistant to splitting, but in many respects works rather like sycamore and beech.

Hornbeam

In southern England, this can be quite common in old, broadleaved woodlands. The tree resembles beech – although usually smaller – but with a diamond-patterned bark and rougher leaves. It differs greatly, however, in its seed, which hangs in bunches surrounded by a light wing-like structure. The wood resembles beech, but is even harder, being traditionally used for cogs in mills and as ramrods for guns.

Box

Box is usually found as a shrub, having evergreen foliage and frequently being used as ornamental hedging. Its wood is very hard and close-grained, being highly regarded for tool-handles and small carvings.

Holly

Holly is another evergreen – also dense and close-grained. Its wood is much whiter than box and is suitable for carving and turning. It can also produce strong, straight shoots which make excellent walking-sticks.

Hazel

A common shrub which is well known for its nuts, although most of the hazelnuts we eat in Britain are imported. It rarely grows to a size appropriate for conventional woodwork, but if coppiced produces straight sticks suitable for walking-sticks, thatching spars or weaving into hurdle fences.

Hawthorn

Hawthorn grows as a woodland shrub, but is most common as a hedging plant where it is trimmed every year. It is similar to holly in that it produces a light-coloured, close-grained wood. Like the hazel, its main use is in the round where it makes a fine walking-stick.

Field Maple

This is the true native member of the maple family in Britain and, as such, is related to the sycamore. However, it is generally a smaller tree with smaller leaves and a very rough bark, even when young. The wood is similar to that of the sycamore, being slightly denser which makes it ideal for spoons or bowls.

Apple and Pear

These may well be found in gardens or orchards and provide close-grained, very hard wood. They make good mallet heads, and if you can find sections without knots these are fine for carving or turning.

Four

The Raw Material

In the previous chapter I described the trees you are most likely to encounter and the main properties of the wood they produce. Summing up, I find ash is generally the most versatile, especially where the ability to withstand flexing forces or shock is important; this is why it is the preferred wood for tool-handles and sports equipment (hickory is reputed to be even stronger, but does not generally grow in Britain). If ash is not available, then for strength I would suggest wych elm or oak – but be careful if oak is in contact with iron or steel which it tends to corrode. Fortunately, ash tends to be fairly widespread in most parts of Northern Europe so it should not be too difficult to obtain.

For most other general purposes, I find sycamore very useful. It is abundant and considered to be a weed in the eyes of the conservationist. Otherwise beech, birch or alder are good general woods. If you can obtain cherry or yew, you will be able to make some very attractive items, cherry being a delightful wood to turn on the pole-lathe.

There are a few occasions when it is preferable to use seasoned wood (see below), but for the vast majority of the projects in this book you will be using green wood: that is, freshly felled wood in log form.

Sources

How do you find green wood?

Obviously, if you have a woodland of your own you need look no further. The species of trees and their quality will determine how much timber you are able to use, but there should usually be some suitable wood in some of the trees to get you started. If you have an orchard or a garden, useful wood may be found there too. I have a 15-feet (5-metre) high maple which I occasionally prune, using branches less than an inch

(25 mm) in diameter to make small spoons.

However, even if you do have some suitable trees, the chances are that sooner or later you may want to supplement your supply with wood from elsewhere.

It might be tempting to take a trip into the nearby countryside and help yourself to a small tree or a few logs – I did it myself when I was younger. However, I strongly advise against this. You might find yourself being shouted at, chased after or possibly shot at (I've met some pretty fierce gamekeepers in my time). If it becomes obvious that people are helping themselves to trees or wood, then it will be that much more difficult for someone else who comes afterwards and who wants to ask for some wood. On the other side of the coin, it is annoying for someone who is responsible for managing trees to find their work being interfered with (I've experienced that too!). A woodland may look neglected to you, but there is a good chance that somebody somewhere has a plan for its welfare.

If you live in a town or city, you might start your search by contacting your local council's parks department. When I set up a workshop at one of the city farms in Bristol, I approached the council's woodland management team who were very interested in the project and were happy to let me have the green wood I needed. Once you gain their interest, you may find that they contact you if some special wood becomes available. You may also find that they ask you to demonstrate your skills, which might even lead to your being offered some premises. Wood from the parks department will tend to come from a wide range of trees, giving you the chance to try out several woods which would be unobtainable from a timber merchant.

Another source of wood in towns might be from tree surgeons who would be glad for you to take it away. In fact, they might give you all they have if you clear it up for them.

Wood from gardens, parks or streets does tend to have more knots than woodland trees. This is because the latter are generally grown close together and forced to grow upwards in search of light; they then put little growth into side branches, and any which are formed will probably soon die back due to lack of light.

In a 'natural' woodland, there will be trees of various ages and sizes: some young and growing, some mature and dominating, some old and dying and some dead and rotting down to nourish the young ones that take their place. Nowadays, in northern Europe, there are very few woods which have not felt the influence of man's activities. Most woodlands have been managed for centuries so as to produce timber in different shapes and sizes for various uses from firewood and charcoal to ships, houses and furniture.

Only during the last half-century has man lost interest in many of the broadleaved woods and these have either been converted to conifers or become the private domain of pheasant shooters. As a result, most of our broadleaved woodlands are in a poor state of health with trees all much the same age – mainly old and dying, or else young and spindly where the older ones have been cleared for firewood.

Woodland owners come in many forms; in Britain, the best-known is the Forestry Commission. Before the last war, woodland crafts were still a significant, if small, part of the forestry industry, and were catered for by the Forestry Commission in the areas where they were carried out. Since the 1950s, only a handful of woodland craftsmen have continued, mostly making use of coppice-grown wood: either sweet chestnut or hazel for fencing and thatching spars.

During that period, the Commission devoted themselves to producing conifers for paper pulp or building timbers with a declining interest in broadleaves. In the 1980s, their attitude changed and now they are again showing an interest in crafts which make use of green wood. The Commission is quite a large bureaucracy, but you could well find that if you approach the right person they will be only too willing to supply you with suitable wood. Even the most modern-minded of foresters has a soft spot for the old woodland craftsman.

A few other national woodland owners such as the Woodland Trust and the National Trust may also be able to provide you with green wood. The Woodland Trust operates a number of 'community woodlands' where local people are encouraged to take part in woodland management and often have the chance to practise some woodland crafts. Also involved in woodland management is the British Trust for Conservation Volunteers, who run tasks for volunteers where you can learn skills such as felling while carrying out practical work. They too would be keen to support any green woodwork project.

There are local naturalist trusts in most counties and a growing number of trusts and other local groups involved in green woodwork in certain parts of the British Isles. Along with those mentioned above, their addresses are given in Appendix 2.

One source I used a lot when I started was firewood merchants. Unlike most of the above organisations, they are usually small-scale operations having to work hard and fast to make a living. Some of them will not want to be bothered with you, but if you can find one who is interested in woodland crafts he may well let you sort through his stack of logs and then sell you what you need at firewood prices: this saves him having to saw, split and deliver it.

Another potential source of timber is a farmer. Farmers often have an area of woodland in their acreage and might be interested in letting you have a tree or two. You could be lucky and find a farmer who is only too happy to have a green woodworker in his woods. Since you might discover one who remembers what he paid for an oak gate-post and expects the same rate from you for a standing tree, you would be advised to sort out the financial side beforehand.

If you start to use larger quantities – a few tons or more at a time – you could try approaching local forestry firms or larger landowners. In this way you might be able to select your wood while it is standing. There is no great practical advantage in this, but I find it a satisfying experience as well as a good excuse for a walk in a new woodland. Moreover, if you are prepared to pay a premium over firewood prices, you will probably find them keen to contact you when some good wood becomes available.

Seasoned Wood

When you make your pole-lathe and bending jigs, I suggest you use wood which has been sawn and seasoned. It is possible to cut all the lathe parts from the log or, if you have a chain-saw, you can cut them to shape with that. I have found, however, that it is much quicker and simpler to use 'processed' timber for at least the bed, the poppets and the tool-rest (see Chapter 6).

If you are using softwood, most timber merchants should be able to supply you. The hardwood may be a little more difficult to obtain, but look through the 'Yellow Pages' and you should find someone selling what you need. You will probably find a smaller country timber merchant cheaper than a large town one, but he may not be able to plane up the wood if that is what you require.

The other principal use for processed timber is in the form of wide planks for the seats of Windsor chairs and stools. I don't know of anyone converting elm planks by hand, apart from the occasional demonstration of how to use a pit-saw. I would not recommend that you tackle such a task without a great deal of determination and patience. Elm is the traditional wood for this job because of its resistance to splitting, and I know of no European woods to match it. The Americans use pine and I suspect that plane might be suitable. If you make your seats 2" or more in thickness, then the tendency for them to split will be greatly diminished and you need not be too choosy.

If you do want elm, then you will have to hunt around and build up contacts. In Britain, the further north you go the later have been the effects of Dutch Elm disease and consequently the greater the availability. Also, the disease has been contained in the Brighton area, and there may be some available there.

On other odd occasions a piece of planked softwood comes in useful, so it is worth keeping your eyes open to see if builders or sawmills are throwing any away. When making the platform for the shaving-horse, a piece of pallet wood is ideal; any

transport firm or warehouse should have something suitable for that job. Always save any reasonable off-cuts to make bending jigs for chair parts.

Selecting Green Wood

As I said earlier, I like to select my wood when it is standing. However, this is more risky as you only have the external appearance to go by and as we are told, beauty is only skin-deep! With time and practice, you should be able to develop an eye for a good tree by taking note of such things as bark, twigs, the ground it grows in and its general form. Like all living things, though, trees are never totally predictable.

For most of you it will be a matter of choosing logs that have already been felled, which in fact makes selection much more reliable. The main factors to take into account when choosing a log are:

1 Rot or stain in the wood.

2 Straightness of the grain.

3 Number of knots.

4 Rate of growth.

Coloration or Rot

Obviously, wood which has started to rot should be avoided. It will feel softer than sound wood and may smell different. If your wood feels firm but is an unusual colour, then you should also take care. In oak, elm, sweet chestnut, cherry and yew, there is a distinct difference in colour between the heartwood and the sapwood. Where this is the case, it is advisable to use only the heartwood as it will be stronger and more durable. There are occasions, however (such as when making oak swill baskets) where the sapwood is used. You may also wish to retain a proportion of sapwood for visual effect.

In the remaining trees listed in Chapter 3 (as distinct from those mentioned above), there is no obvious difference in colour between heartwood and sapwood. However, there are frequently areas of different colour within one log. Beech will often have streaks running through its wood, but this does not affect its strength to any extent. Ash will often have dark sections in its wood known as olive ash or black ash. This dark wood – and to a lesser extent, the white wood in the same tree – may have lost some of its flexing properties, so it is safer to avoid it if strength is important.

Grain

The term grain, when applied to wood, can be taken to have various meanings. I shall use it here to mean the direction in which the fibres and vessels of the wood lie. The grain is easily seen when a piece of wood is cleft in half. If a log is curved, you can be sure that the grain is also curved. If, on the other hand, the log is straight, this means that the grain *might* be straight. With a log from an English elm, the grain is naturally wavy. If it is from one of the other trees, then it might still contain irregularities.

When a tree is young, it will probably have to compete with other trees as well as undergrowth,

and must also contend with damage from the weather or from animals. There is a chance that a leading bud will die and a side-shoot will take over, leaving a kink in the trunk. It is surprising just how quickly the tree will straighten itself out by producing more growth on one side than the other (Fig. 4.1).

Knots

A knot in any piece of wood is formed by the growth of a side branch. The fibres of this branch will run at an angle to the main section and will, therefore, produce a structural weakness. Below are four typical stages in the development of a knot (see Fig. 4.2):

a The young stem puts out a side shoot.

b The main stem grows faster than the side branch, but the size of the knot increases with the growth of the branch. The fibres of the trunk and the branch are joined at the knot. This is called a 'live knot'.

c The branch dies and stops growing. The trunk continues growing and slowly encases the branch, but the fibres of the trunk no longer join with the fibres of the branch. This forms a 'dead knot'.

d The branch falls or is cut off, following which the trunk grows over the end of the branch to prevent the invasion of decay. Within a few years the wood is covered and only an irregular mark on the bark indicates the presence of the knot.

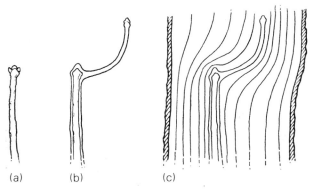

(a)   (b)   (c)

Fig. 4.1   How a tree's growth will straighten.

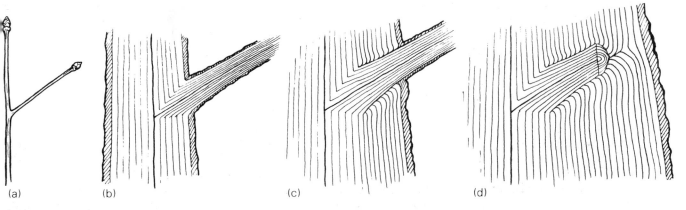

(a)   (b)   (c)   (d)

Fig. 4.2   The stages of knot formation.

If the wood is subsequently converted into planks, the live knots will remain in the plank but the dead knots will probably fall out. In either case, the strength of the wood is reduced.

Whether the irregularity came about through deformed growth or the formation of knots, it is possible over a period of years for it to become disguised to such an extent that there is no obvious blemish on the outside of the tree. If the wood is sawn lengthways into planks, these irregularities may or may not show up, but they will certainly affect the strength of the resulting planks. When such wood is cleft, there is no avoiding any irregularities and the green woodworker will have to cope with them.

If the end product has a curve (such as in an axe handle or an Irish hurling stick), such curves can be used to advantage. The curve in the end product can follow the flow of the grain. Formerly oak trees were deliberately grown with curved branches in order to be used for the curved timbers in a ship's hull. Such curves can also be used in spoon-making. However, in most cases you will be looking for straight-grained sections.

For this reason and also to prevent the logs from cracking (see p. 19), I usually cleave my logs down the middle as soon as I can after felling. It is then possible to see exactly what is happening with the wood and to select sections that are as straight and clean (i.e. knot-free) as possible.

Growth Rate

One other factor to influence your selection, particularly with ash, is that of growth rate. The effects of the rate of growth in ash form a complete study in themselves which is well covered in a pamphlet on the subject, 'Selecting ash by inspection', produced by the Building Research Establishment. Slow-grown ash puts on little growth in the summer and, as a result, contains a high proportion of vessels produced in the spring. It will lack the strength produced by fibres and feels light and brittle.

On the other hand, as the pamphlet states, wide rings *can* cause weak wood 'because the conditions which favour exceptionally rapid growth often result in the production of abnormally thin-walled fibres which render the timber disproportionately weak'. I have experienced this

on a few occasions, but generally I find quick-grown ash to be very tough. However, it is hard to work and can cause problems when steam-bending due to the low proportion of vessels (see Chapter 12).

Quoting again from the Building Research Establishment's publication:

As a general rule, ash with between 4 and 16 rings to 25mm (an inch), measured radially, is likely to be stronger than that of faster or slower growth, and wood with an average rate of growth outside these limits should be regarded with suspicion unless it can be shown that its density is up to specification.

Growth rates can also affect other woods, but as ash is the timber mainly used for strength, the rate of growth in other hard woods is less important.

Storage

Storing logs

Once you have obtained your green wood, how should you store it? The best way is to leave it growing until you need it. Even if the tree has been uprooted, it will usually struggle on growing. Probably you will want to buy a quantity of wood at one time, but be unable to work it all straight away. If this is the case, keep it in lengths as long as you can manage. It will lose far more moisture from the end grain than from the outside. If the wood has to be cut to length, then I find 5 feet (or 1·5 metres) the most convenient. This yields either: three lengths of 20" (50 cm) for chair-legs, combs, spindles, tool-handles and other short items; a 20" (50 cm) and a 40" (1 m) for long handles and back legs for the spindle-back; or a 60" (1·5 m) length for bow-backs.

Unless there is a good reason for removing the bark – such as to use it for weaving chair-bottoms – I find it best to leave it alone.

One way to reduce the radial cracking in a log is to cleave it down the middle (see Chapter 8). This enables the greater tangential shrinkage to take place, with each half of the log closing up on itself, and has the added advantage of making the long logs easier to handle (Fig. 4.3).

These half-logs should now be put into a state of suspended animation and treated like other plant life being stored, such as fresh vegetables:

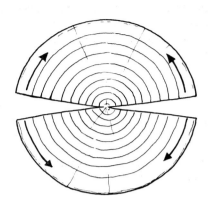

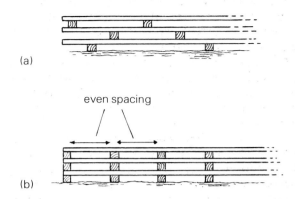

Fig. 4.3   The effect of halving a log.

Fig. 4.4   Storing planks (a) incorrect (b) correct.

not too dry, but not damp; ventilated, but out of the wind; cool, but not frozen for long periods. If you cannot fit them into the bottom of your fridge, then stack them clear of the ground outside, but in the shade. Some woods are prone to staining (especially sycamore) and behave better if stood upright so that the sap is more easily able to drain out of them. If desired, you can seal the log ends with wax or paint, but unless the wood is particularly valuable you can just saw off the few inches at the end when you come to work the log and use the off-cuts for firewood.

Storing planked wood

Seasoning planks freshly sawn from the log requires much care to avoid wastage caused by warping and splitting. Apart from the raw materials for a pole-lathe and a few other small jobs, the only regular use I make of planked wood is for Windsor chair-bottoms. Even these are best if shaped while the wood is fairly green and thus softer. They are bound to warp, but that gives the chair character and can be taken into account when levelling the legs (Chapter 15). Generally planks should be seasoned horizontally, being separated by a number of ½" (12 mm) square dry softwood strips known as stickers. As each plank is laid down, the stickers should be vertically in line to help keep the planks flat (Fig. 4.4). As with green wood logs, the planks should be kept out of sun and rain, although increased ventilation will be an advantage if you want them to dry out.

Five

Tools and Tool Care

As we shall see in the following chapters, all the processes and their associated tools can be summed up under nine headings:

1   Measuring

2   Sawing

3   Cleaving and trimming

4   Shaving

5   Turning

6   Drilling

7   Gripping

8   Hitting

9   Sharpening

For some projects, such as Windsor chairs, you will need tools from all of these categories, some of which are quite specialised. However, you need not go out and buy all the tools in the following lists at one time. For example, with a bow-saw and an axe you can not only make fence-posts but also quite usable tent-pegs or spatulas. Add to this a knife and a gouge, and now you can whittle spoons. With a brace and bits you can assemble simple stools and make a shaving-horse. Then with a drawknife, a

Fig. 5.1   Plasters, hammer, file, burnisher, scraper, waterstone, oilstones, slipstone, protractor, pencil, 18 in (45 cm) steel rule, 10 ft (3 m) tape, sliding bevel, 8 in (20 cm) G-cramp.

pole-lathe and a few turning tools, you can tackle most of the projects in this book. This was roughly the way I progressed, picking up an old tool here and being given a present there until – steadily and without too much pain – I had kitted out my green woodwork shop.

1 Measuring

One of the first operations in green woodwork is to measure your raw materials. Quite often the exact dimensions are not crucial, in which case you can use parts of your body to take the measurements. For example, the end joint on my index finger is an inch; my size 8 boot measures a foot, and from the tip of my outstretched hand to my chin is a yard. Presumably we also have some metric parts to our bodies! Another possibility is to hold an object of the desired length up against the raw materials and transfer its length. If this measurement is to be used often, you could cut a stick to size or make a special measuring stick with notches at particular intervals. If you do this, it is worth putting some red paint on it or else it may well end up on the fire!

When writing a book or running a course, I have little option but to use standard units of measurement. One is then faced with a choice between the imperial and the metric. Having trained as a pure mathematician, I like to keep figures as small as possible so, for example, I prefer 150 mm as 15 cm but better still as 6 inches. However, a twist drill measuring $5/64''$ means much more when expressed as 2 mm. As a result, I use a combination of both systems, measuring in millimetres until I reach 10 mm (about $3/8''$) and from then on in inches (or fractions of an inch) and feet until I reach 10 ft (about 3 metres), and from there on in metres. This means that I buy twist drills in millimetres and auger bits in inches. I purchase planks by the cubic foot and green wood by the cubic metre. Therefore, I find it best to use instruments marked in both metric and imperial units.

A modern tape measuring up to 10 feet (3 m) is very useful. For detailed work, and especially chairs, an 18'' (45 cm) steel rule is invaluable. For measuring angles there is a multitude of choices, some of which can cost up to £150. A device with an adjustable angle, such as a sliding bevel, will be needed, as will a protractor to measure this angle precisely. A spirit level is also helpful when constructing a shaving-horse or a chair as this gives you a good way to drill consistently in one plane. You should be able to find a tool which combines at least two of these into one unit, if not all three together. However, you may discover that it is cheaper to get all three separately.

To mark your measurements you will need a pencil, preferably a sturdy carpenter's pencil. You can use a stick of charcoal from the fire or even a bit of mud, but a pencil is the most reliable and makes less mess when you tuck it behind your ear!

2 Sawing (Fig. 5.2)

To fell your trees or even to reduce your logs to a suitable size, you will need a large bow-saw. I like to use one with a 36'' (90 cm) blade, preferably with 'raker' teeth. Most modern Western cross-cut saws have triangular teeth 'set' alternately on

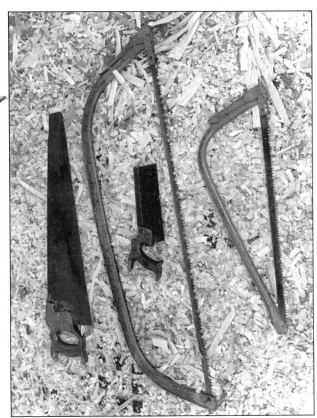

Fig. 5.2 Sawing: panel saw, 36 in (90 cm) bow-saw, dovetail saw, 21 in (53 cm) bow-saw.

41

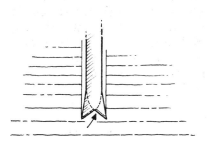

Fig. 5.3   Splayed saw teeth.

opposite sides of the blade. This means that when you look along the blade, the teeth are splayed outwards, the cutting point at the outside edge.

The idea of this is that the kerf – that is, the slot cut into the wood by the blade – is slightly wider than the blade itself, which avoids the edges of the saw blade rubbing hard against the wood. Such a blade works well in seasoned wood, but when the wood is green it tends to clog up in the triangle formed between the saw teeth (shown with an arrow in Fig. 5.3). To clear this, pairs of raker teeth are spaced along the blade, enabling the cutting teeth to cut more effectively (Fig. 5.4).

Fig. 5.4   Raker teeth.

The large bow-saw is best used with a person at each end, which is how the old fashioned cross-cut saws were operated in the days before the chain-saw. If you find a cross-cut saw in good condition, then you could of course use it instead of the large bow-saw.

Although stressing the advantages of working without powered machines, one that I do some-times use is the chain-saw. It is dangerous and noisy and a new one will cost more than all the other tools put together, but it can make life a lot less strenuous. If you do intend to use a chain-saw, please ask somebody to show you how to use it safely.

You will also need a saw for smaller work such as cutting beams to make the lathe or the bending jigs, and cutting smaller pieces of wood to length. A standard woodworking panel saw is good for seasoned wood, but a small bow-saw is better for small cleft sections and branchwood. It is useful, but not essential, to have both. If you really want to save your money, you could use a 30" (75 cm) bow-saw for all the jobs mentioned, as long as you are not dealing with logs much over 9" in diameter.

A tenon saw will be essential when you come to chair-making, but even during the earlier pro-jects it can be very useful. Such jobs as sawing slots for wedges in tool-handles are not only awkward, but quite dangerous with a larger saw.

To saw planks to shape for Windsor chairs, you will require a turning saw. This you can make yourself, and it is described in detail in Chapter 12.

3   Cleaving and Trimming

Cleaving is one of the main operations that sets green woodwork apart from 'twentieth century' woodwork. Since it is the process which enables us to make use of fresh logs without needing powered tools, some kind of cleaving equipment is essential (Fig. 5.5). If you start with large logs, a yard (metre) or more in length, it will be useful to have a pair of steel wedges. The ability to cleave a 5 ft (1·5 m) log down the middle where it has been felled might make the difference between being able to carry it away and having to leave it to rot. If you buy wedges, look out for those with an even taper rather than those with a separate bevel; they will go into the wood more easily (Fig. 5.6). To avoid having to use wedges, you can start the split with an axe and then open up the log by using a pair of wooden wedges or 'gluts' (see Chapter 7).

Traditionally, the tool used by the chair-bodger for splitting out his leg-blanks (or billets) was a cleaving axe or cleaver. Its main function is not to chop the wood to shape, but to act like a wedge with a handle. Most small modern axes or hatchets are suitable for this purpose. None of the cleaving tools needs to have a razor-sharp edge, so you should be able to use any modestly priced axe as long as it has a wedge-shaped section.

Fig. 5.5 Cleaving and trimming: turner's axe, cleaving axe, froe, felling axe, hewing axe, wedges.

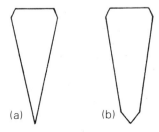

Fig. 5.6 Wedge bevels (a) correct (b) incorrect.

A more specialised cleaving tool no longer manufactured in Britain is called a froe. This tool is best used in conjunction with a cleaving break to guide the split in a long piece of wood, and is still employed in the production of chestnut paling fences. Its dimensions vary according to its particular use. A 'general purpose' froe might have a blade 10" (25 cm) long, 2" (5 cm) wide and

¼" (6 mm) thick. At one end is an 'eye' into which is fitted a strong cleft ash handle about 18" (45 cm) long. The froe is struck into the log with a wooden club and then used to lever the wood open. It should have a slightly convex taper towards the edge to allow it to rock up and down in the split (Fig. 5.7).

Fig. 5.7 Section through a froe blade.

Once you have cleft a length of wood, it will need to be shaped. A rough shaping process called 'trimming' is best carried out with a sharp axe removing large chips of wood. Where possible, it is best to use a side-axe: that is an axe sharpened with a bevel on one side only, the other side being flat (Fig. 5.8). You are then able to cut the wood with more of a vertical stroke than would be possible with a double bevel.

Traditionally, side axes came in various shapes and sizes according to their use. Chair-bodgers used a turner's axe weighing 3–4 lbs (1·5–2 kg) and fitted with a short cranked handle. This shape is suited to working on a block at waist height, where most of the work is done by the

Fig. 5.8 Section through a side axe.

weight of the axe rather than by taking a hearty swing. For heavier work, such as squaring beams, a weightier 'hewing axe' was used with a handle 18"–24" (45–60 cm) long. This can be used with either one or two hands. Like the froe, side axes are no longer manufactured in Britain, but you can still buy a variety of double-bevelled axes. Provided you sharpen them to a fine angle and remove any shoulder on the bevel, these are quite satisfactory.

The most common axe-head is a simple wedge shape which, as I mentioned, is ideal for cleaving (Fig. 5.9(a)). For trimming, I prefer the Kent pattern which has a longer cutting edge and a more slender blade (Fig. 5.9(b))

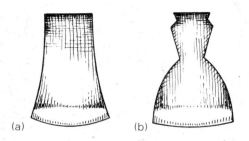

(a)   (b)

Fig. 5.9 Axe patterns (a) wedge (b) Kent.

Apart from cleaving and trimming, an axe may be needed for felling too. Normally a felling axe has a double bevel and a handle 30"–36" (75–90 cm) long. It is also useful for severing awkward fibres when cleaving open a log.

Ideally you would obtain a selection of axes, adapting one for each job, but at first you will be limited by what you are able to find. If possible, have a separate cleaving axe as its blade will inevitably become blunted through hitting the ground from time to time. You may find that you can use a 4 lb (2 kg) Kent axe for trimming, hewing and, to some extent, for felling. (See Chapter 9 for instructions on making your own handles.)

4 Shaving (Fig. 5.10)

This again is an essential operation, not only in chair-bodging but in most other aspects of green woodwork. The tool for this is a drawknife, which is nearly always used in conjunction with

Fig. 5.10 (right) Shaving: Swedish training knife, French folding knife, steel spokeshave, wooden spokeshave, German drawknife, English drawknife.

the shaving-horse. Despite the fact that you work the tool towards yourself, it is really quite safe. A drawknife consists of a blade usually about 10" (25 cm) long with a bevel along one edge; at either end is a wooden handle at right-angles to the blade. This tool was produced in a variety of shapes and sizes according to the craft for which it was used. It is still manufactured nowadays, with a distinct difference between the lightweight German style with short stubby handles and the sturdier English pattern. Which you choose is a matter of taste.

For finer work such as spoons, and for finishing shaved work which will not be turned, you will also need a spokeshave. Traditionally this consisted of a small blade, like a miniature drawknife, fitted into a wooden-handled body. It does the same job as the drawknife, only with a controlled depth of cut. Nowadays spokeshaves are made of steel, more like a plane with an adjustable blade. Wooden ones can be picked up quite cheaply, but I must confess I usually prefer the modern steel ones for most jobs.

A cabinet scraper is essential for making Windsor chairs, but is also useful for the final smoothing of any work that is not turned, such as the handles for axes, adzes and spoons. In its simplest form, this is just a flat piece of steel with a 'burr' formed on one or more edges. These can be cut out of old saw-blades.

A knife will frequently come in useful. You are unlikely to need one with dozens of gadgets, but one which can be folded and put into a pocket is an advantage. If you have a tool-kit with you all the time, you could use a standard wood-carving knife such as a Swedish training knife.

5 Turning (Fig. 5.11)

I have been using a pole-lathe for thirteen years, but am still changing my ideas as time goes on. The chair-bodgers usually had their tools specially made by the local blacksmith to suit their own particular way of working. If you intend to turn bowls, you can use standard modern turning

Fig. 5.11   Turning: 1¹/₄ in (32 mm) firmer gouge, ¹/₄ in (6 mm) spindle gouge, ¹/₂ in (13 mm) skew chisel, ¹/₄ in (6 mm) carving gouge, 2 in (50 mm) firmer chisel, gimlet, 2 in (50 mm) bevel-edged chisel.

tools, but the best results will come from specially hooked tools as described in Chapter 16. For chair-bodging and other spindle-turning (i.e. with the grain of the workpiece running between the lathe centres), I shall describe tools which are still manufactured although not necessarily specifically for wood-turning.

Green wood, as we have seen, is much softer than seasoned wood so the tools we use – like our produce – can be lighter in weight and more delicate than normal turning tools.

The first tool required is a gimlet. A small tool resembling a corkscrew, but with just a small screw at its tip, this is used to enlarge the centre holes in the workpiece before mounting it on the lathe. It is not essential, but it does make the workpiece less likely to fly off the lathe. The first process is to 'rough out' the work: that is, to remove the drawknife marks to produce a smooth cylinder. A shallow gouge, 1" (25 mm) or more in width, does the job well. The ideal is a 1½" (37 mm) gouge, but a narrower one will do.

To smooth the surface, a wide chisel is used; traditionally this would be up to 3" (70 mm) wide, but nowadays the widest made is a 2" (50 mm) carpenter's chisel. I find this works very well and prefer it to the standard large skew chisel used by most wood-turners today. There are two types of carpenter's chisels: the bevel-edged and the firmer. The bevel-edged type has a lighter feel and the angled surface along the side makes it easier to hold correctly on the tool-rest. You could use narrower chisels down to 1½" (37 mm) if that is all you can find, or alternatively fit a handle to an old plane blade. Those who already have standard turning tools, such as a roughing-out gouge and a large skew chisel, may be happier continuing with these.

The Chiltern bodgers did most of their patterning with a V-tool called a 'buzz' or 'bruzz'. These are good for the simple High Wycombe 3-bead pattern, but rather limited for general use. They also have a tendency to pull into the wood and can be tricky to sharpen. I prefer a slender ½" (13 mm) skew chisel for any smaller convex shaping; this is a standard wood-turning tool.

The final tool I suggest is a small gouge either ¼" (6 mm) or ⅜" (10 mm) according to choice. I have a slight preference for the ¼" (6 mm) size. The ideal lies somewhere between a straight carving gouge and a heavier turning gouge. I use both, choosing the latter for heavier work and the carving gouge for lighter, more delicate jobs.

I started working on a pole-lathe using standard turning tools, but slowly discovered that the lighter carpenter's tools felt better. I am now exploring the use of the even lighter carving tools; these tend to be more expensive, but will give you increased sensitivity. If possible, try out a range of tools before buying. The joy is that you can use virtually any chisels on the pole-lathe without coming to any harm.

If you really want to economise, it is in fact possible to make a simple chair-leg using only a good sharp axe. With practice you can cleave, trim (miss out the shaving), rough out and smooth the leg with this one tool!

6 Drilling (Fig. 5.12)

Another operation which becomes essential in green woodwork when you want to joint together two pieces of wood is drilling. Except

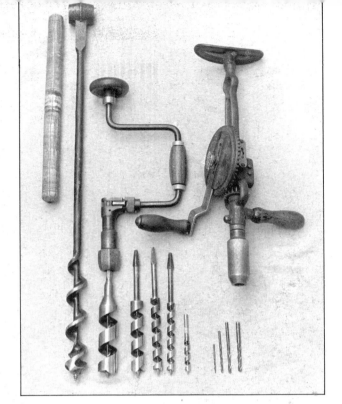

Fig. 5.12 Drilling: breast drill, twist drills – 8 mm, 5 mm, 3 mm, 2 mm, 1½ in bar auger (and handle), auger bits – ⅜ in, ½ in, ⅝ in, ⅞ in, 1¼ in, carpenter's ratchet brace.

when making the lathe and some of the jigs, all the joints in this book are round mortise and tenons – i.e. a round piece of wood fitted tightly into a round hole. The tool we shall use most is a carpenter's brace, together with a variety of bits. It will be a help, if not essential, if this is a ratchet brace which will enable you to drill holes where you cannot completely turn the brace.

Various types of bit can be used, e.g. spoon-bits, shell-bits, centre-bits and auger-bits. The most common nowadays is the auger-bit, which has a channel spiralling up its length to clear the waste wood. Among auger-bits there are several subtle variations and you will have to choose what suits you best. Try if possible to avoid the modern 'combination bits' which are supposed to fit into powered drills as well as a brace. From my experience, they do neither properly and may even damage the chuck in your brace. The range of sizes that will suit most purposes is ⅜" (10 mm), ½" (13 mm), ⅝" (16 mm) and ⅞" (22 m). You may prefer 1" (25 mm) to the ⅞" (22 mm) if you have not yet built up your faith in the strength of cleft wood. I have more to say about this subject in Chapter 11 on chair joints.

For drilling larger holes, you can get a 1¼" (32 mm) or even a 1½" (38 mm) auger-bit. You will find these strenuous to use when drilling into hardwood, but I have survived for many years with the 1¼" (32 mm) bit (and built up my chest muscles). A 1½" (38 mm) bar-auger will make life easier. Instead of using the brace to turn it, there is an eye at the top through which you fit a wooden handle.

Sometimes you will need to drill smaller holes and for this a hand-drill is useful. This should be used with twist drills; the kind normally used in power drills; 2, 3, 5, and 8 mm ($^{3}/_{32}$", ⅛", ¼", $^{5}/_{16}$") will give you an adequate selection. A larger version of this is the breast drill which will also be able to take the smaller auger-bits. Some old ones have a built-in spirit level, which is ideal when drilling some of the chair joints.

8   Gripping

Nearly all the gripping devices will be made out of wood and are described in Chapters 7, 8 and 12. However, one that is worth buying is a clamp or cramp of some sort. (Why some are called clamps and some cramps I do not know.) There is a rapidly growing range available on the market, but I still prefer the standard G-cramp with at least an 8" gap. If you are planning to make a spindle-back or comb-back chair, you are likely to need a good strong cramp for the job. Better still, but not so mobile, is a good bench vice, but even second-hand these are expensive. A possible alternative to the bench vice is a bench-holdfast for holding wood on to the surface of a bench. If you are not planning to use a clamp for bending wood, then you could get by with one of the sliding clamps on the market or even make one yourself.

9   Hitting

This operation is another important part of green woodwork, but again you can make most of your hitting tools yourself (Chapter 7). One that is useful – as much for removing nails from scrap wood as for knocking them in – is a claw-hammer; you may well have one already. For knocking joints together you can buy hide mallets which have a head made out of animal hide, and this will avoid damaging your work. I prefer instead to lay a piece of softwood on to the work as protection.

10   Sharpening

This may be one of the less exciting processes, but is nonetheless vitally important. Using blunt machinery makes the job take longer, but working with blunt hand tools is exhausting and very soul-destroying. There are two main operations involved in sharpening: grinding and honing (see Fig. 5.13). On carving tools you may require a third stage of burnishing and polishing.

Usually when you buy a new tool – and nearly always with a second-hand tool – it will need grinding to remove any nicks in the blade and to bring it to the bevel *you* require. This can only be done satisfactorily on some form of abrasive wheel. Traditionally, this was carried out on a sandstone wheel (rotated with a treadle or by hand) which was lubricated with water. Nowadays most are electrically powered and usually come with a coarse and fine stone, although you can buy electrically-powered wheels with a man-made 'sandstone' wheel in a water trough. If you cannot find an old-fashioned wheel in good condition, then you will have to compromise with modern technology and either buy a powered grindstone or save up your grinding for, say, once a month and borrow someone else's. For coarse sharpening of axes and adzes (again an infrequent occurrence) a large fine file will produce a good even bevel. A few small files will be needed occasionally for sharpening drill bits, and if you sharpen your own saws you will require a diamond or triangular file.

After grinding your tools they will all, with the exception of cleaving tools, require honing. For this you will need one or more bench stones. There are many to choose from and a good summary is given in *Sharpening and Care of Woodworking Tools and Equipment* by John Sainsbury (GMC Publications Ltd, 1984).

When you start out, you could use one of the combination stones available, coarse on one side and fine on the other. A good alternative is a Japanese water-stone. Although comparatively expensive, you can get by with just one grade – say 800 or 1,000 grit – and you will not need any special honing oil as with an oilstone. For sharpening gouges, one or more slipstones will enable you to remove the burr on the inside edge. For a really fine finish, I use a Welsh slate stone. You could go one step further and polish the bevel with a 'strop' of leather, felt or rubber.

To raise the burr on a scraper, you will need a tool called a burnisher or ticketer. This is simply a length of hard steel in a handle which can be either round, oval or triangular. I prefer the latter.

First-aid Kit

Although not strictly a tool, I strongly advise you to carry a first-aid kit. Cuts are not infrequent, but with sharp hand tools they should be clean and heal quickly. The very least you need is a few plasters. While it is unlikely that anything more serious will happen, an approved first-aid kit is a useful precaution.

To summarise, here is a list of what I consider to be the basic tools for green woodwork. Those in brackets will be needed at some stage, but you could leave acquiring them until later.

Measuring

10 ft (3 m) tape or 18" (45 cm) steel rule

pencil

(sliding bevel)

(protractor)

(spirit level)

Sawing

large bow-saw

tenon saw

(small bow-saw or panel saw)

Cleaving and trimming

cleaving axe or froe

trimming axe(s)

(steel wedges)

(felling axe)

Shaving

drawknife

knife

(spokeshave)

(scraper)

Turning

gimlet

roughing-out gouge

square chisel

skew chisel

small gouge

Drilling

brace

⅜, ½, ⅝, ⅞" (10, 13, 16, 22 mm) bits

1¼" (32 mm) bit or 1½" (38 mm) auger

(hand drill with bits)

Gripping

(G-cramp)

Hitting

(hammer)

Sharpening

bench-stone

slipstone(s)

(grindstone)

(slate stone or strop)

(files)

(burnisher)

First-aid kit

Even if you had to buy everything new, you could obtain the essential tools for well under £200 (1989 prices). This is about the same as a work-bench, a dust-extractor or a cheap powered lathe with no tools.

As well as the 'basic' list given above, we shall encounter a number of specialist tools used for particular projects. These will be covered in more detail as they crop up, but overleaf is a summary, alongside the projects in which they are used. Many of them are by no means essential, but are useful luxuries.

Project	Chapter	Special Tools
Pole-lathe	6	spanner, screwdriver,
Bending jigs	12	bench-vice or workmate
Felling	7	breaking bar/turning hook
Cleaving-break	7	spade, punner
Baby's rattle	10	spoon-bit chisel, hooked chisel
Spoons	10	spoon gouge, *twca cam*, Swedish carver's hook
Chairs, general	13, 14, 15	rounding planes
Windsor chairs and stools	14, 15	scooping plane, block plane, boring machine, bench holdfast
Windsor chairs	15	round-bottomed adze, travisher, dividers
Bowls	16	long and strong gouge, ring gouge, hooked bowl chisels
Tent-pegs	17	bench knife
Gate hurdle	17	twybil, ½" (13 mm) mortise chisel
Wattle hurdle	17	bill-hook
Hay rake	17	tine cutter, stail engine

Where Can You Buy These?

I struggled long and hard in my early days, knowing neither what tools to use nor where to find them. At least the first question should now be answered. I have tried where possible to recommend tools which are still generally manufactured. It is now up to you to buy them, to keep up a demand for them so that they will stay in production. Because green woodwork falls between forestry and woodwork, so do the tools. Most manufacturers produce well-illustrated catalogues of their goods from which you can choose what you need. Bristol Design now stock a range of tools specifically for green woodwork and chair-making and are continually expanding their range. Alternatively, you may wish to order from one of the specialist firms (see Appendix 2 for addresses).

If you like to be able to see your tools before purchasing, as opposed to mail order, searching around the local tool shops in your area should enable you to find a fair proportion of what you need. Better still, go to one of the woodworking shows that take place around the country where most of the tool-makers display and demonstrate their wares – but check your bank balance before you go – there will be many tempting offers!

There are also a number of specialist second-hand dealers, some of whom stock a wide selection of tools. Many people consider these to be superior to modern equipment and there is some truth in this, not necessarily because all old tools were better made but because those which were no good have long since been thrown away and only the best have survived. Certain tools which were once common but are no longer in demand may be much cheaper in such shops. Braces and hand-drills fall into this category. However, be very careful when selecting old saws and drill bits, as you may never be able to restore them into good condition if they have at some time been abused.

A very pleasant way to find tools – if you have the time – is to tour the farm sales, car-boot sales, auctions or flea markets where occasionally you might come across a real bargain. Unfortunately, old tools are often collected nowadays to hang on walls rather than for any practical purpose. This means that anything rare which looks interesting – such as a boring machine – can cost as much as or more than a modern powered equivalent (although, hopefully, it will not burn out as soon!).

For really obscure devices, you will probably have to track down a good blacksmith who is used to working with tools. Tine cutters, twybils, hooked bowl chisels and a bench knife will fall into this category. You may find that he can also provide you with a froe cheaper than an imported one. If he is like the blacksmiths I have met, it will make a pleasant change for him from producing wrought-iron railings.

Sharpening

Before describing how to work with these tools, here are a few more details on sharpening. When you are the one and only source of power, it is vitally important that all the cutting tools are kept sharp: that is the axes (other than for cleaving), the shaving tools and the turning tools. Fortunately wood is much softer when green than it is when seasoned, so the tools will hold their edges very much longer.

The section of a blade which has been sharpened is known as the bevel. With most carpentry chisels, the blades are ground to one bevel (about 25 degrees) and then honed to a slightly steeper secondary bevel (about 30 degrees) (Fig. 5.13).

Turning tools on the other hand are always ground to a single bevel. For turning seasoned wood on a powered lathe, the angle is usually between 40 and 70 degrees, but with green wood on a pole-lathe we can use the same grinding angle as

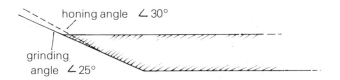

Fig. 5.13   Grinding and honing angles on carpentry tools.

with carpentry tools (25 degrees). It is still important, however, to retain one straight bevel *without* producing a secondary honing bevel.

If you grind the tools on a stone with a water trough, there is little danger of their overheating. On a dry electric grindstone, however, great care should be taken to move the blade quickly to and fro across the stone and not to press the tool hard on to the wheel. If you are not careful, a brown patch will appear on the tip of the blade indicating that the tool has 'lost its temper' – meaning that it will become blunt more quickly. In such a situation it is often best to frequently dip the blade into cold water.

With the turning tools (especially the square chisel), it will help if they are hollow ground. This is the effect where the bevel is slightly concave, and is achieved by using a grinding wheel with a fairly small diameter.

A slight burr detected on the back of the blade along the whole length of its edge will tell you when it has been sufficiently ground. You may be able to see this if the light is good. Otherwise, remove the blade from the wheel and run your thumb down the back of the bevel to feel the burr. When honing the blade on a bench-stone, it is quite easy to feel when the front and back of the bevel are both sitting on the stone. After a few strokes along the stone, a fine surface will be achieved without having to remove any steel from the middle of the bevel (Fig. 5.14).

When honing on an oilstone, a thin mineral oil should be used to carry away the particles. You can buy a special honing oil or, failing that, one part of engine oil can be diluted with 1–2 parts of paraffin. If you use a water-stone, it should be kept in water whenever it is not in use so that it holds the necessary lubrication. But do not let it freeze, or it will crack.

To hone the gouges, you can set aside a special

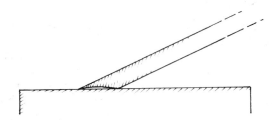

Fig. 5.14   Honing a hollow-ground chisel.

bench-stone and wear a channel into it for each curve of gouge (Fig. 5.15). Alternatively, you can hold the gouge steady and rub a slipstone over the bevel as shown (Fig. 5.16).

It is important to keep one stone with a flat surface for honing the chisels as well as spokeshave and plane blades.

Grinding drawknives is quite straightforward on a large sandstone wheel. Gently play the blade to and fro across the wheel until you can just detect a burr on the back of the blade along its whole length. On an electric grindstone with a wheel at each end, it is virtually impossible to run along the length of the blade because the handle (or your fingers) will bump into the other wheel. You can hold the blade at an angle to the machine, but this tends to round off the edge of the stone. Otherwise you can use a large fine file. Fortunately, a good drawknife rarely needs grinding and it is usually sufficient to hone it with

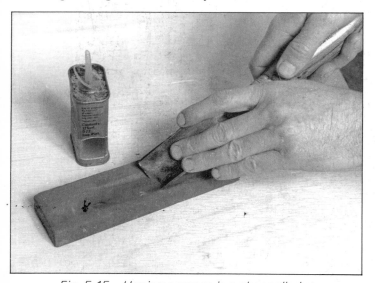

Fig. 5.15   Honing a gouge in a channelled stone.

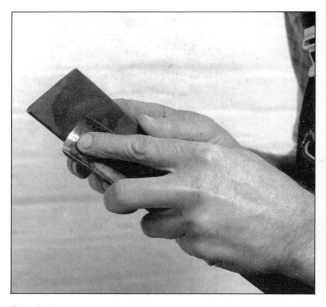

Fig. 5.16   Honing a gouge with a slipstone.

a flat stone; in this case, hold the tool steady (in a vice or shaving-horse) and move the stone. Make sure you keep your fingers out of the way during this operation (Fig. 5.17).

Using a file is also a good way to restore the edge on an axe. You may need to grind an axe-blade when first you get it in order to round off the shoulders of the bevel. After that you should aim to keep a smooth, slightly convex contour to the edge of the axe. A final honing to the edge should keep it to a razor finish.

Most bow-saws nowadays have specially hardened teeth which hold their edge for a long time. When they finally become blunt, you simply fit a replacement. Some panel saws are also 'disposable', which seems rather a waste of steel. Most panel saws and tenon saws, however, can be resharpened, but to carry this out successfully you will need a tool called a saw-set to produce the required splay of the teeth. If you buy one of these, it should include full instructions for sharpening your saws; otherwise, it is probably best to take it to a 'saw-doctor'.

Sharpening an auger bit is also a job requiring some care. The outside edges should remain parallel, so you should never put a bevel on the outside of the spurs. A gentle honing on the inside edge of the spurs, however, will make it cut more cleanly into the wood.

Carrying Tools

Having carefully sharpened your tools, it would be a shame if they were knocked around before you have a chance to use them. You are likely to need to carry them outdoors into the garden or the woods, so some kind of tool crate will be a great help to both you and your tools. Its shape and size will depend on what you have to carry, and will also have to change as you acquire new equipment. I have shown just one example to give you an idea (see Fig. 5.18).

The curved handle is a piece of ash bent to shape while green, without the need for steaming. Sheets of plywood or softwood off-cuts are probably the best form of base for such crates. A detachable section for a set of lathe tools would be useful, so that it can be bolted on to the lathe when the tools are in use.

Fig. 5.17   Honing a drawknife.

Fig. 5.18   Tool crate.

Six

Making a Pole-lathe: Introduction to its Use

By now you should know the theory and be itching to try it out in practice. To start with, I suggest that you make a pole-lathe (see Fig. 6.1). This is a fairly straightforward carpentry project which bridges the gap between working with seasoned wood and green woodwork. In fact, a pole-lathe is not essential for working with green wood. Indeed, only a few traditional crafts – notably bowl-turning and chair-bodging – relied on them, and one can even make perfectly good country chairs without a lathe. But for me, using a pole-lathe is a pleasure in itself. In my youth I experienced the thrill of activities such as sailing and ski-ing. I have found great satisfaction in photography and walking in the hills, and more recently I have taken up the meditative martial art of Tai Chi. But somehow the delight of rhythmically treadling away behind a pole-lathe on a clear spring day, removing ribbons of fresh cherry to reveal yet another unique chair-leg, combines all the pleasures of my other hobbies into one.

The pole-lathe is an ancestor of the modern electric lathe used by many woodworkers for shaping cylindrical objects such as chair-legs and bowls. It consists of a 'bed' which holds two uprights into which are fixed two metal points. The workpiece spins between these points with a cord wrapped several times around it. This is where the pole comes in. One end of the cord is tied above the lathe to a springy pole, the other end is tied below to the treadle. The turner pushes down on the treadle, cutting the wood with a chisel as it rotates towards him. When he relaxes his leg, the pole pulls the cord back up, rotating the piece of wood backwards and lifting up the treadle along with the turner's foot, ready to start again.

This sounds feasible. However, the turner not only has to think about holding the chisel correctly (difficult enough in itself!), but must simul-

taneously pump up and down with his foot. On top of that, the piece of wood is spending half its time going backwards. It can't be very efficient!

At least that's what I concluded when I read about it in Herbert Edlin's *Woodland Crafts in Britain* while I was studying tree surgery. However, I thought it might be fun to try it out on bits of amputated tree. I was given a beginner's set of turning tools and soon discovered just how effective a pole-lathe can be.

After several decades of being a museum piece, the pole-lathe has recently made a comeback. In fact, it has many advantages over its powered relations:

1 It can be set up without requiring an electricity supply – e.g. in a garden, field or the woods.

2 Being powered by the operator, it has an instantaneous on/off control which makes it very quick to stop and easy to see how the work is progressing. This is also an excellent safety aspect making it ideal for teaching.

3 It has an infinitely variable speed from 0 to as much as 2000 rpm. It changes gear automatically, increasing the rpm as the diameter of the workpiece decreases.

4 When working green wood properly, there are no splinters or dust, thus making masks and goggles unnecessary.

5 It is simple and comparatively cheap to build and makes a pleasant project for parents to carry out with their children (my 10-year-old daughter has now been using a lathe for half her life).

6 It keeps the operator warm, which saves on heating the workshop!

Fig. 6.1 An indoor pole-lathe.

There are no two identical pole-lathes. Different versions of traditional pole-lathes are illustrated in several books on woodland crafts, but very rarely have detailed plans for its construction been written down. It is a very personal machine and one that plays a central role in my work. I have always advised people to try out a variety of pole-lathes and then make their own, drawing on the elements they preferred from my lathes and adding personal touches.

However, I was finally tempted to describe how to make a pole-lathe for an article in the magazine *Woodworking International* (February 1989), and now run courses where people make their own lathes. My early lathes were hacked out from logs with a chain-saw and erected in the woods using a long ash pole.

I now accept that for most people it is more convenient to use planked and seasoned wood and to substitute elastic cord instead of the springy pole. This enables the green woodworker to set up his pole-lathe in an area 5 ft square be it in a back room, a garden, a craft fair or a woodland.

The pole-lathe described in this chapter does in fact use two poles, but the spring is provided by the 'bungy' cord. It is a lightweight lathe designed mainly for spindle turning (e.g. chair-legs and tool handles). I shall also describe how it can be used with a springy pole, and in Chapter 16 there are details of a variation which is better suited for turning bowls. Do not forget, though, that it is easy to adapt these plans to make use of whatever wood you are able to lay your hands on.

Making a Pole-lathe

Requirements:

Seasoned hardwood (beech or ash)

3 ft (90 cm) length 5 × 2" (13 × 5 cm) section

8–10 ft (2·5–3 m) length 5 × 1½" (13 × 4 cm) section

2 ft (60 cm) length 5 × ⅞" (13 × 2·2 cm) section

3–4 ft (90 cm–1·2 m) length 2 × 2" (5 × 5 cm) section

Seasoned softwood

20 ft (6 m) length 3 × 2" (8 × 2·5 cm) section

20 ft (6 m) length 1½ × 1" (4 × 2·5 cm) section

Any plank 1" (2·5 cm) or more thick 18 × 10" (45 × 25 cm) or larger

Two poles 8 ft (2·5 m) long, 1½–2½" (4–6 cm) diameter

Other materials

18" (45 cm) length of ½" (1·2 cm) threaded bar

6 m (20 ft) length of 3–4 mm (⅛") nylon cord

2 m (6 ft) length of 6 mm (¼") elastic shock-cord

two strips of leather 6 × 1" (15 × 2·5 cm)

one 5½" (140 mm) long coach bolt 10 mm (⅜") diameter

four 5½" (140 mm) long coach bolts 8 mm (³/₁₆") diameter

The bed of the lathe consists of two 5 × 1½" (13 × 4 cm) beams (preferably beech or some other hardwood) fixed to either side of a pair of uprights 4–5 ft (125–150 cm) in length (Fig. 6.2). A 4-ft (125 cm) bed will enable you to turn items up to 30" (75 cm) in length, which will be fine for the majority of projects. If you want to turn long handles or the back legs for post-and-rung chairs, then you will need a 5 ft (150 cm) bed.

After making most of my lathes quite low, I now find it most comfortable if I can lift my leg underneath the bed; a 40" (1 metre) clearance between the bed and the ground is just right. Those who have operated a powered lathe may find this a peculiar height, but after a while you will probably learn to appreciate the ability to have a close-up view of the work. If you are likely to be working with children, it is a good idea to have a second setting lower down.

Traditionally the uprights, or legs, of the lathe would simply be the stumps of two trees cut about 4 ft (125 cm) high. If you are able to work in a woodland, you might find such an arrangement is possible. However, for most of you this will not be feasible, so you will need to make a pair of uprights; this will also enable you to move the lathe around – for example, into the sun or out of the rain – and to transport it from place to place. I used to use two inverted T-shapes for the

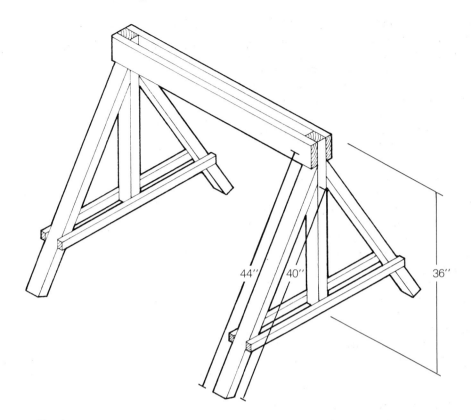

Fig. 6.2   A-frame and bed.

uprights, but now prefer a pair of A-frames which are sturdier and provide a good anchor for the poles supporting the elastic cord.

To construct the A-frames, you need 20 feet (6 m) of 3"×2" (8×5 cm) softwood to make the sloping sections and the uprights, as well as 12 feet (3·6 m) of 1½×1" (4×2·5 cm) softwood (large roofing batten is fine for this) for the horizontal bracing. Before assembling the frame, which can be either nailed or bolted, you should drill the holes for the bolts which will hold the two beams of the bed in place. I use 8 mm (5/16") coach bolts 5½" (14 cm) long and drill 10 mm (3/8") holes. This allows for a slight inaccuracy when aligning the positions of the holes. The frame can then be nailed together as shown, using 4" (10 cm) nails at the top of the frame and 2" (5 cm) nails for attaching the bracing. If you wish to be able to dismantle the A-frames, then you should use bolts here too. You can now bolt together the A-frames and the bed.

On to the bed you then attach two poppets so that these can be slid along to cater for different lengths of work. The poppets (see Fig. 6.3) are

Fig. 6.3   A poppet.

57

two short uprights into which are fixed the two metal points which will hold the wood to be turned.

On a traditional bowl-turning lathe, one of the poppets was often incorporated into one of the uprights that support the beam. You could adopt this approach, but I find two adjustable poppets more versatile.

These poppets are made out of two 18" (45 cm) lengths of 5×2" (13×5 cm) hardwood. The wood to be used here is important; I suggest beech or ash, for reasons which will be explained later. Ideally, the 2" (5 cm) dimension of the poppets should be a few millimetres less than the 2" (5 cm) of the softwood frame, to enable the poppets to slide freely along the bed. If the softwood is left with a sawn finish and the wood for the poppets is planed, that should give you the right sizes.

Next take a piece of 5 × ⅞" (13 × 2·2 cm) hardwood, 2 feet (60 cm) long, and cut it as shown in Fig. 6.4. Take the parts marked **a** and plane the sloping edge to a semi-circle (Fig. 6.5). These will be used as mortise keys to wedge the poppet tightly on to the bed. Take one poppet and mark the position of the bed on to the wider face with 4" (10 cm) below the bed and 9" (23 cm) above it. Now remove the poppet and ¼" (6 mm) above the bottom line, drill a hole of ⅞" (22 mm) diameter at right-angles to that face. A second hole with centre 1½" (4 cm) below the line should be drilled, sloping upwards at the same angle as the sloping edge of the key. I have used ⅞" (22 mm) wood to fit the ⅞" (22 mm) drill bit; you could of course use 1" (25 mm) if you prefer (Fig. 6.6). Clean out the wood between these two holes; that is the slot for the key. Try it out to make sure the key fits smoothly. On the two narrow faces, cut two recesses for pieces **b** and **c** as shown. Screw **b** and **c** into place, making sure that their bottom edges are parallel to avoid the poppet rocking in use. Now repeat this for the second poppet, only putting **b** and **c** the other way round so that both **b** pieces will face each other when the poppets are in place.

The tool rest is best made from a length of 2×2" (5×5 cm) hardwood 1 ft (30 cm) shorter than the length of the bed. You will need to saw it lengthways as shown in Fig. 6.7, and this undoubtedly requires the use of either a bandsaw or

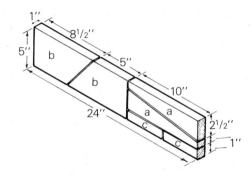

Fig. 6.4   Cutting parts for the poppets.

Fig. 6.5   A key.

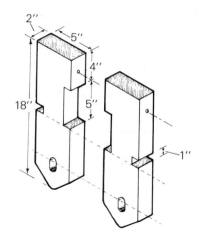

Fig. 6.6   Cutting the poppets.

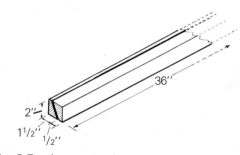

Fig. 6.7   A sawn tool rest.

a circular saw with tilting beds. This will give you one long tool rest; the other half can be cut to produce two shorter ones. The top edge should now be rounded off with a plane or a spokeshave. If you don't have access to the appropriate machinery, then take a length of 2×1½" (5×4 cm) and plane it down to a similar shape.

The tool rest now sits on the two tool-rest supports (b). It is useful to loosely attach the tool rest to one poppet so as to stop it sliding around. For work over 2" (5 cm) diameter, you will also need to put in some spacers between the tool-rest and the poppets. You can probably leave this job until you have tried out the lathe, then you will be able to turn your own wooden pins for the job which can be located into holes in the top surface of the tool-rest supports.

You will now need two lengths of iron to make the 'centres' to hold the workpiece as it revolves. This is the only part where you may require the expertise of a blacksmith or someone else with welding equipment. One of the centres should be adjustable, so you need a length of threaded bar or studding. In Britain nowadays most studding is sold in metric lengths. I use an 8" (20 cm) length of 12 mm studding welded to a bent iron bar as in Fig. 6.8. To avoid welding, you can simply bend

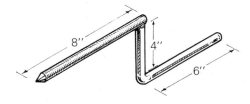

Fig. 6.8   A threaded crank.

an 18" (45 cm) length of studding to the same shape. Grind or file a point as smoothly and evenly as possible to the end of the threaded section; if this point is rough, it will tend to drill into the workpiece when the lathe is in action.

Now drill a horizontal hole through the centre of the narrow face of the right-hand poppet (if you are right-handed), level with the top of the tool rest. This should be 2 mm less than the diameter of the crank (i.e. a 10 mm hole for 12 mm studding). If you do not have metric auger bits, you should use a ⅜" bit for 12 mm studding

which will give you a tight fit. If you use imperial ½" studding then a ⁷/₁₆" hole is better. Take care that this hole runs exactly parallel with the lathe bed. As you can see, the height of the rest cannot be adjusted, so its position in relation to the centres has to be a compromise. You may prefer to make the centres rather higher or lower than I suggest.

Screw the crank into this hole, removing it and waxing it frequently. I once made the mistake of using a beautiful lump of oak for the poppets and it soon started corroding the crank, resulting in a loose fit. I also found that sycamore wears too quickly. I have not tried softwoods, but I doubt they would last. As stated earlier, I have had most success with beech and ash poppets. The crank will be stiff at first, but should ease as you use it; it will also be affected by atmospheric humidity.

The other centre need not be adjustable. For this you can use a ⅜" (10 mm) coach bolt 5½" (14 cm) long, ground to a smooth point at its end. When you grind the point, make sure that the nut is screwed on to the bolt. Removing it will be difficult, but this will clean the thread and enable you to replace the nut later. The bolt can then be knocked through a ⅜" (10 mm) hole in the other poppet in a position matching the cranked centre; you can fix it tightly with the nut.

Next round off all sharp edges and protruding corners and coat the whole lathe with linseed oil. You may find that in use the corners of the tool-rest supports get in the way and you might wish to trim them off. It is quite liberating to realise that you are able to saw corners off your machinery!

Now the main body of the lathe is complete and the next stage is the treadle. Again there are several different ways of tackling this. Basically you want some form of structure hinged at ground level on to which you can comfortably place your foot. Another A-frame is a good solution and I suggest you make this approximately 4 ft (1·2 m) long with the foot-rest about ¼–⅓ of the way up it. This will give you plenty of movement at the end of the treadle (and thus plenty of revolutions) without having to lift your foot more than about 15" (40 cm) up and down. When carrying out heavy work (such as bowls) you will need to adapt the treadle to obtain more leverage (but fewer revolutions). This frame can be made

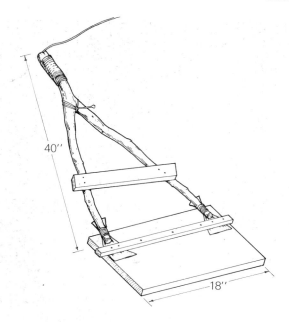

40"

18"

Fig. 6.9   A forked treadle.

out of lengths of straight-grained 1½×1"
(4×2·5 cm) softwood nailed, screwed or lashed
together, or by using a natural fork as illustrated
(see Fig. 6.9).

The frame should now be hinged to a base on
which you will stand while operating the lathe.
The simplest form of hinge is obtained by using
two strips of leather 6" (15 cm) long and 1½"
(4 cm) wide which can be cut from a pair of old
boots. The base should be at least 18×10"
(45×25 cm) and an inch (2·5 cm) or more thick.
Place the bottom of the treadle on the edge of the
base board, mark the line of the hinge and saw
the ends of the A in a straight line.

Fig. 6.10   Fixing the treadle hinge.

Turn the treadle upside down and place the
leather strips on to the end 3" of the treadle arms.
Cut two small pieces of thin plywood and nail
them down to hold the leather strips in place,
then lash them tightly. Turn the treadle the right
way up and place it just resting on the edge of the
base board. Using either more plywood or
another softwood strip, clamp the loose ends of
the leather to the board, having first shaved back
the leading edge of this clamping strip to allow
the treadle to pivot up and down (see Fig. 6.10).
So long as the leather is oiled occasionally, it will
last for several years. You could use metal hinges
or hooks and eyes instead. If you use a natural
fork for the treadle, this can be fixed as in Fig. 6.9.

At this stage you will need to find your pole or
poles. If you use the elastic cord method, you will
require two straight poles each about 8' (2·5 m)
long and 1–2" (2·5–5 cm) in diameter. Since the
spring is provided mainly by the cord, the type of
wood used is not important. As mentioned in
Chapter 4, do not be tempted to cut down the first
sapling you find; look for an overgrown hedge or
a crowded thicket and ask the owner for your
poles before cutting them. You might also find a
suitable fork for the treadle and a straight stick
1½–2" (4–5 cm) in diameter for your first piece
of turning.

You now need two types of cord. For the
spring, a piece of ¼" (6 mm) shock-cord 2 ft
(60 cm) longer than the lathe bed (to allow for
tying knots) is best. This can be purchased from
specialist rope suppliers or ships' chandlers.
Alternatively, two roof-rack 'bungies' or even a
bicycle inner tube could be used. The second cord
is to run from the treadle around the workpiece
and up to the spring. Traditionally a leather
thong, hemp rope or catgut was used for this, but
I find ⅛" (3 mm) nylon cord ideal for the job.
Take about 20 ft (5 m) of this cord, tie one end to
the shorter arm of the treadle, then wind it
around the longer arm and run it through a slot
cut into the very end of this arm. Thus when a
section of the cord eventually frays, you can
remove the frayed end and unwrap some fresh
cord from around the treadle.

Form a loop in the other end of this cord
through which you pass the elastic shock-cord.
Now tie the shock-cord to the tops of the two
poles so that when it is not stretched, the distance

Fig. 6.11 A pole-lathe in the woods.

between the poles is equal to the length of the bed. Place the bottom of one pole between the two cross supports on one of the lathe uprights next to the vertical section; then spring the other pole into a similar position at the other end of the lathe. Place the treadle between the uprights with the base to the operator's side of the lathe and the 3 mm cord running up to the shock-cord on the side away from the operator. You may need to lash the poles into place on the A-frames (see Fig. 6.1).

The lathe I have described should enable anyone to use a pole-lathe in virtually any situation. However, if you have the space and are able to obtain a suitable pole, then I suggest you try a 'real' pole-lathe, as in Fig 6.11. The 'correct' pole is a subject of much debate among green woodworkers. To my mind the ideal is a straight coppice-grown ash (grown from the stump of a felled tree with no large side branches). It should be 15–20 ft (4·5–5 m) long and 2½" (6 cm) diameter at the base, tapering to 1¼" (3 mm) at the top. Having said which, I have heard practised pole-lathe turners recommend larch, alder, willow, birch and beech, so if you can't find ash it is not the end of the world. You may get on well enough with a crooked 10 ft (3 m) beech pole.

Traditionally, the base of the pole would be fixed outside the bodger's hut, resting on a horizontal rail with the thin end hovering over the lathe to receive the cord attached to the treadle. If you are going to work in the woods or in a garden shed, then this is a good method to use.

The base of the pole is fixed either at ground level or to a post up to 4 ft (1·2 m) high. A good tight lashing should do, but it could be slotted and pegged, or even wedged. It will have to with-stand considerable forces, so anchor it well.

Should you intend to set up your lathe in the open, then the pole can be supported somewhere near the middle on a simple prop made by locking or pegging two short poles together, or by making use of a natural fork (Fig. 6.12). You may find that this support has to stand on a hard surface or a precious lawn, in which case you can make a

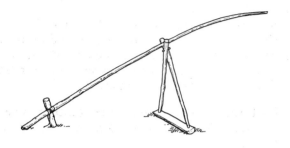

Fig. 6.12 Supporting the pole.

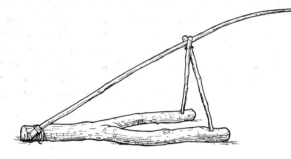

Fig. 6.13 An alternative pole support.

wooden base as shown (Fig. 6.13). If, when in action, the pole feels rather weak and with little spring, then either make it shorter or support it nearer the thin end. If it is hard work to bend the pole, then move the support nearer to the base.

Another spring mechanism involves a horizontal bow suspended above the lathe. Having tried this a few times with a short, slender ash pole, but with little success, I had concluded that it was a clever but impractical idea until I saw a photograph of it in one of Roy Underhill's books. It is based on an eighteenth-century French design which utilises the techniques of the bowyer. One method is to assemble the bow from a number of slender strips to create a form of leaf spring. The other method is to cleave the bow from a 5" (13 cm) diameter log with the sap-wood to the outside of the bow and the heart-wood to the inside. To add to its efficiency, a whirling flywheel can be incorporated on the string of the bow. An amazing device, but personally if I cannot use a long ash pole I think I'll stick to the shock-cord!

Of course, the simplest method of all is to make use of a hanging branch and set the lathe up beneath the tree. Given the right branch, this works well although it takes a while to get used to the different feel. Whatever form the spring takes, set up the lathe so that the driving cord is always moving in a vertical plane at right-angles to the line of the lathe bed (Fig. 6.14). This will help to prevent the cord tangling up in itself as it runs around the workpiece.

It is also important, if using the springy pole, that its tip should never project over the lathe

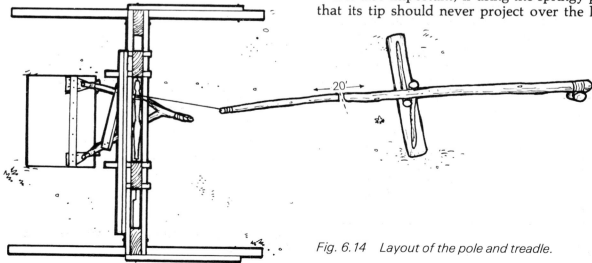

Fig. 6.14 Layout of the pole and treadle.

bed, or you will feel the power of your new machine when the pole hits you on the head. (You now know why I am usually seen wearing a woolly hat!)

You may wish to erect a support of some kind to lean against while working. For heavy work such as bowl turning, this will be a significant help, but for lighter work such as chair-legs it is more of a luxury. One option is to position the lathe so that you can lean against a wall or a work-bench.

When demonstrating the pole-lathe, I often notice somebody watching who is obviously deep in thought. Later he might come up to me – I've yet to have a woman suggest this – and go into great detail as to how I could convert it to continuous motion. This must be how the treadle lathe was invented, and indeed I have one in the woods myself. But for spindle turning, a treadle lathe (or a powered lathe even more so) loses that sensitivity and instant responsiveness which is peculiar to the pole-lathe. My treadle lathe has long since been converted to operate a grindstone.

The Measuring Gauge

One accessory which you will find very useful is the measuring gauge (Fig. 6.15). This can be made from any flat piece of wood, drilling along it a set of holes of the sizes you are likely to use for joints (start with 1¼, ⅞, ⅝, ½, ⅜″ (32, 22, 16, 13, 10 mm respectively), but you may well add others as you need them). Cut away some wood so as to create a U-shape at each hole. I find it useful to cut this U with a slight taper because when shaping a round tenon on a piece of green wood, you will have to leave some extra to allow for shrinkage. If the width of the mouth of the U is 15–20 per cent more than the actual hole drilled, that will give you the size to turn the wood when it is green.

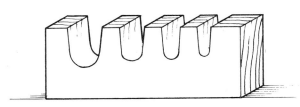

Fig. 6.15   The measuring gauge.

The Lathe in Action

I am sure you are now dying to try out your new lathe. If you already have a standard set of turning tools, you could certainly make use of some of them on the pole-lathe. One tool you will not need, however, is a scraper. Remember, you are the only source of power and there is no point – and certainly no satisfaction – in scraping away at a piece of green wood and turning it into a fluffy pulp.

There are three general rules of spindle-turning which apply whether you use a powered lathe, a treadle lathe or a pole-lathe. The only difference is that on a pole-lathe your muscles will soon let you know if you are working inefficiently.

1   **Rest the bevel on the wood (except when cutting with the long point of the skew)** (Fig. 6.16).

By holding the tool with the bevel at a tangent to the wood it will be cutting at its finest angle, thus removing the wood most efficiently and in the process polishing it and leaving a smooth surface. In other words, the difference between peeling a potato and scraping it! The only exception to this is when carrying out deep cuts with the long point of the skew (see p. 68).

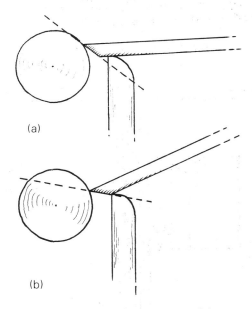

Fig. 6.16   Rest the bevel on the wood (a) correct (b) incorrect.

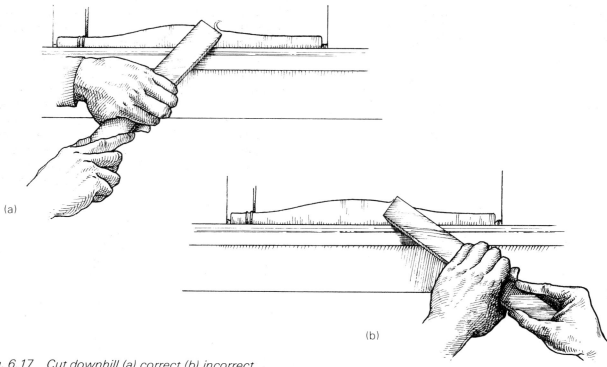

Fig. 6.17   Cut downhill (a) correct (b) incorrect.

2   **Cut downhill (i.e. from thick to thin)**
(Fig. 6.17).

In spindle-turning, the fibres of the workpiece run along its length. If you cut the wood
from a thin section to a thick section, the tool
will be lifting the fibres away from the workpiece and will leave a ragged edge (Fig. 6.18).

By cutting from thick to thin (downhill),
the fibres are forced down into the wood and
will be cut cleanly (Fig. 6.19).

If you are not convinced, try folding over
the pages of a phone book and rubbing your
thumb across them in both directions to feel
the difference (Fig. 6.20).

3   **Keep the tool rest as close to the workpiece as
possible** (Fig. 6.21).

The delicate control required for accurate
work comes from holding the tool precisely.
The nearer the tool rest is to the cutting edge,
the greater the leverage at the handle to resist
the force of the wood against the blade.

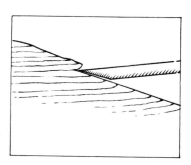

Fig. 6.18   Tearing the fibres.

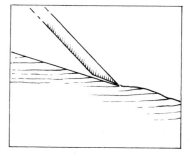

Fig. 6.19   Cutting down on to the fibres.

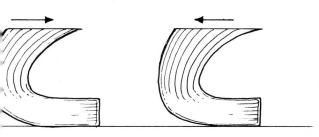

Fig. 6.20   Trying it on a phone book.

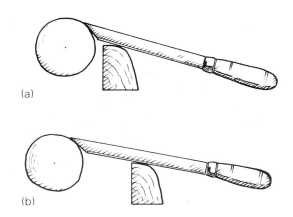

(a)

(b)

Fig. 6.21   Keep the tool rest close to the work (a) correct (b) incorrect.

horse – these will be revealed later. In making this pin, you will have scope to practise with the four main turning tools and with any luck will have something useful at the end of it.

Take a straight freshly-cut stick 1½–2" (4–5 cm) diameter and cut it to 14" (35 cm) in length. You will see at each end the soft area of pith in the centre which was formed when it was a twig in its first year of growth (see Fig. 6.22). Place a drop of thick oil on this point at each end to act as a lubricant when it spins on the lathe.

Fix the poppets of the lathe so that the two metal centres are 14" (35 cm) apart. Take the lathe

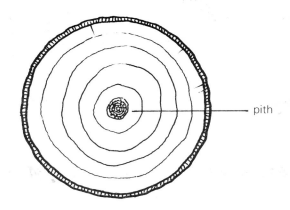

pith

Fig. 6.22   Pith centre of roundwood.

On a powered lathe the inexhaustible electricity supply, the heavier tools and the use of sandpaper make it quite easy to ignore these rules. Using green wood on a pole-lathe your tired limbs, rattling tools and 'furry' surfaces will force you to learn it properly. Once the techniques have been mastered, however, the sensitive control, delicate tools and silken finish will signify a skill which can then easily be transferred on to a powered lathe (although by that time probably you will see no point in deserting the pole-lathe!).

It doesn't really matter what you make first on your pole-lathe. You may well just want to practise away with no specific aim in mind. However, it can help if you have a particular shape to aim for, even if at first you don't achieve it. A good project is to make the pivot pin for a shaving-horse (Chapter 8). At this stage, you don't really need to work out the details of the rest of the

string and hold it between yourself and the piece of wood to be worked on. Now wrap the string twice around the workpiece, which you then mount on to the lathe with the metal centres going into the pith. Wind up the crank so that the workpiece rotates freely, but does not rattle.

Depress the treadle and release it several times. This will cause the centres to wear into the workpiece, so tighten the crank to take up the slack. When it is running freely, put the tool rest in position. Place the roughing-out gouge on the tool rest, holding the handle with your right hand if you are right-handed or with your left if you are left-handed. Rest the ball of your other hand (the soft part between little finger and wrist) on the tool rest, lightly gripping the metal part of the gouge with your fingers (see Fig. 6.23).

Before bringing the gouge up against the workpiece, just get the feel of the rhythm. I tend to support myself slightly with my hand on the tool

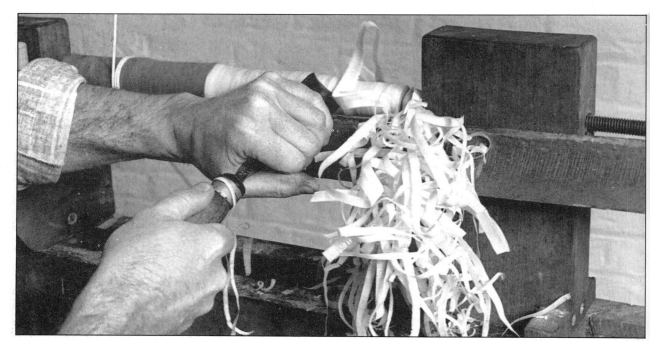

Fig. 6.23   Holding the roughing-out gouge.

rest while balancing on my right leg and treadling with the left foot; this is not as awkward as it may sound.

The length of the treadle and the springiness of the spring or pole will give you the rate at which to treadle – between one and two beats a second. (Try to tune it to your heartbeat to gain the full therapeutic effects.) When the foot comes down, the tool cuts; when the leg relaxes, the spring should lift both the treadle and your leg back up; the workpiece then reverses and you must

remove the tool a fraction. It is much easier to work when the workpiece is rotating evenly, so it helps if the piece of wood you are turning is as straight and even as possible.

Make the first cut about 1 inch (2·5 cm) in from the end furthest from the string, holding the gouge at a tilt as shown in Fig. 6.23. By looking at the silhouette of the workpiece, you can see when you have cut it down to a complete cylinder which has no part of its surface uncut (Fig. 6.24).

Work back in 1" (2·5 cm) steps to about two-thirds of the way along the workpiece, taking care to keep the blade away from the cord. Now measure the diameter with the measuring gauge

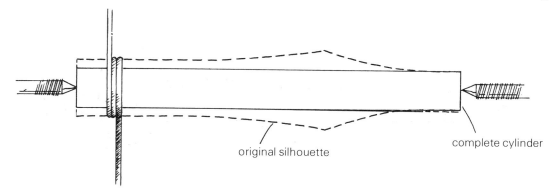

original silhouette

complete cylinder

Fig. 6.24   Silhouette of the workpiece.

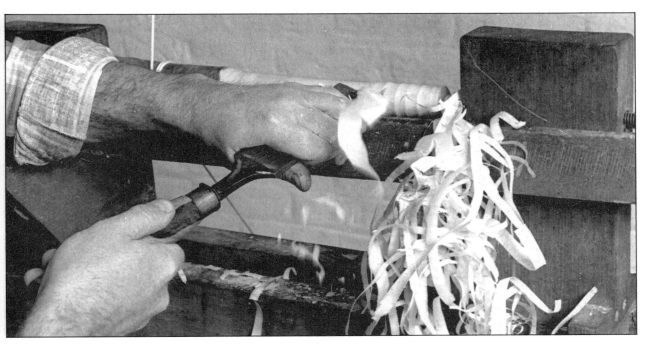

Fig. 6.25 Holding the square chisel.

and rough out to between 1" and 1¼" (2·5–3 cm).

Take the square chisel and, *holding it at a skew to the workpiece with the bevel down* (Fig. 6.25), turn this section down to ⅞" (22 mm). With the chisel, make the cut in one steady sweep from the centre towards the end, rather than in steps as with the roughing-out gouge. Keep the top point of the blade well clear of the workpiece. Sooner or later this point will bite into the wood, taking a chunk out of the smooth finish you have just worked so hard to achieve. This is certainly annoying, but not such a disaster as it might be when operating a powered lathe. A pole-lathe cuts out immediately, thus avoiding hurling the chisel into the distance. When this section is down to size, just put a slight taper on the end.

Depending on how you have set up your lathe, you now need either to turn the workpiece around between the poppets or to move the string to the other end. I prefer to turn the workpiece rather than to move the treadle and the pole. Rough out from the smooth section backwards, stopping an inch or so from the end. This last section should now be turned to a ball shape to form a knob. To do this, take the small gouge and

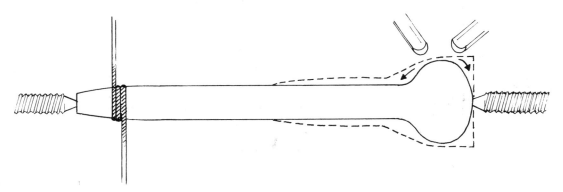

Fig. 6.26 Turning the knob with the small gouge.

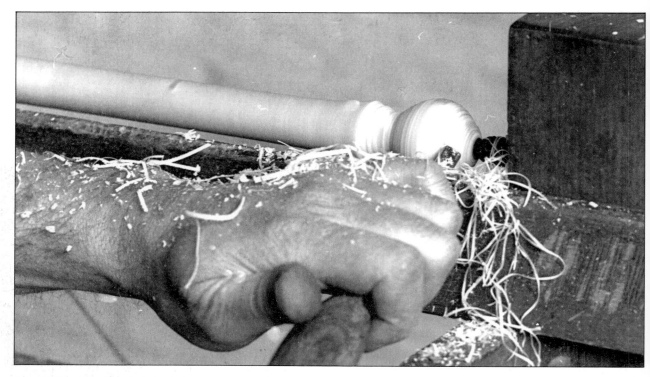

Fig. 6.27   Small gouge in action.

roll it from the high point of the knob first down
one side and then the other (Figs. 6.26, 6.27).

If you want to practise with the skew chisel,
you could use it now to run over the knob, going
over the cuts made by the small gouge. Much the
same applies to the skew chisel as to the square
chisel, except that it is already positioned skew to
the workpiece (Fig. 6.28). When carrying out a
cut steeper than 45 degrees, I suggest you use the
sharp point rather than the blade. This is where
you should depart from the rule of rubbing the
bevel on the workpiece; in this instance you are
using just the tip of the blade, more like the tooth
of a saw than the blade of a chisel. If you allow
the actual blade of the chisel to come in contact
with the wood, there is a distinct danger of it
biting in and spiralling right through the ball.
This is probably the most tricky operation in
spindle-turning, so if it doesn't work straight
away take a rest and try again another time. You
can then clean up the rest of the pin, working
with the flat chisel towards the base of the knob.

This completes your first project on the pole-
lathe. It will be nothing like perfect, so perhaps

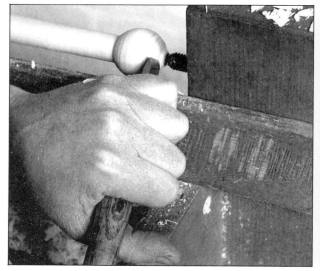

Fig. 6.28   Skew chisel in action.

you should make a few more attempts. When
you have made a pin with which you are happy,
put it to one side to dry out and shrink. It will be
going into a ⅞" (22 mm) hole and needs to be a
loose fit, so after a few days in the warm it should
be just right.

Seven

Making Use of Round Wood

One reason for starting off the practical projects with the pole-lathe is that it is a good way for the conventional woodworker or do-it-yourselfer to begin working with green wood without completely losing touch with the tools and materials to which they are accustomed. On the other hand, you might be coming to green woodwork as I did, more from the woodland side of things, being involved in tree surgery, woodland management or conservation. If so, you will feel more at home with this chapter. Of course you may be neither a woodworker nor a tree-worker, in which case it will *all* be exciting to you!

If you own your own woodland or have been given free rein in someone else's wood, then you will be felling some trees yourself. As mentioned earlier, most woodlands have been managed at some time in their history, and if this management suddenly ceases the state of the wood deteriorates. So even if you don't want to make use of the timber you should be felling some of the trees in order to thin them out. This is where you will be faced with a dilemma. Should you select the trees with straight unbranched trunks which are ideal for green woodwork, or should you use the spindly, crooked, branched ones and leave the better trees to grow on into valuable timber?

There is no easy answer and you will have to decide your own priorities and make the necessary compromises. Where two good trees are growing close together, then you could choose one of them. Another tree might produce many branches quite low down the trunk, but have a short clear length at the bottom. From the point of view of the potential timber, there would be little to gain in letting such a tree grow on, so you could fell it and make use of the trunk and possibly some of the branches. There are several good books on woodland management available, or

Fig. 7.1   Work-break, gluts, club and maul.

you could seek advice from your county forestry adviser (most county councils have one).

Having decided what to fell, you will need to fell it.

Felling

Felling a tree correctly can only be learned satisfactorily under the eye of an expert and requires a lot of practice to do it well. There are so many variables such as the lean of the tree, the proximity of neighbouring trees, the direction of the wind and the possibility of rot, all factors which can affect your approach. My advice is to go along on a tree-felling task with a conservation group or, better still, to attend a specialist course in tree felling.

With that word of warning, you should be able to tackle trees up to 8" (20 cm) diameter using

69

hand tools without too much danger, but do go with someone else who can give you a hand. This, then, is the theory:

First, decide the intended direction of the fell (usually determined by the lean of the tree), then establish your 'safe' areas accordingly (Fig. 7.2).

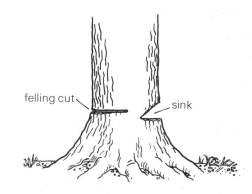

Fig. 7.3   Felling cuts.

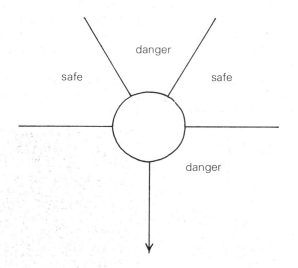

Fig. 7.2   Safe areas when felling.

It is obvious that in front of the tree is unsafe, but danger directly behind it may not be so apparent. Sometimes, if the tree is leaning heavily, it can split up the middle and the back portion can fly out with alarming speed (believe me!).

Start work by removing the 'sink' or 'bird's mouth', usually as low as possible. This is a wedge of wood cut from the side of the tree on which it is intended to fall. Use the large bow-saw for this job and, if you have one, a felling axe. If you are using the saw only, start with the angled cut first; it is easier with two people, one at each end.

Cut until you are ¼–⅓ of the way through, then saw the horizontal so that it meets the first cut in a straight line. Those of you who are skilled with a felling axe will already know how to remove the sink without a saw. If you have a felling axe but have not had much practice, you could first cut the horizontal with the saw and then remove the sink with the axe. You will need a sharp blade and it can be very dangerous, so

take care of yourself and whoever is standing nearby.

The felling cut (see Fig. 7.3) should be made on the opposite side of the trunk at least an inch or so above the first horizontal cut, which will help to prevent the trunk kicking backwards as it falls. Continue this cut until about 1" (2·5 cm) short of the 'bird's mouth'. The uncut portion of wood then acts as a hinge and the tree should fall just where you want it. If, as is likely, the tree becomes caught up in its neighbours, then you will have to lever it back with a log until it is free; this can be back-breaking work. There is a tool called a breaking bar/turning hook which you can use to lever the tree over, and also to roll it round if it becomes caught up. This is worth having if you intend to do much felling.

If the tree seems not to want to fall, you can drive your steel wedges into the kerf (the saw-cut) after removing the saw blade. If the blade is jammed, you will have to try to wedge the cut open and pull the blade out after disconnecting one end from the bow. As I said, it is best to have some expert guidance!

It is more likely that you will start out by obtaining your green wood ready felled – most probably in log form. Should you not be used to woodland work this is doubtless as well, saving you both the worry of deciding which tree to fell and the effort involved in felling it. The next step is to decide what you are going to make out of it. If you select the tree standing, it is worth knowing beforehand what use it will be put to. Here then is a list of green wood projects that will get you under way (see Fig. 7.1):

70

1   a chopping-block

2   a club

3   a pair of gluts

4   a maul

5   a work-break

Some of these items will be in constant use, others just used for a particular process, but they are all simply made and provide a good opportunity to get the feel of green woodwork. Some are better made of one type of wood; others are better made from another, while some are best made from a combination. I will outline the options as we go along, but bear in mind that you should not be put off if you have only a limited choice. At this stage, it is important to try various options and learn for yourself. As time goes on, you will discover things not mentioned in this or any other book and your contacts will widen, opening up the possibility of new knowledge, new tools and new woods.

1   Chopping-block (see Fig. 9.4)

If you have just felled your tree, go to the butt end and square it up with the large bow-saw. A useful height for a chopping-block is about 30" (75 cm); if your tree was less than 12" (30 cm) in diameter, you will need to anchor your block by partly burying it in the ground, so allow an extra 6" (15 cm) in length, sawing it square across 3 ft (90 cm) from the end. Partly bury it in a convenient place and there is your chopping-block. It is good to assemble a few blocks of various sizes for different jobs.

When using ready-cut logs, choose a couple – ideally up to 18" (45 cm) in diameter – and try to get someone with a chain-saw (or a two-man cross-cut) to cut one to 30" (75 cm) and the other to 15" (38 cm) long.

Another option open to you if you can find a section in the tree where three branches emerge from one point is to use this to form a three-legged block.

Beech is a very good, hard wood for a chopping-block, and elm will make a block that will never split. Failing these, you can use any other wood available.

2   Club

The following description is based on a club I was given by an old craftsman who was cleaving chestnut for paling fencing. Take a log about 14" (35 cm) long and 5–6" (12–15 cm) in diameter; 6" (15 cm) from one end, saw all the way around the log to about 2" (5 cm) deep. Then using an axe, split away this outer ring to leave a core about 2" (5 cm) in diameter. This is the handle of the club. Shape it with the axe until it fits the hand comfortably, and you now have a very useful tool (Fig. 7.4).

The wood selected for a club can be any heavy hardwood, with ash, elm, beech, hornbeam, thorn or a fruit wood preferred.

Fig. 7.4   Trimming a club handle.

3   Gluts

Gluts are simply wooden wedges which can be used instead of steel wedges to open up a split in a log once it has been started. They have the added advantage that if you need to sever the fibres with an axe, it will not blunt if it hits a wooden glut.

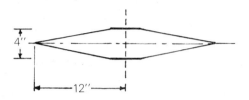

Fig. 7.5 *Taking a pair of gluts from the log.*

(To see this in action, see Chapter 8, The Shaving-horse.)

To make a pair of gluts, find a straight-grained length of wood 3–4" (8–10 cm) in diameter and about 2 ft (60 cm) long. A hard wood is necessary here, so look for hornbeam, beech, yew, thorn, apple, pear or even rhododendron. Use the side axe and the chopping-block to taper each end down to a wedge shape as shown, leaving the central section round (Fig. 7.5).

Saw this squarely in half to give you two gluts. Chamfer off the edge of the top face and the

Fig. 7.6 *Chamfering the corners.*

corners on the sharp end (see Fig. 7.6), so as to prevent undue fraying. Ideally, leave these to dry out slowly for as long as possible. If you are in a hurry to use them, make a spare pair and use the first ones as firewood once they wear out.

4 Maul

This is an important tool used mainly for driving the wedges into a log when cleaving it. It can also be used for hitting the cleaving axe, and at any other time when something needs hitting hard. If you have a sledgehammer you could use that instead, but personally I dislike them. Metal hitting on metal makes a jarring noise, and will also occasionally cause splinters of steel to fly off. Not only is this dangerous, but with time it will cause the tops of the wedges to fold over, making them more awkward to use.

Another problem for the beginner is that the head of a sledgehammer is only a few inches across and it is easy to miss the target. A wooden maul avoids all these problems while providing the satisfaction of using an item of home-made equipment.

Start with the handle. I would recommend a straight pole (preferably ash) with as few knots as possible. It should be just over 1½" (4 cm) in diameter and about 40" (1 m) long. As an alternative, you could use a length of wych elm or a straight hawthorn, hazel or even yew stick. If you intend to use your maul straight away, then you must be prepared for the handle to shrink and come loose before long, so you could make a spare one at the same time and let it season before fitting. Once you have set up your workshop, I suggest that you make a new handle out of cleft ash (see Chapter 9), but in the meantime this should get you under way.

The handle will be fitted into a hole drilled into the head; if you have a 1½" (37 mm) auger, use that and whittle the handle down to size. If you intend to use the brace and a 1¼" (32 mm) bit, then whittle the handle to 1¼" (32 mm); but any smaller and the handle will not last long. If the handle is very straight, then you could try turning the end down, using the pole-lathe if this is at hand.

To make the head, find a knotty piece of wood about 7" (18 cm) in diameter. English elm is ideal because of its resistance to splitting, but it does tend to become rather furred on its end grain with time. Wych elm, beech, plane, hornbeam, yew or one of the fruit woods (apple or pear) are all good alternatives.

To drill the hole it is best if the log is held firmly; even better, still attached to the fallen tree. Drill the required hole right through at right-angles to the log, taking care if the log is on the ground that the end of the drill is not blunted by driving into the soil or against a rock. If using a brace and bit, you will probably find that it will not go right through without your having to withdraw it regularly to clear out the wood. You will also find it very hard work – maybe take a break, but don't give up. Where the drill is too short to go right through, you can trim some wood away from the far side of the head until the hole is visible (having first withdrawn the drill!).

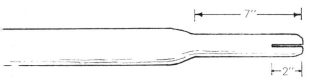

Fig. 7.7   The maul handle.

Slightly chamfer the end of the handle to help it to pass into the hole, then check to see that it will be able to fit right through. Next, using the tenon saw, cut a slot in the end of the handle 2–3" (5–8 cm) deep to enable you to drive in a wedge afterwards (Fig. 7.7).

Now you need a wedge, which ideally is made from a piece of well-seasoned cleft oak heartwood. I usually keep a supply in my airing cupboard ready for use, but if you don't yet have such material to hand then you will have to make your wedge from green wood. Sometimes large splinters of wood can be found during felling or pruning operations, and one of these could be whittled directly into a wedge. Otherwise, sort through the log pile for a straight-grained length 4" (10 cm) or more in diameter and cut it to around 6" (15 cm) long. Oak is the best for this, but it should be heartwood so an oak log would have to be considerably more than 4" (10 cm) in diameter to avoid the sapwood.

If you cannot obtain suitable oak, then try whatever wood is available that cleaves easily. Split it with the cleaving axe just as you would with a piece of firewood. We shall deal with the more precise techniques of cleaving later, but for this job simple chopping is quite adequate. When you have a sliver of wood about 1½" (40 mm) wide and ½" (13 mm) thick, whittle one end into the wedge shape as illustrated.

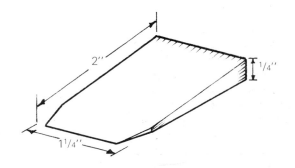

Fig. 7.8   A wedge.

The end result should be about 3" (8 cm) long and the same width as the hole in the head. It should taper from about ¼" (6 mm) to a sharp edge (see Fig. 7.8).

The thin end of the wedge should have as straight an edge as possible. It helps to shave off the leading corners in order to help it guide its way into the slot. If possible, let it dry out for a day or so.

Now drive the handle through the hole in the log, using an axe or any convenient lump of wood as a mallet and making sure the slot is at right-angles to the direction of the grain in the log. Then drive the wedge into the slot as far as it will go. If you have the slot in line with the grain, there is a chance that the wedge will force the log to split. If either the handle or the wedge are still green, leave the wedge sticking out so that it can be tightened up as the wood dries out.

Take your large saw and, holding it parallel to the handle of the maul, saw cleanly through the log about 4" (10 cm) above and then below the handle. This should liberate your maul (see Fig. 7.9). If you have a vice available, then you could saw the head out first and hold it in the vice to work on it.

Fig. 7.9 *Liberating the maul.*

and a drilling post. With apologies to Black and Decker, I shall call it a 'work-break'.

If you are setting up your workshop in the woods, I suggest you set up your work-break nearby. But if your lathe and shaving-horse are to be at home, then you might prefer to have your work-break in a corner of the garden (assuming you have one). It is easier to construct most of it out of softwood logs, as these will normally be straighter and accept nails better than hardwood logs. If you do use hardwood, you may find it better to bolt or lash all the joints.

You will need five logs:

one 6–8" (15–20 cm) diameter, 6½ ft (2 m) long

one 6–8" (15–20 cm) diameter, 5 ft (1·5 m) long

three 4–6" (10–15 cm) diameter, 5 ft (1·5 m) long.

Finally, trim any twigs or branches from your maul and round off the free end of the handle. Sooner or later this original handle will snap or come loose, but by that time you should have a fresh one made which will last much longer.

Like the Irishman's broom, I've had the same maul for seven years now – it has had three different heads and five different handles. If you think you have a good maul head, then you may like to take it to the blacksmith when it is well seasoned and ask him to put a metal ring on either end to prevent it splitting.

5   A 'Work-break'

While carrying out green woodwork projects, there are numerous occasions when you need to grip a piece of wood in order to work on it. When assembling Windsor chairs, it is best to resort to the modern bench vice or a 'work-mate'. For many other purposes, the shaving horse (see Chapter 8) is ideal. There are other times when none of these devices is satisfactory; for example, when sawing logs or cleaving long thin pieces of wood, some other aid is needed.

The craftsmen of old had many different and ingenious ways of gripping wood and one such device is called a cleaving-break. The following is a multi-purpose break which combines the cleaving-break with a saw-horse, a chopping-block

Fig. 7.10 *Cutting out the drilling post.*

Bury the two thicker logs firmly in the ground 20″ (0·5 m) deep and 4 ft (1·2 m) apart. Nail, bolt or lash one of the thinner logs horizontally between the two uprights about 3 ft (90 cm) from the ground. It will help if you flatten this log with an axe where it is fixed to the uprights. Now fix one end of another log on to this horizontal, next to the shorter upright, with the other end on the ground. The final log should now be attached to the taller upright, its top surface being level with the bottom surface of the first horizontal; its other end should be at the same height and fixed on to the sloping pole (see Fig. 7.1). This now gives you a useful cleaving-break and the shorter upright can be used as a chopping-block.

Saw horizontally half-way through the taller upright just above the higher of the cross poles. Make a series of similar cuts at 6″ (15 cm) intervals up the post and then cleave out these sections. Clean up these vertical faces, first with an axe and then with a drawknife, checking as you work that the faces are truly vertical. This now gives you a useful drilling post (Fig. 7.10).

Now drill a 1¼″ (32 mm) or 1½″ (37 mm) hole

Fig. 7.11   Sawing large logs.

Fig. 7.12   Sawing small logs.

into the sloping pole about 1 ft (30 cm) above the ground, and shape a peg to fit. This can be used to support large logs while you saw them to length (Fig. 7.11). Smaller logs can be gripped between the two cross-poles for sawing (Fig. 7.12). As with all devices in this book it is up to you to improvise and make it serve your own requirements.

Eight

The Shaving-horse

Fig. 8.1   A shaving-horse.

Now comes your first major green wood project: making a shaving-horse (Fig. 8.1). You should already have a nicely seasoned pin made on the pole-lathe, but before going any further I would like to explore the process of cleaving in more detail.

As mentioned earlier, cleaving is the process of splitting wood along the grain in a controlled manner. It is basically the same as chopping firewood, only with the intention of obtaining a section of wood of a particular size.

For large logs, you will use wedges and gluts which are driven into the wood with a maul (or a sledgehammer), usually with the log laid on the ground (see Fig 8.8). For smaller logs it is easier to stand them on end and split them with the cleaving axe (also called a cleaver) which is struck with the maul, the club or a mallet depending on the amount of force required (see Fig. 9.2). For long, thin work you should use the froe in conjunction with the cleaving-break (see Fig. 8.19).

To explain the theory of cleaving, I shall consider the example of using a cleaving axe to split out the blanks for chair-legs (known as billets) from a log about 18" (45 cm) long. The general rule of cleaving is to split in half and in half again until you get down to the right size. As the cleaver is driven into the wood, so the fibres will have to flex apart to allow it to enter the log.

Where there is an equal amount of wood on both sides of the cleaver, then the wood will open up evenly (Fig. 8.2). If there is more wood on one side than the other, then the smaller side will bend more, which often has the effect of shearing across the fibres on that side and causing the split to run off in that direction (see Fig. 8.3).

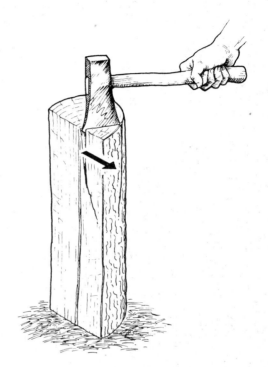

Fig. 8.3   Cleaving a log causing it to 'run off'.

It is best to split the wood radially – that is, with the split running towards the centre of the log. If the log has grown evenly, the centre will coincide with the pith (see Fig. 8.4): that is, the very centre ring created by the first year's growth. The split will then be making use of the weakness of the wood along the line of the rays.

However, if the log has grown unevenly the pith may lie off-centre which invariably causes problems (see Fig. 8.5). First, there will be uneven stresses in the wood which will cause it to warp along its length as it dries out (see p. 19). Second, these stresses tend to make it more resistant to cleaving. Third, it is more difficult to cleave the

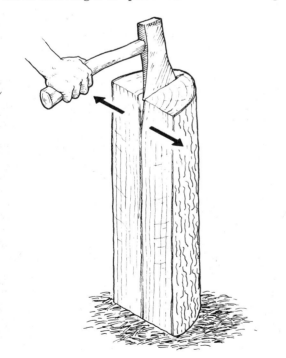

Fig. 8.2   Cleaving a log straight.

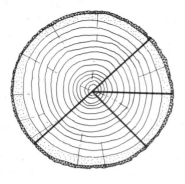

Fig. 8.4　The centre coincides with the pith.

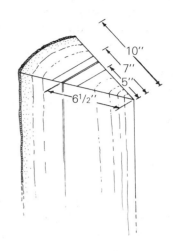

Fig. 8.6　Cleaving tangentially.

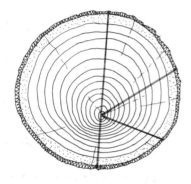

Fig. 8.5　A log which has grown unevenly.

wood into even halves; each section will be a different shape and thus more likely to split unevenly. If possible, therefore, try to use wood where the pith is fairly central.

Having cleft the wood radially into eighths, it can then be cleft tangentially; the exact position of this split is not so easy to arrive at. Take a section from a log with a perfectly circular cross-section and a radius of 10" (25 cm) (Fig. 8.6). To obtain two halves, each containing the same volume of wood, we should make the split 7" (18 cm) from the centre. However, the section in the centre will be of a more rigid shape as well as being more rigid in any case due to the heartwood. So it is necessary to split it rather nearer the centre. If we come in to half-way, there is only a quarter of the wood on the inside section and it is most likely that the split will run inwards. Depending on the species of wood, the

difference between its heartwood and sapwood and many other factors, the split should be made somewhere between these two points. A general rule of thumb is to try just inside two-thirds of the distance out from the centre. With time and experience, you will learn just where to split what wood, but the delight of working with a substance like wood – especially while it is still green – is that you can never expect to get it right every time: you will always be learning.

Obviously, depending on the shape and size of your end product, you could stop after splitting the wood into half or continue splitting further. There may also be times when, despite the general rule of splitting in half and half again, you decide it is better to split into a number of unequal sections. Again, experience will tell you when you can and cannot get away with it. Generally, the longer the wood to be split in proportion to its width, the more danger there is of a split running off.

If you want to cleave long pieces of wood, then the best way is to use a froe and a cleaving-break. My rule of thumb is that if the wood to be cleft is more than 6 times longer than it is wide, then I use the froe and the break – otherwise there is little chance of guiding the split and it is quicker to split it vertically with the cleaving axe.

You will now have a chance to practise the various methods of cleaving in making your shaving-horse. This can be made completely out of wood, virtually all of which is green, and while making it you have the opportunity to learn many of the skills involved in chair-making. It is also a highly versatile device which, unlike the pole-lathe, was used in many of the traditional woodland crafts.

There are two main components to any shaving-horse:

1   a bench with legs

2   a swinging arm pivoted on the bench

The craftsman sits astride the bench (as on a horse), and with his feet operates the swinging arm to grip a piece of wood. He then has both hands free to shape the workpiece, usually with a drawknife or a spokeshave. The shaving-horse has several advantages over the modern bench and screw-vice:

1   it grips and releases much more quickly

2   it is light enough to be carried

3   the craftsman can sit down while working

4   it is easy to make without having to buy special materials

There are two main 'breeds' of shaving-horse: the single arm (more common in the central European tradition and subsequently taken to America) and the twin arm or frame (which seems to be peculiar to the British Isles).

With the single arm version, the arm is slotted through the bench and then through a platform fixed above the bench at which point it is pivoted. At the bottom of the arm is a foot (for the craftsman to push his feet against), and at the top is a bulbous head with jaws that grip down on the workpiece (see Fig. 3.5, p. 28).

This breed of horse has a very strong grip due to the height of the pivot, greatly increasing the pressure of the foot by the principle of leverage. It is especially suited to working thin pieces of wood such as roofing shingles or slivers of wood for spale baskets. The major drawback I find with the single arm version is that it requires a lot of axe work to shape the arm and a certain amount of work with a mallet and chisel to cut the slot through the body.

If you want to try it, then you can get the general idea from Fig 3.5, and adapt the method described for making the frame type. Otherwise, its construction is well described by both Drew Langsner and Roy Underhill in their books (see Appendix 1).

To my mind, the frame construction of the British design has more in common with country chair-making and gives more scope for making use of the pole-lathe (an opportunity not to be missed!). One version of this type of shaving-horse can be seen in books by Fred Lambert and Jack Hill (see Appendix 1). Over the years I have evolved a variation of this which makes as much use of the pole-lathe as possible.

Making a Shaving-Horse

Requirements:

1 clean straight log 8–10" (20–25 cm) diameter, 4½ feet (1·4 m) long

1 straight log 3" (8 cm) diameter, 30" (75 cm) long

4 sticks 2 ft (60 cm) long, approximately 1½" (4 cm) diameter

1 straight stick 14" (35 cm) long, 2" (5 cm) diameter

the pin you made in Chapter 6 – or you can use a straight ash or hazel rod ¾" (2 cm) diameter, 14" (35 cm) long

1 softwood plank ¾" (2 cm) thick, 4–5" (10–12 cm) wide and 2 ft (60 cm) long (a piece of pallet wood, skirting board etc.)

The Body

The body of the horse is made from a log split in half. Most woods can be used but a soft light timber is best, e.g. willow or poplar. Lay the log on the ground with one end up against a rock or some other solid object. Hold the cleaving axe with its blade across the centre of the log.

Now swing the maul against the cleaver (Fig. 8.7). If it does not 'bite' first time, make sure that the cleaver is in exactly the same spot and try again. When a split has started to open up along the side of the log, insert one of the wedges into the crack a few inches from the end and drive it in (Fig. 8.8).

As the crack moves along the log, drive in the

Fig. 8.7   Starting to split the log.

Fig. 8.8   Driving in the wedge.

Fig. 8.9   Severing the fibres.

(13 cm) and put it to one side to be used as a wedge to support the platform of the horse. You will probably notice a spiral on the cleft surface of the log (Fig. 8.10) – this is just the way trees grow. You are aiming to make this surface level, so if the spiral is pronounced you may need to try another log.

To level out this spiral, you will have to remove some wood from the two opposite high corners. If you already have an adze, you can anchor the log firmly on the ground and level out the surface with the adze – but please take care of your lower legs and your feet! Somewhat safer is to lean the half-log on a low chopping-block and chop off the excess wood with an axe (Fig. 8.11). A hewing axe (a heavy side-axe with a straight

second wedge, at which point the first wedge should come loose. Leapfrog the two wedges along the log until you reach the other end. If you have a good log, it will open up and fall into two halves; if not, you may have to sever the remaining fibres with an axe (Fig. 8.9). Be very careful not to let the blade of the axe hit the steel wedges or any stones on the ground.

Take one of the halves, saw off the end 5"

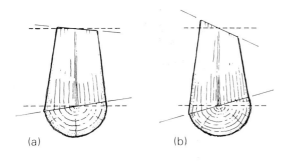

Fig. 8.10   Spiral or 'wind' on the cleft surface:
(a) usable (b) reject.

Fig. 8.11   Trimming the top of the log.

handle about 12–18" (30–45 cm) long) is perfect for this. Otherwise use a turner's side axe, a sharp cleaving axe or a felling axe.

When you have this surface roughly level, it is a good idea to remove some of the excess wood from the opposite side of the log; to do this, lay the log face down and drive a wedge into the end about half-way from the centre (Fig. 8.12). If you are very lucky, this will run cleanly along the log; if you are very unlucky, it will run off towards the surface you have just cleaned up and you will have to start again. It is most likely to tear off towards the bark side.

Chase the split back with the wedges or gluts, finally pulling it right away. Then repeat this from the other end. Now clean up this new surface in the same way as before so that you end up with a rough plank approximately 8" (20 cm)

Fig. 8.12   Cleaving off the bottom of the body.

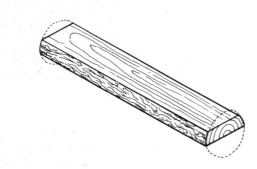

Fig. 8.13   A rough plank.

wide, 4" (10 cm) thick, and 4 ft (1·2 m) long (Fig. 8.13). Naturally, if you manage to get hold of a plank this shape by some other means, then make use of it.

Now you need to drill the holes for the legs. I much prefer a three-legged horse as it is unable to wobble if placed on uneven ground. When in use, your weight will be towards the rear, so that is where you should position the pair of legs, with the third one at the front. I also find it useful to be able to remove the legs when I transport the horse, so for that reason I suggest drilling the leg sockets right through so that you can drive the legs out by hitting them through from above.

Support the plank with the wide surface upper-most and its underside clear of the ground. If one end is wider than the other, choose that for the rear of the horse. At this end, mark the centre line and measure 5" (13 cm) in from the end. Two inches (5 cm) to either side, mark two points which will be the centre for drilling the leg holes. Through each of these points, draw a line at 60

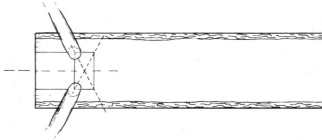

Fig. 8.14   The direction in which to drill the rear legs.

degrees to the centre line (see Fig. 8.14) This will give the direction to lean when drilling. Now set the sliding bevel at 25 degrees from the vertical and place it on one of these lines to show you how much to lean when drilling. This will result in the legs splaying both outwards and to the rear. To drill the holes, use the brace with a 1¼" (32 mm) bit, but if you have a 1½" (37 mm) auger it will be easier to use and will make a sturdier horse (Fig. 8.15). It will assist if you are working with a partner who can help to hold the body steady and also line up your drilling. Make sure that you don't blunt the auger bit on the ground when it comes through.

Before drilling the front hole, give your chest muscles a rest and make the legs. At this stage, the simplest way is to use three sticks 2 ft (60 cm) long. Later on, it is a satisfying project to shave a set of legs or even turn them. I like my horses to be taller than was traditional practice in order to have as long an arm as possible – thereby maxi-mising the leverage and therefore the grip on the workpiece.

Shaping the legs repeats the process of shaping the handle for the maul. Accuracy is rather less critical in this case, because when the horse is in use the legs will be forced into the body thus

Fig. 8.15 Drilling the rear leg hole.

Fig. 8.16 Drilling the front leg hole.

tightening the joint. However, do leave a tapered shoulder to stop the leg poking too far through the body.

Test the two rear legs in the hole and see how they look. You may find that any difference in the drilling angles can be compensated for by rotating one or both of the legs. When you are happy with this, knock them in lightly with the club but be careful not to split the body. Turn the horse the right way up and prop the front on a suitable block (or part of the work-break), making sure that the rear legs are standing on a level surface. If necessary, trim one of the legs so that the body of the horse is level.

Mark the position for the front leg on the centre line 5" (13 cm) from the end. Set the sliding bevel at 15 degrees from the vertical and place it on the centre line. Drill through (Fig. 8.16), making sure that the horse is steady and that you do not lean to left or right; if you do, then the horse

may tend to tip over to one side. You can now fit the front leg and the horse should stand firm. If any of the legs protrude, saw them or trim them with a gouge until they are flush with the body.

Now you have an idea how to make a three-legged stool, and you already have quite a useful bench! Another venture into the field of chair-making is to shape yourself a seat. Starting with an axe, chop out a hollow just to the front of the back legs. When this is about an inch deep, follow up either with a shallow gouge and a mallet (or club), or with a round-bottomed plane if you have one. Test it for comfort by regularly sitting on it to see how it feels. You want the part on which you sit to be as wide as possible, becoming narrower where your thighs are.

On the front half, level off the top surface and trim up the sides so that they are vertical. It should roughly resemble the shape as shown (see Fig. 8.17).

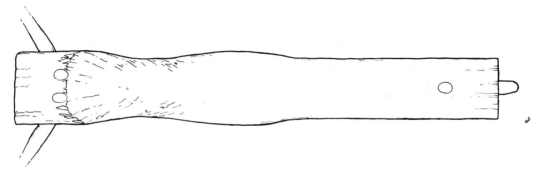

Fig. 8.17   View of the body from above.

The Frame

Start with the arms and find a log of ash about 3" (8 cm) diameter and 30" (75 cm) long. If ash is not available you could try any other wood, but it is important that it has no large knots. It can have a curve, but this must only be in one plane and not a compound curve. If you have a froe and have made the cleaving-break, this will provide an opportunity to try them out.

Stand the log on a solid surface and drive the froe into one end with the club until the back of the froe blade is flush with the log end (see Fig. 8.18). Lift the log into position as shown. Now press down on the froe handle, levering the log open. Insert a piece of wood in the crack to keep it open, then remove the froe and put it into the crack further down the log (see Fig. 8.19).

If the split has started to run off in one direction, position the log so that its thicker half is at the bottom. By pressing down on that half at the same time as levering open the split, you can

Fig. 8.18   Driving the froe into a log.

Fig. 8.19   Cleaving with the froe.

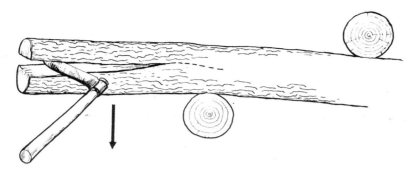

Fig. 8.20 Forcing the split downwards.

force the split to run back down to the middle of
the log (see Fig. 8.20).

Always try to keep the log in such a position
that the point at which the split is just opening is
directly above the point of leverage. Knowing
just how much pressure is required to keep the
split running straight comes with practice. A
good clean log will readily run straight, with no
need to direct it. Awkward logs require more
manipulation; the longer and narrower the log,
the trickier it is to cleave straight. You may need
to cleave a few logs until you have a matching
pair roughly the same size and without too much
spiral.

If you have no cleaving-break and froe, you
should be able to split the log by using wedges in
the same way as cleaving out the body. Those
who have access to a powered workshop could
saw the log down the middle, or you could even
use two pieces of sawn 3 × 2″ (8 × 5 cm) softwood.

Now mark the distances from Fig. 8.21 down
one arm.

Cramp the two halves together again and using
the brace and ⅞″ (22 mm) bit, drill the top hole
right through at right-angles to the arm (see Fig.
8.22). Insert a peg or straight stick (your turned
pin might do if it hasn't shrunk too much) into
this hole to act as a guide for drilling the two
centre holes. These must be drilled in exactly the
same plane as the first. Now with the 1¼″
(32 mm) bit, drill the bottom hole for the foot-
rest, again keeping at the same angle. It is easy to
be a few degrees out of line, and this will cause the
frame to be twisted when it is assembled. This
could be an opportunity for you to try out one of
your drilling posts. Use a G-cramp to grip the log

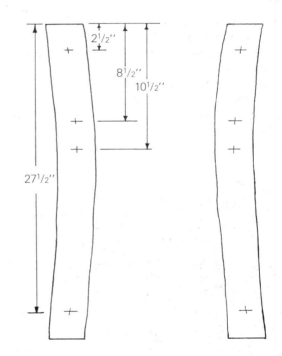

Fig. 8.21 Distances down the arms.

against the flat face of the post so as to hold it
steady while you drill. You may need to remove
some wood from the back of the post to make
room for the G-cramp. Now you should smooth
the inside faces of the arms.

To make the foot-rest you require a 20″ (50 cm)
log about 1½–2″ (4–5 cm) in diameter. You now
need to shape the ends down to 1¼″ (32 mm)
either on the pole-lathe or by whittling them with
a knife. Leave a swelling in the middle which is

Fig. 8.22   Drilling the arm.

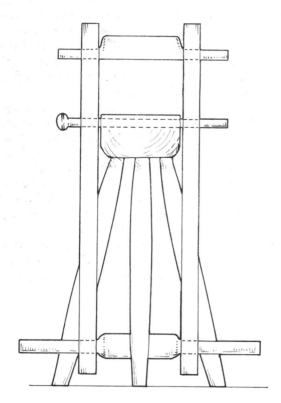

Fig. 8.23   The arm in position.

equal in length to the width of the body of the horse. This will provide a shoulder to keep the arms in place (see Fig. 8.23).

To make the top grip, take a 14" (35 cm) log 2½–3" (6–8 cm) in diameter and split it down the middle. Mark out on this the width of the body, and using the tenon saw cut out the shoulders. First with an axe and then with the knife, whittle down the tenons to ⅞" (22 mm) diameter to fit the top holes in the arms. You can now fit the foot-rest and the grip into the appropriate holes in the arms to make up the frame. The flat side of the grip should face downwards.

The next task is to drill a hole through the body to take the pin. Sitting astride the horse, mark a point 4–6" (10–15 cm) in front of your knees and draw a line across the body. This will be the line of the hole. It should be as high on the body as possible, so mark its centre about an inch (2·5 cm) from the top surface. Using a spirit level – or with the help of a friend to sight it – drill a ⅞" (22 mm) hole right through. Your drill bit will probably be too short to go straight through, so you will have to withdraw it regularly to clear out the waste. If you have faith in your accuracy, you could drill from both ends and hope to meet!

I suggest one pin passing straight through in preference to a pin from each side. It is then easy to remove it to change the height of the frame for different sizes of work, or to remove the frame if you have to transport the horse.

Now lift the front of the horse, pass the frame over the body to the correct position and hold it in place with the pin. In the meantime, the pin should have dried out and shrunk to make it an easy fit. If it is too tight, you can put it back on the lathe and turn it down a little; if so, you should notice how much harder the wood now is. Assuming that everything has gone right, the frame should just clear the ground when at the lower of the two settings. If there is no clearance, you will have to make longer legs or saw an inch or so off the bottom of the frame.

When you are happy with the frame, you can fix it together by fitting in some pins. Roughly whittle four slightly tapered ⅜" (10 mm) pins about 3" (8 cm) long (oak, ash, beech or hawthorn are best, but anything straight will do nicely). If they are perfectly round either they fit or they don't; if they have odd corners, these will crush slightly when they are knocked into place and make a tight fit. Leave them to season for a few days in the warm. When the pins are dry, remove the frame from the horse and drill four holes ⅜" (10 mm) diameter, as shown in Fig. 8.24, into the appropriate parts of the frame. Then tap in the pins.

This should give the frame much more rigidity.

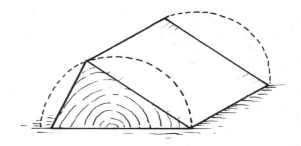

Fig. 8.25   Cleaving the wedge.

would be fine, about 2′ × 5″ × ¾″ (60 cm × 13 cm × 2 cm). Failing that, you could cleave a length of log and trim it up with the axe. I prefer a softwood for the platform, so that it will 'give' slightly when gripping the workpiece. It is fixed to the body by a simple wooden peg. Put the wedge and platform in position as shown, and drill a ⅞″ (22 mm) hole at right-angles into the plank. Continue this hole a few inches into the body. Whittle or turn a 4″-long (10 cm) peg to fit tightly into the hole in the body, and drive it into place. Trim down the protruding part so that when the platform is placed over it, there is sufficient play to enable you to alter the angle of the platform. Then drill a ⅜″ (10 mm) hole through this peg and whittle a tapered pin to fit through it so as to hold the platform in place.

You should now have a functional shaving-horse. As time goes on, you may wish to make some adjustments to suit your particular way of working. For example, if it is to be used by children you should add an extra foot-rest at a height suitable for shorter legs. If it is to be left outdoors, it should be well coated with linseed oil. You may also want to make some spare legs and cross-pieces out of cleft wood, ready to replace any parts that may break or come loose. The reason for doing this and the techniques involved are explained in the following chapter.

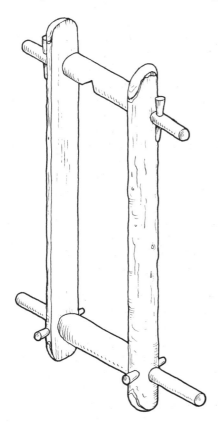

Fig. 8.24   Position of the pins in the arm.

The Wedge and Platform

Using the froe or cleaving axe, take the offcut from the end of the body and split off the edges to form a triangular wedge as shown in Fig. 8.25. Aim for the three sides to be different lengths so that you can turn it to raise or lower the platform. You may need to trim up these surfaces with an axe.

The platform is best made from a piece of pallet wood (admittedly not green wood, but just right for the job). Otherwise any other softwood plank

Nine

Making Tool Handles

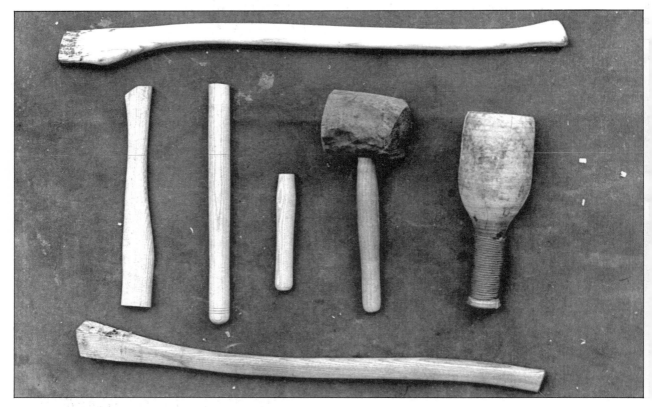

Fig. 9.1 Handles for an adze, felling axe, cleaving axe, froe and chisel; two mallets.

Up to this stage, any handles or legs have been shaped by whittling an appropriate stick down to size. Such wood retains much of the tubular strength of the tree which has, after all, evolved to maximise this strength. A round-wood log over 4" (10 cm) in diameter compares well with a section of wood of similar dimensions which has been cleft from a log.

Unfortunately, the cells formed during the first few years of growth are comparatively thin-walled fibre cells. This 'juvenile growth' makes up the bulk of any round-wood less than 2" (5 cm), resulting in it being proportionately weak. For this reason, if maximum strength is required, it is better to replace the round-wood components with cleft parts where the juvenile wood will be discarded.

Now you have a shaving-horse, you should be able to produce such components by going through the processes of cleaving, trimming, shaving and (if you wish) turning; these are the four processes involved in chair-bodging. A good project in which to try them out is in making a handle for a froe which, as described earlier, consists of a heavy blade with a handle at one end.

Bodging a Froe Handle

You need a good ash log at least 4" (10 cm) in diameter with growth rings spaced at 4–16 rings to the inch (25 mm) for maximum strength (see p. 38). Cut out a knot-free section 18" (45 cm) long. Stand the log on end, preferably on a chopping-block or other hard surface, and cleave it in half using the cleaving axe and the club (see Fig. 9.2).

Cleave one of these halves into half again, and so on until you have a 'billet' large enough to yield a 1½" (4 cm) diameter handle. Take this billet to a

Fig. 9.3   *Trimming with the axe.*

Fig. 9.2   *Cleaving a log.*

Fig. 9.4   *Shaving the billet.*

chopping-block and with a trimming-axe, remove some of the surplus wood (see Fig. 9.3). First make a series of nicks into one edge of the billet, starting at the bottom and working up at about 1–2" (2·5–5 cm) intervals. Then, with a few vertical strokes, remove this wood. By doing this in two stages, you avoid the axe becoming buried in the wood. Work your way around the billet, removing any protruding ridges.

Having trimmed one end, turn it over and trim the other. Be sure to keep your fingers behind the wood, and do not be tempted to trim all the way up to the top without turning it round – you might just lose a finger! Do not worry about the bark at this stage; it does no harm to leave it on.

Along with a drawknife, take the billet to your shaving-horse and place it on the platform and beneath the grip. Sit on the horse and push with your feet against the foot-rest; this should then force the grip down on to the billet, holding it firm. If it doesn't feel right, try moving the block forwards or backwards or putting the pin in the other set of holes on the frame (see Fig. 9.4).

When using the drawknife, there is no right way up. Some drawknives feel better bevel up and some bevel down (the bevel being the part of the blade that you sharpen). Generally for concave (hollow) work or with awkward grain, it is better to hold it bevel down. This enables you to rock the blade on the back of the bevel in order to lift it out of the wood if it is cutting in too deeply (see Fig. 9.5).

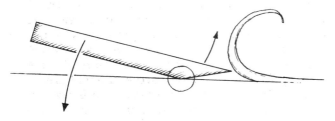

Fig. 9.5   Rocking the drawknife out of the wood.

When working on long level or convex surfaces, you may get a smoother feel by holding it bevel up with the blade itself flat on the wood.

Work away on one end, regularly releasing your grip and rotating the billet so as to shave the wood evenly on all surfaces. Be careful not to release your grip while you are still working on the wood, or it will slip out and butt you in the stomach – in which case it can wind you, but this is the worst that can happen. The drawknife does look dangerous, especially as you are breaking the cardinal rule you were always taught: that is, never to cut towards you. But while you have both hands on the handle, it is very difficult to cut yourself. If you are accident-prone, however, be careful when picking up the tool or putting it down and *never* hold it by the blade. (If you can

get away with doing that, then it's not sharp enough!)

Continue shaving the billet until it is roughly cylindrical and make sure that it is not curved along its length. Banana-shaped billets are the curse of the novice bodger. It is important to bear in mind at each stage the shape of the finished object. You have to be able to see it in the log when you cleave it, and then to liberate it from the billet without damaging it. As you probably found out when making the pin for the horse, any deviation of the blank from a straight line will be accentuated when it spins on the lathe. This is one reason why you have to be much more careful to select straight wood to start with. A second reason is that you are cleaving the wood in order to maximise its strength by following the flow of the fibres. If, having cleft it, you now proceed to cut through all these fibres in order to make a crooked piece of wood straight, you will be defeating your object.

Now you have to centre it up – the single most critical stage in the craft of bodging. Centring up a squared piece of timber is easy: all you have to do is draw two diagonals on to the ends which meet at the centre point. But with a billet from the shaving horse, this is not possible. You can try to do it by eye which, if it works, is the quickest and simplest approach. Otherwise, a suitable method for the novice is as follows:

Set the poppets of the lathe the correct distance apart to receive the billet (so that the threaded crank projects about an inch (2·5 cm) from the poppet). Let us assume that you have set up the lathe for right-handed use (i.e., with the crank at the right-hand end of the lathe). Imagine the centre of the finished handle at one end of the billet, then gently push this spot on to the fixed metal point at the left-hand poppet. Keeping the billet in place with your left hand, tighten up the crank until it just bites into the centre of the right-hand end. Tighten up the crank a little and then slacken it just enough to allow the billet to spin freely. There must not be any friction. Now give the billet a *gentle* spin. If it rotates evenly, you have found the correct centres. If it rotates in a

Fig. 9.6   An off-centre billet.

'lumpy' manner, then let it settle at its lowest point. When this happens, it should be clear that there is more wood below the centre line than above (see Fig. 9.6). Holding the billet again with your left hand and keeping it steady by resting a finger against the cranked poppet, slacken off the crank enough to *just* release the billet. Now raise that end a little and wind up the crank again. Repeat this procedure once or twice more if necessary until it rotates evenly.

When you have settled for a centre at each end, make sure you can remember which they are and then remove the billet from the lathe. Now, using the gimlet, enlarge these holes. You could omit this stage, but there is always a tendency for the metal points to wear into the wood. If you do not regularly tighten up the crank to avoid the billet coming loose, it will soon wear an uneven centre and eventually fly out of the lathe. By drilling out these centres beforehand, this problem is less likely to occur (it will happen often enough anyway at first).

Lubricate the centres with a dab of wax or thick oil (linseed, chain-saw, engine or cooking oil are all fine). Now proceed as with the pin on p. 63.

For a froe handle, you will need only a simple shape. If you have the time, it is best to turn it about 15 per cent oversize and then leave it to season. Then it can be remounted on to the lathe using the original centres, and the blade end can be turned to fit exactly into the socket. You will notice that the handle has turned slightly oval, demonstrating the differential rates of shrinkage.

When in use, the handle will be used mainly to push the blade into the workpiece, so it should have a slight shoulder where it leaves the eye and be wedged in the end in much the same manner as the maul handle (p. 73).

Wedges

Now is a good time to build up a stock of material to be seasoned for use as wedges. To my mind the best wood for wedges is oak heartwood but, failing that, hornbeam, beech, yew, thorn, holly or box would serve the purpose. None of these will cleave as well as oak, so you may find it easier to saw them directly to shape.

If using oak, try to find a log 1–2' (30–60 cm) in length, 12–18" (30–45 cm) in diameter and straight-grained. Using the cleaving axe, split out

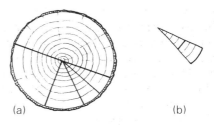

Fig. 9.7 *Splitting a log (a) radially (b) tangentially.*

radially an eighth segment, then split this in half tangentially (see Fig. 9.7 (a) and (b)). To split further, you may need to use the froe and cleaving-break.

With oak you will probably find that about half of the outer section is sapwood, so cleave it again and discard the sapwood. Cleave the remaining segments further until you have a number of strips approximately 3/8" (10 mm) thick and ranging from 1–3" (2·5–8 cm) wide. This will give you wedges suitable for small chair parts up to large axes. It doesn't matter too much if they run off when you are splitting them, but it will give you some very good practice in using the froe and the cleaving-break. I prefer to split the wood radially in order to make use of the lines of weakness caused by the rays, but you might like to try splitting them down further tangentially.

This is basically the same process as is used to make ceiling laths (the forerunner of plasterboard to act as a base for plaster), and in the making of oak swill baskets which were commonly used for carrying coal and potatoes. According to the 'swillers' who made these baskets, some oak preferred to be cleft 'lat-way' (radially) and some 'back-way' (tangentially) (see Mary Barratt's book, Appendix 1).

Now you have obtained your strips of wood, take them indoors to dry. Anywhere up to 60° Centigrade is ideal to dry them thoroughly – above that temperature, the wood can start to deteriorate. Leave them there until they are required. When you need a wedge, take your seasoned strip to the shaving-horse and shave one end down, using the drawknife to make as clean a wedge as possible. Saw it off about 1" (2·5 cm) longer than necessary, trim it down to the right width with a knife, chamfer the leading corners slightly and you have a tailor-made wedge (see Fig. 7.8).

A New Maul Handle

This is a good chance to apply your finesse on the cleaving-break to a heavier job. For this you need a length of good ash (4–16 rings per inch (2·5 cm) straight and knot-free), 2½–3 ft (75–90 cm) long and 6" (15 cm) or more in diameter. This will also give you wood of the right dimensions for axe handles. The very best wood for such purposes is what I like to call 'toffee-ash' – the bottom section of the trunk where the grain is more interwoven; this does make it rather more difficult to cleave and the cutting tools tend to get stuck when you cut it – hence the name – but I find it well worth the struggle. I broke the previous handle on my felling axe when trying to lever open an ash log (something I am always being told not to do), which told me that I had a piece of prime toffee ash. When at last the log decided to cooperate, part of it became a new handle and I have been happily using it to lever open logs ever since. One good source of such wood is large coppice-grown ash – often found where they were felled in order to plant conifers and have successfully fought for their survival.

If the log is large in diameter (8" (20 cm) plus), start by cleaving it with the wedges or the cleaving axe. Then cleave the final stages (or the whole process if using smaller wood) using the cleaving-break, until you have a section 1½–2" (4–5 cm) in diameter. With ash, there is no effective difference between heart and sapwood, so you can use any part of the log as long as it is straight-grained.

Trim it with the side axe if needs be, then shave it down using the shaving-horse and drawknife just as with the froe handle. Try it out occasionally to see how it feels, then smooth it off with the spokeshave. You will now be able to feel the fibrous quality of good ash, and should develop a technique with the spokeshave of flicking it back should you feel the grain running deeper than you intend. This is similar to the technique used with the drawknife when rocking it back on its bevel, and will give you some much needed practice for making an axe handle.

If the wood is very straight, you may be able to turn down on the lathe the end which will go into the head. Remember to leave it oversized and allow it to season. When you feel like replacing the original stick handle, you can try to drive it out if it feels loose, otherwise you will have to drill it out using the brace and ⅝" (16 mm) bit. This will be enough to loosen the old handle. It is for this reason (and to save money!) that I dislike using the small metal wedges which one can buy to tighten up tool handles. If you do the job properly, your wooden wedges should be quite adequate. Having removed the old wedge, you can replace it with the new one using the method previously described.

Axe Handles

While you have a supply of good cleft ash, it is an opportune time to make some axe handles. If you have bought axes with commercially made handles, there is a good chance that they will break at some stage as they are not made from cleft wood. Making your own handles will enable you to utilise any broken axes you may acquire and to tailor their handles to your own requirements. If possible, try to find a handle of the shape you want and then use it as a pattern. Otherwise you can use the outlines shown in Fig. 9.8 (a), (b), (c), (d) and (e).

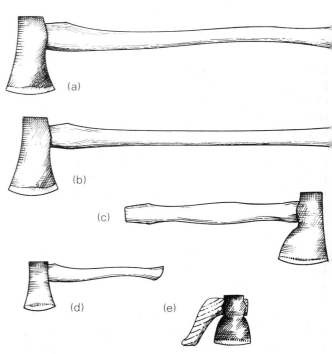

Fig. 9.8 Axe handles (a) fawn-foot felling (b) straight felling (c) hewing (right-handed) (d) cleaving (e) turner's.

To make a handle for a felling, hewing or cleaving axe, the procedure is similar to that of the maul handle but requiring much more attention to the shape. Remember that an axe handle is made from one piece of wood – once you have made a cut, that is final. So when you are starting out, reduce the wood steadily and err on the side of caution.

If you take an eighth or sixteenth segment of the log (depending on its size and the handle required), this will give you a good start towards the shape you need (Fig. 9.9). Where the axe is going to be used for striking against the wood, as with a felling or hewing axe, there is a heavy shoulder on the top of the handle, just behind the

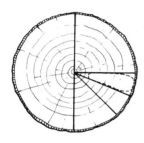

Fig. 9.9   Cleaving for axe handles.

head, to absorb the shock. On a felling axe which is going to be swung continuously in a large circle, the rest of the handle should be as light as possible, ending up with a swelling at the end to help prevent it from sliding out of your hand.

The most common style nowadays is the fawn foot handle, which looks elegant and feels good to the hand. A basic version, which was more usual in earlier days, just has a straight handle and is easier to make.

The hewing axe will often be used two-handed for hewing flat surfaces on to logs, or one-handed for trimming up billets. It therefore needs a handle that feels comfortable to the hand at any point along its length, so it will be bulkier than that of the felling axe.

The handle on a cleaving aze is used mainly to hold the head steady while it is being struck and then to minimise the shock. If this is the only axe you can afford to buy, then put on a handle similar to that of a hewing axe so that it can be used for a variety of purposes without being too

weak. If you intend to use it just for cleaving, then you can make the handle rather smaller all round.

Whichever handle you are making, take the segment of ash and roughly draw the outline you desire along one face. Try to make use of any curves in the grain so that they coincide with any curves in the handle. Rough out this shape (using the axe you already have), then shave it down on the shaving-horse – first with a drawknife and then with a spokeshave. This is where you will find that a V-shaped notch in the grip of the horse comes in useful. Another way of holding the handle while you work on it is to grip it tightly between the centres of the lathe.

Take great care with the section that is to fit into the axe-head; it should eventually fit snugly into place, so avoid tapering it towards the end. At this stage, it should be left about 15 per cent oversize to allow for shrinkage. Leave it in the warm to dry for as long as you can wait, ideally for a month or two in an airing cupboard.

When it has seasoned, shape the head end with a spokeshave until it is nearly down to size. Now put a chamfer on the very end to assist it into the eye. If you try it for size you should see a mark in the wood where it rubs on the metal, so remove some wood at this point and try it again. This stage can be quite time-consuming at first, but when you have fitted several axe handles you will become much quicker.

Some people prefer to use files and rasps to take the handle down to size. It makes little practical difference, but I prefer the feel of the spokeshave. When you have achieved a good tight fit, with the handle just able to project from the other end of the eye, you should smooth off the rest of the handle. A cabinet-scraper is good for this job, but scraping it with a knife will also work. You may choose to finish it off with sandpaper, but do not waste time and paper by trying to sand down a rough surface; you should be able to achieve a reasonable finish by scraping it first.

Saw a slot into the end of the handle to about half to two-thirds of the depth of the eye. Now shape up a wedge from your supply of seasoned strips. Fit the handle into the axe head and, holding it clear of the ground, drive the handle into the eye. You will find that the weight of the head holds it steady while the handle is being driven in; there should be no need to hold it up against anything. Keep hitting the handle with moderate force until it will go no further. Provided it has come out at the other end of the eye, you can then drive in the wedge.

I find it helpful to use some glue to hold the wedge in place, but this is not essential. When the glue has set, you can saw off any excess handle projecting from the head and – to finish it off nicely – clean up this cut with a spokeshave or a sharp knife. It gives me great satisfaction to see the contrast of a dark oak wedge against the clean white of an ash handle in the eye of an axe. Finally, clean up the end where you hit the handle and coat it liberally with linseed oil.

Turner's Side-axe Handle

The handle for a turner's side-axe is rather different in that it should curve to about 70 degrees (Fig. 9.8 (e)). This is best made from the very base of an ash tree where a root buttress starts to flare out. Alternatively, you might find a suitable piece of wood in a curved branch. Obviously it will be strongest if the grain and the curve of the handle actually coincide. If that is not possible, you could either reduce the angle of crank in the handle or to some extent go against the flow of the grain (Fig. 9.10).

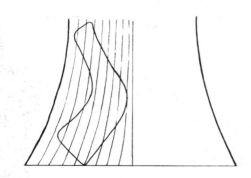

Fig. 9.10   Selecting a handle for a turner's axe.

Because the handle is not long, it is unlikely that an element of short grain will weaken it to the extent that there is a chance of it breaking. Apart from this consideration, follow the same instructions as with the other handles.

Mallets

One way to make a mallet is to use exactly the same method as with the maul, only scaling it down to the size you want (see p. 72). This can be modified somewhat by having a removable

Fig. 9.11   Making a mallet.

handle, as with a pick-axe (i.e. one that can be slid in and out of the head).

The choice of woods to use for the head is similar to that for the maul, but because of its smaller size (4–5", 10–12·5 cm) it should be easier to find a suitable piece of fruit wood or even thorn, holly or box, all of which are comparatively dense, hard woods. If the chance arises, use a section from a log which has been cut for a year or more, so long as it has not started to rot. It will then be well on the way to seasoning and is less likely to crack.

The handle should be turned from the same stock of toffee ash about 15" (40 cm) long. It is difficult to predict exactly how much any piece of wood will shrink as it seasons.

I find that with ash, the quicker it has grown the more it will shrink and the more oval its shape will be. If you turn the handle with a very gentle taper from 1¼–1½" (32–38 cm) when green, the thin end will certainly pass through a 1¼" (32 mm) hole when dry and the thick end definitely will not. You may then be able to use the seasoned handle without returning it to the lathe. Slide it into the hole in the head, with the long side of the oval pointing towards the ends of the mallet (Fig. 9.11). This will give a tight fit without putting pressure on the sides. If it is still too large, reduce it a little with the roughing-out gouge so that the head sits neatly at the thick end.

Traditionally, the chair-bodgers would use a tool called a beetle or bittel, which is a cross between a mallet and a maul. The head was usually bound with two rings of iron to prevent it splitting, as was otherwise inevitable when it was in constant use. In warm, dry weather, the head would shrink and the rings would come loose, which would be a nuisance to the bodger. He could either soak the head to swell it again or try to fix the rings with nails or screws. Often he would tend to leave the rings off and the tool was then known as a summer beetle, as opposed to a winter beetle which had its rings on.

A different version can be turned out of a single piece of wood to make a bottle-shaped carver's mallet. This should be 10–12" (25–30 cm) long and about 4" (10 cm) in diameter and, again, is best made from a dense wood such as apple, pear, holly, beech or hornbeam. It is less likely to crack if cleft from a large log, but you could take a chance by starting with a piece of roundwood and drying it slowly. If it does crack, it is best to bind the handle with some twine or pole-lathe cord (see Fig. 9.1).

Chisel Handles

To make chisel handles involves much the same process as for the froe handle, only fitting it into a ferrule instead of the eye of the froe. A ferrule is a metal ring (usually brass) that fits over the end of a handle to stop it from splitting. These can be bought cheaply from specialist tool suppliers, or else made by cutting short lengths of copper pipe.

You may buy some of your turning tools without handles, or you may pick up some good, old tools which either have damaged handles or no handles at all. Also, it looks neat if all your handles match. For chisel handles I usually use ash, but beech is just as functional (if not as attractive). If you can get hold of it, box is regarded as the best, especially if you will be hitting the handles with a mallet.

I must admit that the powered lathe turner has the advantage at this point. Having made his handle, he can set a drill into one end of his lathe and drill out a hole perfectly in line with the handle. If you happen to have a pillar drill, you could set up a jig to hold the handle vertically beneath it and drill it out with that. But if you have neither a powered lathe nor a powered pillar drill, then I suggest the following simple approach for which you will need a twist drill and some bits.

Fig. 9.12 Drilling a chisel handle.

Cleave and rough out the blank for the handle, ready for the lathe. Before centring it, drill a hole into it as near in line as possible to the centre-line of the blank (Fig. 9.12). With the drill still in the blank, rotate it slowly and you should be able to accurately line up a point on the other end which is in line with the hole you have drilled (Fig. 9.13). That point will be one of the centres and the drill hole will be the other. You can now proceed to turn the shape of the handle to completion, apart from the actual point where the ferrule will fit. As with the other handles, leave it to season thoroughly.

Fig. 9.13 Marking the other centre.

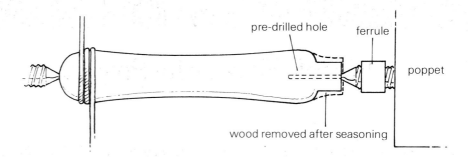

Fig. 9.14 Fitting a ferrule on a handle.

When you remount it on to the lathe to turn down the ferrule section, slip the ferrule over the metal centre of the lathe (Fig. 9.14). Now square off the ferrule end of the handle with the tip of the skew chisel and measure back exactly the length of the ferrule; with the tip of the skew, make a clean square shoulder at this point. With the small gouge, turn down this last section until the ferrule very nearly fits; you can test this by offering the ferrule up to it every now and then. It does not matter if the surface of this part of the tool is not smooth; this will in fact help the ferrule to stay in place. Before fitting the ferrule, it helps to warm it slightly to make it expand.

When the ferrule is in place, enlarge the hole you drilled previously with a drill marginally smaller than the tang of the chisel. Heat up the tang (be careful not to heat up the blade, thus losing its temper) and holding the blade in a vice or with a G-clamp, drive the handle on to the tang. Finally, just punch a hole into the ferrule with a nail, to locate it in place on the handle.

You can if you wish avoid the use of a ferrule by screwing a jubilee clip over the head of the handle while driving on to the tang of the tool. The clip can then be removed. This avoids the need to season the handle before using it.

It is possible to turn chisel handles from wood which has already seasoned in some other form such as chair-legs. This is a good way to use up surplus stock and avoids having an oval handle – an advantage or disadvantage depending on your viewpoint. You will soon find, however, that turning seasoned wood on a pole-lathe using the light tools I recommend is not as enjoyable as starting from scratch.

Drawknife handles

These follow the same principles as chisel handles. One difference is that you may be able to drill right through the handle before turning which gives you completely accurate centring. When fitting the handles, the tangs should come right through the handles and then be peened (hammered flat) over a tight-fitting washer to make sure that they do not pull off when in use (Fig. 9.15).

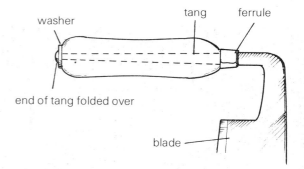

Fig. 9.15 Fitting a drawknife handle.

Ten

Simple Pole-lathe Projects

If you have got on well with the turned tool handles, you will now be able to carry out some other turning projects.

1 Rolling-pin

I had been using a pole-lathe for many years before I heard about using a wide chisel for finishing. Until then, my only chisel was the ½" (13 mm) skew, which in retrospect was an excellent – if rather frustrating – way to learn how to use a turning chisel. The slightest lack of concentration and the long corner would bite mercilessly into the smooth finish I had been struggling to obtain.

Fig. 10.1 Two spoons, a spatula and two rolling-pins.

It may not be obvious, but a rolling-pin was one of my greatest challenges in those days and still requires my concentration and a steady hand. A Windsor chair-leg is all curves and grooves – making it hard to notice any slight error – whereas a standard rolling-pin should be flat. It is analogous to the difference between trying to draw a curve and a straight line freehand.

The best wood to use for all kitchen utensils is sycamore. It looks clean, has an even, close grain, but no smell or taste. Its close relation, field maple, is also good for such purposes, as are beech and birch. All these are very pleasant to work on the lathe when green, producing long soft ribbons as you cut the wood.

At the outset, you are faced with the decision as to whether to settle for an oval rolling-pin or to

turn it in two stages allowing it to season in between. At home, I use an oval one in which I left the centre holes in case I wanted to round it off. I find that for my level of cooking it works well enough as it is, and I can always blame the pin if the pastry comes out wrong!

If you decide to make your rolling-pin in two stages, then just rough it out at first and let it season gently for a few months before returning it to the lathe. Then you will need to rough it out again before applying the finishing tools.

There are two possible designs (see Fig. 10.1).

a   A straight rolling-pin with simple round handles at each end; and

b   A tapered pin with a gently curved profile and no separate handle (apparently used for rolling out chapatis).

The more complex type which has separate handles fixed to each other and a dowel running through the middle is more difficult to make and to my mind has no practical advantage.

2   Candlesticks

This project gives you scope to try out a variety of different shapes. You can turn them straight out of a round log, leaving the base with its bark on. Be prepared for it to crack, although you will probably find that the base will split but not the turned section. A similar effect is gained by turning a cleft piece of wood and leaving the base with the cleft surfaces untouched. This is less likely to split and creates an interesting contrast between the two finishes, the cleft and the turned. However, it is awkward to rough out and the sharp corners tend to wear the cord of the lathe. In both cases, turn the shape you want and then turn a very slightly hollow base so that it doesn't rock. The hole for the candle can be drilled out with a brace and bit. If you want to finish off the job properly, insert a brass liner in the hole to avoid any danger of the candle burning the wood.

An alternative method is to turn the candlestick in two parts, with an upright turned on the lathe and inserted (when seasoned) into a piece of wood for the base. Later on, in Chapter 16, we shall see how to turn a dish on the lathe – which would of course make a suitable base for a candlestick.

Fig. 10.2   Candlesticks, from laburnum roundwood and cleft oak.

3   Baby's Rattle

The first time I saw a baby's rattle being made was at a demonstration by a fellow Bristol craftsman, Don White, on a powered lathe. At the time, I could not imagine that such an intricate job could be carried out on a pole-lathe. With a little patience and concentration, however, it is not such a difficult job. In fact, a talented 10-year-old managed it on a one-day course. How's about that, Don!

Before you start, it will help to add to your turning tools a small hooked tool to cut under the rings. I have found a spoon-bit chisel the best standard aid for this job. But if you cannot obtain such a tool, you can get by with the long nose of a skew chisel.

Cherry is a lovely wood to use for this, but any fairly dense, diffuse porous wood will be fine: in particular holly, box, field maple, plane and beech. You need to start with a 6½–8" (16–20 cm) length cleft from a log at least 3" (8 cm) in diameter and roughed out to a 1" (2·5 cm)

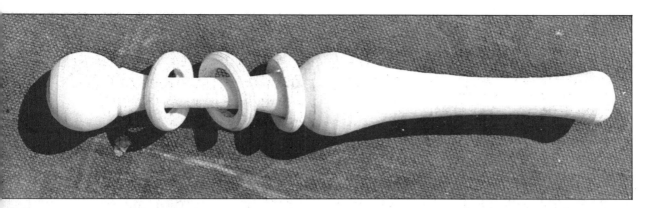

Fig. 10.3   Baby's rattle.

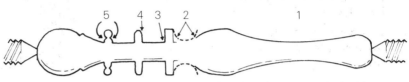

Fig. 10.4   The stages in making a baby's rattle.

cylinder (you could start with a piece of 1½" (6 cm) roundwood, but it will be a little weaker). The longer the piece you start with, the more margin you will have for error. Too long, though, and it will start to whip on the lathe.

The pattern I shall describe is based on one that Don kindly gave me at a woodworker show, which I have adapted slightly for the pole-lathe.

Start with the roughing-out gouge 3" (8 cm) from the end to form a handle (Fig. 10.4). Use the skew chisel to round over the tip. Re-set the wood in the lathe so that the cord runs around the handle without running off the end on to the metal centre. Mark out the position of the three rings with the point of the skew chisel, each ring being ³/₁₆" (5 mm) wide with ½" (13 mm) between them, starting 4" (10 cm) from the tip of the handle. Clean out the waste between these with the small gouge and use the tip of the skew chisel to square up the sides of the rings. Then, using the blade of the skew, round off the corners so that there are now three deep square-edged 'beads' (a bead being the technical name for such a shape). Burnish them with a handful of clean shavings.

With either the hooked tool or the tip of the skew chisel, cut away steadily underneath the first of these beads to produce the ring. You must be sure to pull the tool well back on each reverse stroke of the lathe to avoid it catching on to the wood. Try to make the cuts on both sides meet at the same point. The ring should now come free.

Hold it with your hand and smooth off its inside face by rubbing it on the rest of the rattle. Repeat this for the other two rings.

Hopefully, they will come free without breaking, but if one should break you may have enough spare wood at the end to try another. Push all the rings to one end and, using the roughing-out gouge, clean up the stem beneath the rings. You could leave this as a simple curve, or alternatively crisp up the lines by cutting a flange at each end with the skew chisel.

Shape the end of the rattle with the skew chisel. If you have some spare wood, you could part it off. Finally, burnish the whole thing (the handle should already have been well burnished by the cord) and rub in a harmless finish such as vegetable oil or beeswax.

If it worked – well done! If not, then try and try again. This makes a wonderful demonstration piece (if your nerves can stand it!).

4   Spoons

Another of my favourite projects is making spoons, if only for sentimental reasons, as it provided my first income as a green woodworker in 1978 when I sold a dozen cawl spoons to a craft shop in Cardigan (Fig. 10.5).

These are elegant lightweight spoons used for eating the traditional broth in West Wales from which their name is derived. They are about 12"

Fig. 10.5   A cawl spoon.

(30 cm) long, with a simple tapering handle and a deep bowl about 2" (5 cm) in diameter.

Traditionally, these were carved out of sycamore with a small axe, a hooked tool called a *twca cam* (Fig. 10.6), a spokeshave and a knife. I have asked several blacksmiths to make me a *twca cam*, but I have never got on well with it. There is a smaller Swedish version which one can buy that I find useful for finishing off the bowl of the spoon. Generally, however, I prefer to use a modern spoon gouge for the bulk of the hollowing.

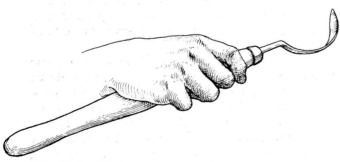

Fig. 10.6   *The* twca cam.

You can start with a sycamore log either 2" (5 cm) in diameter or 5" (13 cm) or more. The other woods as suggested for the rattle could also be used. If you have a 2" (5 cm) log this should be split down the middle and you can then use its semi-circular shape as a basis for the bowl. With a larger log, split it into eighths and work from that as shown (Fig. 10.7 (a), (b)).

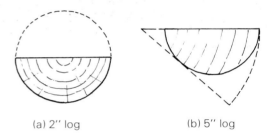

(a) 2" log   (b) 5" log

Fig. 10.7   Spoon blanks from (a) the round (b) a cleft log.

Spoon Method One – Carving

If you are fairly confident with the turner's axe, you can remove most of the surplus wood with this alone. Stand the blank with the bowl end resting on the chopping-block and chop off the corners at about 45 degrees. Turn it round and trim back with the axe as far as the shoulders of the bowls. For the uppermost cuts, it is better to rest the side of the blank on the edge of the chopping-block (Fig. 10.8).

If you are not too happy with this, saw out the shoulders with a tenon saw (better safe than sorry) and then split along the handle to meet these cuts (Fig. 10.9 (a), (b)).

At this stage, before continuing with the handle, carve out the bowl. I like to grip the spoon in the shaving-horse just below the bowl and carve it out with the spoon gouge and mallet.

It is useful to make a simple jig by carving a hollow in one end of a length of softwood. The

Fig. 10.8   Axing the shoulders of a spoon.

Fig. 10.10   Gripping the spoon in a softwood jig.

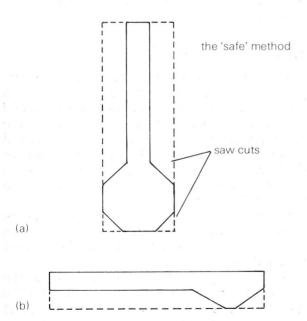

the 'safe' method

saw cuts

(a)

(b)

Fig. 10.9   Sawing the spoon blank from (a) above (b) the side.

bowl of the spoon can then rest in this hollow, which will prevent it from slipping around and also support the handle where it is gripped by the horse (Fig. 10.10).

Start by hollowing out across the grain to avoid the fibres tearing out. You can then clean up the front and back of the bowl by sweeping down into this hollow. As you cannot see the inside and outside of the bowl simultaneously, gauge the thickness by feeling it with your thumb and forefinger. (Remember, vision is but one of your senses.)

Having removed the bulk of the wood from the bowl, finish it by just pushing the gouge without using the mallet. Remember always to work down into the bottom of the bowl – never work up the sides, or you will tear the grain. This is where you could use a hooking knife. Whenever possible, try to anchor the hand that is holding the tool against either the other hand or the shaving-horse to stop it slipping. Now, with either the spokeshave or a knife, smooth off the outside of the bowl and then the handle. When using the knife, hold it steady with one hand, using the fingers of the other hand to grip the spoon and the thumb to push the back of the knife blade. This will give you greater control and reduce any risk of the knife slipping (Fig. 10.11).

Fig. 10.11   Supporting the knife.

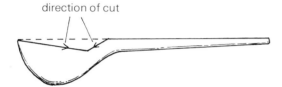

Fig. 10.12   Shaping the top of the bowl.

To finish off a cawl spoon, take the knife and cut downwards from the handle towards the bowl, and a more gentle slope along the top of the bowl to meet this cut, giving it a much more interesting and functional shape. Then trim up the inside of the lip of the bowl to make a fine edge (Fig. 10.12).

Within a few days this will have dried out, and you can scrape it smooth and then finish it off with fine sandpaper. After sanding it once, wipe it with water to raise the grain and then, when dry, sand it again. Rub with an edible oil and it can be used straight away.

Spoon Method Two – Turning

An alternative method makes use of the pole-lathe while avoiding the rather tricky axe work. You need a blank with a perfectly straight grain for this job. Rough out a 2" (5 cm) diameter circle and turn a shape, starting with the handle so that you have a silhouette the same as that of two spoons held face to face. You will need to leave stubs at the very ends to avoid the marks caused by the metal centres (Fig. 10.13).

Fig. 10.13   The spoon blank on the lathe.

Cut off these stubs with the knife and, holding the blank with the bowl end uppermost, take your courage in both hands and cleave it down the middle (Fig. 10.14). If you chose your wood well, you will now have two spoon blanks. If not, the worst which can happen is that you will have one spoon-blank and a very small bowl-blank! Now proceed as with *Method One*. (I believe this is how the Welsh spoon carvers did it, but I have yet to find any reference to it.)

Fig. 10.14   Splitting apart two spoons.

Small spoons can be carved out of large twigs pruned from a suitable tree or shrub. Large ladles can be made either by carving or by using the lathe. The bowl of a large ladle can be turned by employing the techniques used in bowl turning (see Chapter 16). If you take to making spoons, look out for one which you like the look *and* the feel of, and work out the best way to copy it.

5 Spatula

Although you do not need a pole-lathe to make it, I would like to include the spatula (see Fig. 10.1) because it is so simple to make and provides a good use for any leftovers of sycamore or beech.

Split the log down to narrow segments, then cut out the shape of the handle with a small axe. Gripping the rough handle, shave the blade of the spatula using the drawknife with the bevel up (as with the wedges for tool handles). Either use the spokeshave to clean up the handle while gripping the blade in the horse, or whittle the handle using a knife. You should be able to produce a spatula in a few minutes.

I have outlined my favourite simple pole-lathe projects, but when you have mastered these you will be able to try out any other spindle-turning projects where the finished article is up 40" (1 m) long and 4" (10 cm) in diameter. Here are a few suggestions:

1 Light pulls – using sections to be parted off from a larger job.

2 Foot massagers – simply a series of rounded-off V-shaped grooves in a length of wood hollowing slightly in the centre. Leave a smooth section at one end for the cord and then part it off.

3 Cricket stumps and bails – copy a commercially-made set and use good straight ash.

4 Drumsticks – a good exercise in turning long thin objects (see Windsor chairs, p. 156).

5 Bodhran tappers – a short drumstick with bulbous ends used on an Irish version of the drum.

6 Spirtle sticks – a device for stirring porridge.

7 Plant dibbers.

8 Skittles – you will need a heavier skew chisel and roughing-out gouge to make these. Season them slowly in good ventilation afterwards.

9 Baseball bats.

10 Lace bobbins – a good exercise in applying a tender touch.

Eleven

Chair Joints

I managed to amuse myself on the pole-lathe for several years making simple one-piece objects. Sooner or later you will probably – like myself – want to tackle the craft for which the pole-lathe is most renowned – namely chair-making (Fig. 11.1). Before starting on the projects, however, it is worth discussing some of the issues which arise during chair assembly.

Country chairs and stools are functional items which were originally fashioned by rural craftsmen using simple techniques with locally grown materials. Wood was certainly the major raw material, though some chairs had woven seats of rush, straw, rope or bark, but rarely were they upholstered. Their joints were generally constructed by tightly fitting a round piece of wood (the tenon) into a drilled hole (the mortise). Most of the components were shaped while the wood was green and the joints were then finished when they had dried out.

Windsor chair-legs, for example, were made in the woodland from timber which had been freshly felled, and were then stacked in the fresh

Fig. 11.1   A selection of country chairs: spindle-back chair, frame stool, comb-back and bow-back Windsor chairs, Windsor stool.

air with a cover to keep off the rain until they were seasoned. Apart from the advantages already mentioned in Chapter 2, this also meant that the waste wood did not have to be transported to the workshops in town. The larger shavings were in fact either used in building the bodger's hut or else sold as firewood. The legs also weighed much less when seasoned, again reducing the burden of transport.

Although each region had its own identifiable style of chair, they usually fell into one of two direct categories:

1 Windsor (slab-and-stick);

   or

2 Post-and-rung

1 Windsor (Slab-and-stick)

The key component of the Windsor construction is a fairly thick solid plank seat into which the other components are socketed.

There are many theories put forward to explain the origin of the term Windsor chair, but the most likely explanation stems from the rapidly increasing population of London during the eighteenth and nineteenth centuries. They all needed chairs, many of which were produced in the East End of London, but steadily the production of chairs – especially the cheaper ones – shifted to around High Wycombe in the Chilterns. Many of these were traded at Windsor market before arriving in London as 'Windsor' chairs.

The 'slab-and-stick' style evolved from the earliest country stools or benches in which three or four sticks were driven into holes bored in a simple plank or half log.

As the style developed, the legs were made from wood which was cleft and shaved. Then backs were added, again by socketing the components into the plank seat. During the eighteenth century, the refinements were introduced which have continued in use to this day. Legs were turned on a lathe and were supported in the chair by 'stretchers'; these are cross-members fixed so as to force the legs apart and increase the rigidity of the structure. Then the *bow-back* was developed, being formed by placing a slender length of wood in a container filled with steam until supple enough to bend into shape. In the English tradition, a splat was often used; this is a decorated flat panel, usually in the centre of the back. The best known version is the *wheel-back*, which is still commonly used in mass-produced chairs for pubs and restaurants. There are also many elaborations including arm-chairs and rockers.

Post-and-rung

In contrast, the post-and-rung chair is based on a frame with two different sets of components: vertical posts and horizontal rungs. There are four posts into which a number of holes are drilled to form the mortises. The rungs are shaped to size and driven into the holes to create a rigid structure. A seat is then woven on to the framework out of rush, straw, bark or some similar soft material. An alternative to the woven seat is to cut slots into some of the components to hold a thin plank of wood.

A stool has four short posts of equal length, whereas a chair has the rear posts about twice the length of the front ones. Different methods can be adopted to fill in between the rear posts of a chair. A *ladderback* (common in Northern England and in American Shaker chairs) uses a series of horizontal slats. A *spindle back* has a number of vertical spindles supported between two or more horizontal rungs. Other variations involve adaptations of one or both of these methods and, on occasions, incorporate a woven back. By making the front posts longer, arms can be added and, as with the Windsors, they can be designed as rocking-chairs.

Mortise and Tenon Joints

Whether the stool or chair is of the post-and-rung or slab-and-stick variety, its construction is based on the round mortise and tenon joint. In cabinet-making, these mortises and tenons can take a variety of shapes according to their purpose. In making country chairs, the joints are usually round. The mortise is drilled out and the tenon can be either whittled or turned to fit; it is a very quick and simple method of jointing wood.

Unfortunately, due to the different rates of shrinkage of wood (see p. 18), any fluctuations in moisture content will cause movement with a corresponding loosening or tightening of the

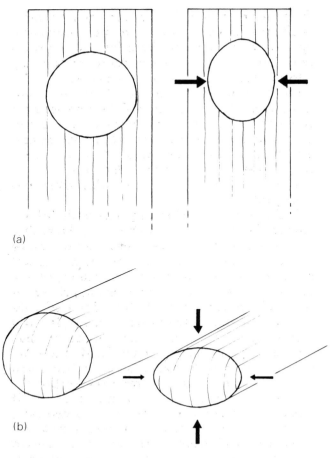

(a)

(b)

Fig. 11.2   (a) Shrinking mortise (b) shrinking tenon.

joint. If the wood dries out, both mortise and tenon will shrink to an oval shape (Fig. 11.2 (a), (b)). By aligning the grain so that both ovals are in the same direction, the problem will be minimised.

The radial face is the face at right-angles to the growth rings; on a wood with prominent annual rings, the lines will be parallel and fairly evenly spaced (Fig. 11.3). The tangential face lies parallel to the annual rings. Whenever a curved surface has been shaped, or where the grain is not exactly straight, V-shaped patterns appear on this tangential face where the growth rings have been cut through (Fig. 11.4).

In a post-and-rung joint, the optimum arrangement is as shown, with the mortise drilled into the tangential face. The tenon is then inserted with its radial faces to the side (Fig. 11.5).

Let us consider an example where such a joint is made between a post and a rail of the same type of wood and with a similar moisture content. If the joint dries out, the *sides* should move together and remain a good fit, but the *upper and lower surfaces* may lose contact due to the greater rate of shrinkage of the tenon. Should the joint gain moisture, then again the sides will remain snug, but the tenon will expand against the end grain of the post. If this is not excessive, the tenon will become slightly compressed, resulting in an even tighter joint. As it subsequently dries out, the joint will return to its original state and still be a

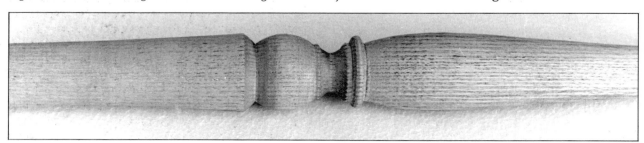

Fig. 11.3   The radial face.

Fig. 11.4   The tangential face.

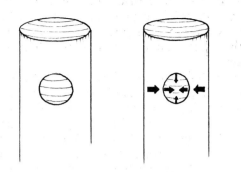

Fig. 11.5 Optimum grain alignment for a joint.

good fit. If the movement is excessive, however, there is a danger that the upper and lower surfaces of the tenon will become crushed to a point at which the cells lose their elasticity. In such a case, when the joint dries out again the undamaged cells in the tenon will shrink, the crushed cells will remain crushed and the joint will then become loose.

Not only can all this happen in a vertical plane, but problems also arise with regard to a horizontal section through the joint.

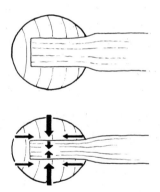

Fig. 11.6 A mortise shrinking along the tenon.

We can now see that if the joint dries out, the length of the tenon will hardly change, but the depth of the mortise will decrease as the post shrinks. The walls of the mortise will creep slightly along the length of the tenon (Fig. 11.6). If a brittle glue was used in the joint, this rubbing between the two surfaces will cause the bond to crack.

In a maritime climate such as the British Isles,

the extremes in humidity are rarely encountered (well, one extreme anyway!) and the joints held up well in common furniture for many generations. Any tenons were well dried before fitting into the mortises, and nothing would ever dry out enough to cause the kind of problems just mentioned. Now that central heating is more common, these joints are subjected to far greater fluctuations in moisture content than ever before. The result is that chairs which have lasted for centuries are now starting to fall to bits.

How can the green woodworker overcome these problems?

In America, where in many regions there have always been wide fluctuations in humidity, country chairmakers have often used a technique which involved fitting a dry tenon into a wet mortise. The idea is that as the chair dries out, the mortise shrinks more than the tenon, gripping it tighter the more it dries out. When I started making chairs – especially post-and-rung style – this seemed to provide the answer. But as we have now seen, a dry rung which is fitted into a wet mortise will quickly absorb some moisture and swell. There is a chance therefore either that the mortise will be split open, or that the cells of wood in the tenon will become crushed and, when it dries out again, the joint will come loose.

After several years of trial and error, heated discussion during courses and quiet contemplation of the relevant literature, I have adopted the following range of techniques to overcome these problems. By the very nature of wood, the joints can never be perfect, but by combining these techniques I am now able to make a chair well capable of holding together when subjected to normal wear and tear. Some of these methods apply primarily to post-and-rung construction, some mainly to Windsors and some to both. They will be mentioned again when we come to the projects themselves. You may think that many of these are not worth the trouble, and of course you may wish to try out other methods which I have not mentioned.

There are several other interesting approaches put forward by American chairmakers such as Dunbar, Alexander and Sawyer, and the debate still continues. Whatever you decide, I suggest you make a note of the technique *you* use. Your great-grandchildren might just be interested when the joints in one of their chairs finally work loose!

1 Correct Grain Alignment

This technique has already been covered on p. 107. By aligning the grain as shown in Fig. 11.5, you minimise the likelihood of gaps appearing between the surfaces of a joint due to fluctuations in humidity. Of course, this may not always be possible; as for example, where two joints are made into a post at right-angles to each other. Compromises must be made, but remember this point while you work out your solution.

2 Moisture Content

Although a completely dry tenon in a completely green mortise will cause problems, it is an advantage if the tenon is *somewhat* drier. As long as the joint can tighten without actually crushing any of the cells beyond the limits of their elasticity, this can only be an advantage.

There are small, battery-operated devices called moisture meters which you can use to measure the moisture content of your chair parts. I know a number of green woodworkers who use them, though I consider such a device rather a luxury.

When I started making chairs, I used to place the wood in my airing cupboard and weigh it at regular intervals until the weight became stable. I then knew that this was as dry as I could get it. The drying time varies – according to the diameter of the wood – between a few days for 3/8" (10 mm) diameter spindles and several months for 1½" (38 mm) diameter chair-legs. Fortunately the tenons are always at the end of a length of wood, and will therefore dry out before the centre which is where any mortise is likely to be made.

These drying periods can only be taken as very rough guides, and it is best if you experiment with the conditions you encounter in your own workshop or home.

3 Grooved Tenons

If the mortise is likely to shrink, you can make the most of this by shaping a groove on the circumference of the tenon. As the mortise dries, it will be able to close into the groove and thus lock the tenon in position (Fig. 11.7). Even if it does come loose, it should not pull out.

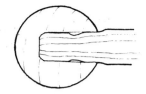

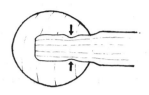

Fig. 11.7 The grooved tenon.

4 Assembling Joints Under Tension

As mentioned earlier, the Windsor chair is constructed so that the stretchers force outwards against the legs. This results not only in the joint between the stretcher and the leg being under tension, but equally the joint between the leg and the seat (Fig. 11.8).

This will force the bearing surfaces into contact, increasing their grip on each other. A similar effect is gained in a post-and-rung construction if the holes are not exactly in line as shown.

When the frame is assembled, the two rungs will be pulled into line in order to be fixed into the opposite post. This again will impose a certain amount of tension on the whole system (Fig. 11.9).

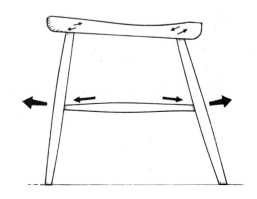

Fig. 11.8 Stretchers stretching.

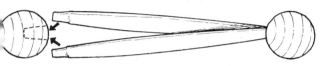

Fig. 11.9   Tensions in post-and-rung construction.

Obviously, this principle should not be over-done in either of these examples. Once the natural elasticity of the wood has been ex-hausted, some of the cells will become crushed and the joint will become weaker. However, it does suggest that slight human error when drill-ing holes in a post can add to the strength of a chair.

The approach involving the building of tension into the construction is also employed when using steam-bent components. There is always an element of unpredictability in steam-bending. When the bow is removed from the former, it may spring open or it may actually close up; rarely does it stay exactly the desired shape. When it is fitted into place, it will have to be forced into shape and will retain some of this tension thereafter.

5   Deep Blind Joints

Mortise and tenon joints can be of two types:

a   through, where the tenon emerges at the far end of the mortise (Fig. 11.10(a)); and

b   blind, where the tenon stops short of the other side (Fig. 11.10(b)).

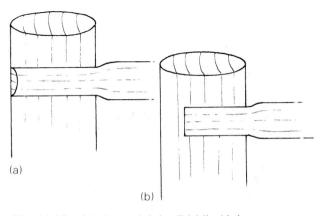

(a)

(b)

Fig. 11.10   (a) through joint (b) blind joint.

If the nature of the construction forces the tenon *into* the mortise, it leads to fewer problems if a blind joint is used. This avoids the possibility of the tenon projecting if the joint dries out; it also reduces the movement in the tenon, as the end grain is not exposed to the atmosphere and will therefore be less able to respond to changes in atmospheric humidity.

This joint should be made deep into the mortise to provide sufficient anchorage. If possible, aim for the depth of the mortise to be about 1½ times the diameter of the tenon, e.g. a ½" (13 mm) tenon should fit ¾" (19 mm) into the mortise. Sometimes this may not be practicable, but you should never make the mortise depth less than the tenon diameter.

If a joint is going to be subject to pulling forces, you may need a through joint held with a wedge (see next section).

6   Pins and Wedges

One way to prevent a blind joint from pulling apart is to drill a small hole through it and drive in a small strong pin. I like to use a piece of cleft oak whittled to shape; its irregular profile helps it grip into the joint so that it cannot itself come loose (Fig. 11.11).

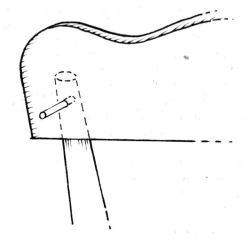

Fig. 11.11   A pinned joint.

Another, more subtle method of securing a blind joint is by using a fox wedge. Here a slot is cut into the end of the tenon, into which a wedge is placed. As the joint is driven in, the wedge will

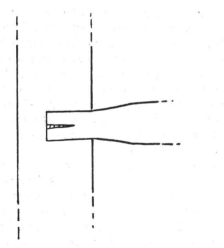

Fig. 11.12   A fox-wedged joint.

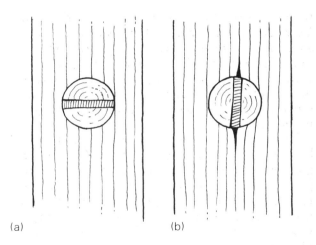

(a)   (b)

Fig. 11.13   Wedge alignment (a) correct (b) incorrect.

hit the end of the mortise and force itself into the end of the tenon, thus tightening the joint (Fig. 11.12). This works best if the mortise hole can be slightly flared away from the opening. If it works, it creates a very strong joint which is unlikely to pull apart.

In practice, however – using modern auger bits, at least – it is difficult to flare a round mortise. Another problem is to make the wedge large enough to do its job properly without being so large as to prevent the tenon from being driven fully home. There is also a possibility that the wedge will break out of the back of the mortise.

A simpler alternative where the joint is under tension is to use a through joint and drive a wedge into the end of the tenon after the joint has been assembled. (This is exactly the method described for fixing a handle into a maul head in Chapter 7.) The important thing to remember is that the slot in the tenon is aligned at right-angles to the grain of the mortise, so that the wood around the mortise is not cleft open by the wedge (Fig 11.13 (a), (b)).

7   Interlocking Joints

When using post-and-rung construction, it is possible to drill the mortises so that one rail will lock another one into place.

After one side of the frame has been assembled, the mortises are drilled for the adjacent side so that the drill will cut away about a quarter of the tenon now located in the post. When the new

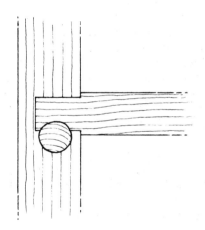

Fig. 11.14   Interlocking joints.

tenon is inserted, it will fill that space and prevent the first tenon from either turning or falling out (Fig. 11.14). It can be argued that this will weaken the post at such a joint. However, in post-and-rail construction there is little sideways pressure on the posts; if the wood has been cleft and the tenons are not too large, this technique should pose little danger of breakage.

8   Combining Different Woods

As we have already seen, various woods have differing properties, e.g. the elasticity of ash and the wild grain of elm. For this reason, different woods are used for different parts of the chair. You can also make use of the varying rates of shrinkage between woods to help keep the joints tight. For example, if a wood with slight movement (e.g. sweet chestnut) is used for the tenon into a wood with large movement (e.g. beech), when the joint dries out the mortise will tighten up on the tenon.

Most of the problems in joints are not caused by the initial shrinkage of wood, but by subsequent movement due to changes in atmospheric humidity some time after assembly. As a result, I see this technique as one of the most useful methods of keeping joints tight. It also provides another excuse for using a combination of different woods to make up a chair.

9   *Use A Glue That Allows Movement*

Provided you use as many of the above techniques as you can, there is a good chance that your stools and chairs will stay together without any need for gluing. If for some reason you have to assemble your chair before the parts have shrunk sufficiently, it is wiser not to use glue but to wait and see if it comes loose and then make some adjustments. Glue would then be a hindrance. Otherwise I see no virtue in avoiding glue, which is one more means of holding your work together.

Accepting the inevitability of some movement in the joints, you should avoid a brittle glue that is likely to crack. For this reason I prefer one of the PVA glues, preferably waterproof, such as Evostick Waterproof Woodwork adhesive. This also has the advantage of taking longer to dry, thus giving you more time to work. Bruce Hoadley has suggested some techniques using rubber-like silicon adhesives, which are better able to absorb the wood movements discussed. Their successful application relies on some sophisticated techniques to ensure the correct thickness of adhesive, but it is possible that future developments may make their use more convenient.

Making the Joints

Mortises

The mortises are made by drilling. For most joints, a brace and bit is the most practical piece of equipment. Only for holes less than 3/8″ (10 mm) is it feasible (without power) to use a twist drill; while only over 1¼″ (32 mm) is it necessary to use the much slower bar-auger. Of course, if you already have a powered pillar drill you can use this for most joints. If you have a standard electric drill you can try it as I once did, but you may find the effort saved by the motor will soon be outweighed by the worry of a slight slip ruining your work.

One piece of equipment – the most expensive in my workshop, costing £65 – which I have found extremely useful, especially during courses, is a boring machine (Fig. 11.15). (That's what it is called, but I find it very exciting!) This, I understand, was designed for drilling out large mortises in building beams. It functions like a two-handled brace, which makes its operation less strenuous than a normal brace and bit. How-

Fig. 11.15   A boring machine in action.

ever, its big advantage is that it can be set at a particular angle and is, therefore, a great help in drilling the leg and back holes in a Windsor chair seat. Mine came with two large diameter auger bits so, in order to use it, I had to adapt the mouth of a normal brace to fit into the boring machine so that it would then accept modern bits. Unless you are likely to make a large number of Windsor chairs, you will probably want to stay with a brace and bit.

Traditionally, chair-makers used spoon-bits which are well described by Michael Dunbar as resembling 'a test tube sliced in half along its length'. It has no lead screw, as with an auger bit, making it easier to alter the angle at which you are drilling as the hole progresses. It is also useful where the depth of the hole is limited, as there is no need to stop short because the lead screw might break through. Similar to this is a shell bit.

Nowadays these are no longer standard tools, although I understand they are currently being made again in Taiwan. If you do manage to acquire a set, with practice they should prove useful. However, in the methods I describe I shall assume that you are using the more common auger bits, which are fine for making post-and-rung chairs as long as you take great care not to split or tear the wood when starting to drill. Even more care is needed with Windsor chairs, because many of the angles are further from 90 degrees and the spurs of an auger bit are more likely to tear the wood. For the smaller holes in bows, for example, I prefer to use a twist drill after having started the hole with a small gouge.

Sharpening auger bits is a very precise job and however well carried out, you will rarely restore one which has been damaged or badly sharpened in the past. If you intend to use old auger bits, make sure they are not worn on the outside edge of the spurs. I have found it worth investing in new ones of good quality.

The one occasion when I find it very useful to have a round or flat bit is when drilling blind mortises for the legs into a Windsor seat. For this job, I start drilling with an auger bit and then finish it off with an old Scotch-eyed bit with the lead spike and spurs removed (Fig. 11.16). I also file a mark on this 1¼" (32 mm) from the end, so that I can see when to stop drilling.

Tenons

There are various ways of making the round tenons of country chairs, the simplest method being to whittle them with a spokeshave or a knife. With the latter, no other equipment is required and it makes a good job to be carried out sitting in front of a log fire. Nonetheless it is time consuming. The slightly ridged surface which results should not detract from the strength of the joint, as the wood will be able to 'give' to some extent to accommodate it.

Another device I have used is a rounding plane or 'rounder' (Fig. 11.17). This works on the pencil-sharpener principle and consists of a solid block with a tapered hole running through it. A blade is held so that its cutting edge just sits on the perimeter of the hole. As a piece of wood is fed into the rounder by revolving it, the blade removes a continuous shaving until the tenon is small enough to pass out of the other end; therefore a cylinder of a given diameter is produced every time.

This is a traditional device, but was developed by Fred Lambert and is now being manufactured by Peter Hindle of Ashem Crafts (see Appendix 2) using cast aluminium. The technique of using rounders in conjunction with geared-down lathes is currently demonstrated far and wide by Jack Hill, who uses them not only to make joints but also to shape complete chair parts.

Using the rounder has the same advantage as whittling, in that it avoids the need to return to the lathe when assembling the chair. If you are lucky you might find some old rounding planes, although they will probably require some renovation. To buy a set of new ones would cost up to £200, but if you intend to use them with a geared-down powered lathe to shape the components as well as the joints, it might be worth it. If you wish to make your own, a detailed drawing is given in Fred Lambert's book (see Appendix 1). To make a tapered hole, you will need a reamer or some other device which you may find difficult to obtain. What you have to do is to set

Fig. 11.16 A round-nosed auger bit.

Fig. 11.17   Rounding planes: on the left, two home-made; on the right, made by Peter Hindle of Ashem Crafts.

a blade into a block of wood so that as the workpiece rotates in the block the blade is cutting in the same way as the flat chisel would do on a lathe. Obtaining just the right cutting angle can be a delicate job, requiring a little shaving off here and adding a shim there. Whether you buy new or old or make your own, it will take a little time and practice before you can make effective use of them.

The third alternative is, of course, the pole-lathe. When you turn the chair components green, they should already be cut to length. There is no rotating metalwork as on a powered or treadle lathe, so the workpiece can be safely turned right up to both ends, avoiding the need to part off (that is, to remove a superfluous section at the end of the workpiece). When the component has dried out, it can easily be remounted on to the lathe, using its original centres with the driving cord in the middle. It is then a matter of seconds to turn the tenon (or tenons) down to size. There is always a danger of removing too much wood and making the tenon undersized, so at first you have to take it very steadily and constantly check with the measuring gauge, but with practice you will develop an accurate eye. Using the pole-lathe also has the advantage that it is simple to chamfer the tips of the tenons to help them into the mortise, and to shape a slight groove to help lock them in place.

When you first try re-turning a dried component on the lathe, you will notice just how much it has become distorted. There is no point in trying to blend the new cuts that you make at the tenon into the original cuts made when the wood was green. Take any antique Windsor chair and look at the shoulder cut at the tenon in the workshops before assembly. You will see that it is quite distinct from – and invariably rougher than – the finish obtained by the bodger in the woods. Until the advent of specialised machinery in the late nineteenth century, tenons were nearly always turned to size in this manner on a pole-lathe.

You must take care that if your lathe is set up outside, you keep the chair components dry. If they spend much time in moist conditions, they will absorb this moisture and start to swell. Choose a dry day (summer or winter) and keep the chair parts in a plastic bag except when you are working on them; then, if possible, return them to a warm, dry environment before fitting them into the chair.

There are also devices called hollow augers described by John Alexander (see Appendix 1), but he admits that to use a pole-lathe for turning the tenons will 'take some learning, but it beats whittling and hollow augering and the slow speed is right'.

Twelve

Steam-bending and Other Chair-making Jigs

Before starting to make any stools or chairs you will need a few extra pieces of equipment. For the stools these are fairly simple. For the chairs, you will require a steamer and some bending jigs. To give an idea of what jigs you need for which projects, here is a summary:

	low-bench	drilling post	turning saw	steamer	comb jig	post jig	bow jig & strap
frame-stool	✓	✓					
spindle-back	✓	✓		✓	✓	✓	
Windsor stool	✓		✓				
comb-back	✓		✓	✓	✓		
bow-back	✓		✓	✓			✓

should aim to use a plank 2–3″ (5–8 cm) thick, 15″ (40 cm) wide and 5 ft (1·5 m) long. It need not be planed or have straight edges, but the top surface should be as level as possible. Elm would be an ideal timber for the job, but because of its scarcity I would rather use a plank like that for better

Although not really a jig as such, one extra item you will require for all these projects is a 1-ft (30 cm) length of softwood, such as roofing batten. This is to be laid on to any chair component before striking it with a hammer, thus protecting the surface. Alternatively, you could use a special 'soft' hammer, but I find the softwood works well enough.

Instead of the low-bench and drilling post, you can use a standard woodworker's bench with a vice or get by with a Workmate; if you have one of these you could start straight away on the frame stool. A band-saw or a good powered jig-saw will take some of the effort out of sawing planks and enable you to make a Windsor stool straight away. For those who have none of these woodworking luxuries, here is how the green woodworker does it.

Low-bench

This is a very simple construction consisting of a heavy plank with four legs mortised into it. You

purposes. Beech, sycamore or plane are all good alternatives. Failing this, you would use a large softwood plank or bolt together several softwood beams. Or if you want to be a purist, try cleaving it out of a large log. You will find, however, that if it cleaves well enough to enable you to do this, it may split when under stress.

Ideally the legs should be ash, but oak or beech would be good substitutes. They should be cleft and 20–24″ (50–60 cm) in length. If you have a 1½″ (38 mm) auger to drill the sockets, this is the best size for the leg tenons; if not, make them 1¼″ (32 mm) but no smaller. Alternatively, you could chisel out square sockets with a mortise chisel, but this is an approach I would rather avoid. I prefer swinging an auger bit to pounding a chisel any day. Besides which, I have not yet found a way to make square tenons on a pole-lathe!

The important thing is that the low-bench should feel solid. It will be used for several purposes: to support the chair parts when you knock them together; to hold planks steady when you saw out seats; to hold these seats as you drill them; and as a base for various jigs. It also makes a useful shelf or coffee table.

If you are working in the open, you could point the legs and drive them into the ground. If working in the woods, you may be able to use one or more tree trunks cut off 2 ft (60 cm) high, on which you can nail or peg the plank. As another alternative, you could bury some posts in the ground and fix the plank to these.

Drilling Post (see Fig 13.7)

This was mentioned in Chapter 7 and you should have a suitable post incorporated into the cleaving-break. Another way of obtaining a solid vertical face is to fix a block of wood at least 20 × 6" (51 × 15 cm) to the frame at one end of the lathe. If you intend to make a spindle-back chair, you will find the post jig described later also serves well as a drilling post.

Whether you use an upright on the cleaving-break, a jig mounted on the lathe or any other convenient vertical post (such as a barn-pole), you should drive in some sturdy pegs as illustrated (see Fig. 13.7). These should be about 6" (15 cm) long and ⅝–1" (16–26 mm) in diameter when seasoned. It is best if they are turned to size along their whole length after having seasoned. Reject chair-legs or stool rungs are always useful for such purposes.

Ensure that the post is truly vertical and that the pins are truly horizontal. This will enable you to drill your mortises at the correct angle (see p. 127).

The Turning Saw

This is a type of frame-saw which operates on the same principle as the bow-saw, with a slender blade held under tension. In addition, the turning-saw is constructed so as to allow the blade to rotate; this makes it much easier to cut curved shapes, such as Windsor seats, out of planks. Traditionally, this was always the tool used for such jobs and was given a variety of different names such as the 'up-and-down saw', the 'dancing Betty' and the 'Jesus Christ saw', 'because I keep on bowing to it all the time I'm using it' (J. L. Mayes, Appendix 1).

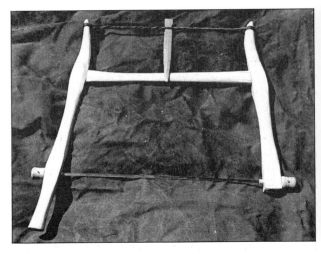

Fig. 12.1   A turning saw.

Requirements:

Green wood

32" (80 cm) good quality ash log 6" (15 cm)+ diameter.

8" (20 cm) dense diffuse porous wood, e.g. hornbeam, box, thorn, apple, pear, beech, holly, cleft from a log 5" (13 cm)+ diameter.

Other materials

30" (75 cm) long *sharp* ⅜" (10 mm) band-saw blade with 6 or 8 teeth per inch.

two 2" (5 cm) round nails.

17 ft (5 m) of pole-lathe cord.

As with most green wood projects, make the components green and leave them to season before assembly. Start with the turning knobs; it is best if these are made from one of the denser diffuse porous woods mentioned above, as they will be better able to withstand the pressure of the nails which hold the blade in place.

Turn them in one 8" (20 cm) length, then part them off when they are complete so that each is 4" (10 cm). The shanks should be 2" (5 cm) long and finish at ⅝" (16 mm) diameter when they have dried out, so remember to leave them oversize at first. Turn the knobs themselves to 1½" (2 cm) diameter, with square shoulders where they meet the shank so that they seat well on the handles. Only the shanks will need to be turned down when seasoned.

From the ash log, shape two arms to a rectangular section 2×1½" (5×4cm), one 32" (80cm) and one 26" (65cm) long. The ash must be quickly grown and straight-grained, as these arms will be subject to considerable stress when the saw is in use. They can be made straight with square edges, though some of their bulk and weight can be reduced if the corners are smoothed off (but leave them square where they will receive the knobs and the cross-piece).

The crosspiece is 26" (60cm) long and 1½×1" (4×2·5cm) in section over most of its length, but leave it round at one end where you will be holding it when in use (see Fig. 14.8). Cut two tenons at the ends 1½×½" (4×1·5cm) to fit 1" (2·5cm) into the arms. Cut the corresponding mortises into the arms of the saw (you can remove most of the wood with a brace and ½" (13mm) bit, then clean it up with a chisel). The stick to wind the cord tight – the toggle – can be a thin piece of ash 1×⅜×12" (2·5×1×30cm) with its corners smoothed off. Notch it slightly where it meets the string.

Assemble the crosspiece and the two arms and wrap the length of pole-lathe cord (3mm nylon) at least four times around the top of the arms, tying it so that the arms are about parallel to each other. In order to drill the holes for the turning knobs, tie some more string round the other ends of the arms and then tighten by the 'Spanish windlass' (rotate the toggle, tightening the cord).

Grip the saw firmly in a vice or to the drilling post, and mark the positions of the turning knobs. It is important that they are in line with each other so as to enable them to rotate properly. Using a brace with the correct bit, drill one hole, lining it up carefully with the mark on the other arm. Repeat this at the other end.

When they have dried, turn the shanks of the knobs down until they fit into their holes so that they can turn freely without being too loose. Carefully saw a slot down the shanks and 1" (2·5cm) into the thicker section of the knob. Into each knob, drill a hole ¾" (2cm) back from the shanks of the right diameter to accept the nails which will hold the blade (I found 3mm holes about right). Take the length of bow-saw blade

and, with the rest of the saw in its correct position, mark the location of the holes to be drilled in the blade. Use the same drill bit as you used to drill through the knobs. If the bit is in good condition you should manage with a hand-drill. You can now assemble the saw and round off the ends of the nails with a file. Remember to slacken the toggle when it is not in use, so as to release the strain on all the parts.

In *The Woodwright's Shop*, Roy Underhill describes a 'sash saw', which is an adaptation of the pole-lathe to produce a 'foot-operated, reciprocating band-saw'. I have yet to come across its use in the British chair-making tradition and, as Roy concedes, it has no real advantages over a hand-held turning saw. I'd like to try it out one day all the same.

Steam-bending

The principle of steam-bending is to soften a length of wood so that it becomes pliable and can be bent to the desired shape. This is sometimes achieved not by steam, but by boiling it in water. For small objects or in specialist crafts such as swill-basket making, this may be the best way. Turning water into steam requires considerable energy. However, the process of condensation (when the steam turns back to water) gives off this energy and keeps the steamed wood hotter for a longer period than if it had been boiled. Wood is at its best state for steam-bending when fibre saturation point has been reached – i.e. when the free water has been lost but the bound water is retained (see Chapter 2). At this stage the cells have not started to stiffen, but the gaps between them are full of air rather than sap, thus making the wood easier to compress.

One advantageous by-product of steaming is that much of the remaining moisture in the wood is driven out and subsequent seasoning is much quicker.

Some woods bend better than others. In this respect we are fortunate in the temperate climates where ash, beech, oak and elm are among the best timbers in the world for the purpose, along with the less common woods like walnut and robinia. One other wood popular for steam-bending is yew, although this is at its best when in the form of small-diameter roundwood.

Fig. 12.2   A steamer.

The Steamer

There are many ways to produce steam: a kettle, a pressure cooker or, better still, one of the specialised gadgets used for steam cleaning or removing wallpaper. Any of these, provided it has one steam outlet point, is fine. You will need a power source – be it electricity, gas or some other kind of flame – which will of course determine to some extent where you can use it. I like to do my bending in the woods, so the most obvious source of heat is firewood.

My first steamer was made when I was working on a woodland project with a team of trainees. I found a 3" (8 cm) diameter iron pipe and a colleague welded a thick plate over one end. Into this we poured a kettle full of boiling water, then placed the length of wood in the pipe, fitted a bung on top and supported the apparatus with the bottom end over a camp-fire. Had James Watt not beaten me to it, I would have invented the steam engine that day! After about 10 minutes, there was an almighty explosion with boiling water and steam propelling the bung half-

way across the woods. So I drilled a hole in the end and tried again, and we sat smugly watching a small jet of steam issuing forth from the bung. It was not until there was a smell of acrid smoke that we removed it from the fire to have a look at our chair-bow. We had now discovered how to make charcoal! With a little practice, though, we were able to use it to make some fairly rough but usable chair-bows.

The next stage served me well during my first courses and consisted of two 5-gallon drums. One had its top removed and a number of holes driven into the bottom; this was the burner. Later on, a door was cut in one side to enable more wood to be thrown in. On top of this was a metal mesh on which stood the second drum two-thirds full of water. I then fitted a copper pipe into a turned wooden bung which was tightly wedged into the mouth of the drum. Fitted to the copper pipe was a length of heavy rubber tube which ran to the 'steam chest': an 8" (20 cm) diameter heavy plastic pipe with a wooden bung at each end, one of which held another piece of copper pipe on to which the rubber tube was fixed. The second bung had a wooden handle and didn't fit very well. By fitting the bung, leaving a gap at the bottom, the steam had to fill the 'chest' before it could leak out of the gap, along with any water which had condensed. A simple rack was fitted inside and the chest was lagged with a pile of straw. The boiler provided about three hours of steam, after which we removed it to boil the kettle for lunch. We then had another steaming session in the afternoon. Of course, the plastic pipe soon began to sag and was replaced by a galvanised flue-pipe. After two years' service, the top drum was leaking badly and eventually the bottom drum collapsed having burned right through.

My current steamer was a joint design with my friendly blacksmith and evolved out of its forerunner (see Fig. 12.2). This is a 40-gallon drum cut two-thirds of the way up. The bottom section has a hinged door through which the firewood can be loaded and this also regulates the flame very sensitively. It has an inner skin to protect the main drum from the heat. The top third was welded on to a heavy steel plate and constitutes the boiler. It has two brackets welded to the plate so that it can sit on the burner. A steam pipe is welded to the top, and on to this is fixed the same rubber pipe. The round flue-pipe was limited in its capacity, so I have now constructed a wooden chest 5 ft (1·5 cm) long and 1 ft (30 cm) square in section (Fig. 12.3). It is made from marine ply which has been well varnished. I have made a rack as shown, which allows me to load all the parts for four of each of the chairs described in the next chapters.

Until the last few decades, steam-bending was the most common way of bending wood. Thonet must have been the greatest exponent of the art, responsible for the production of over 50 million bentwood chairs during the nineteenth century. As a slight diversion, it is interesting to note that these chairs were regarded as inexpensive, 'costing less than the average worker earned in a week' (*Fine Woodworking* on bending wood, see Appendix 1). Would that still be considered inexpensive nowadays?

In most modern production, curved shapes are produced by the process of lamination, whereby wood is sliced into thin flexible strips and then glued back together to the desired shape. Given the equipment to cut the strips, this is easier and generally more reliable. It also enables more

Fig. 12.3   A steam-chest.

dramatic shapes to be achieved and has led to some interesting designs. However, there are some craftsmen – notably David Colwell in Wales and Stuart Linford in High Wycombe – who still rely on this remarkable ability of wood to bend.

One surprising phenomenon of steam-bending is that the more gentle the curve, the more likely the bent component is to spring back. On the other hand a severe curve – like that of the bow-back – can often close up even more as it dries out. Two of the following jigs are gentle curves and must, therefore, be over-bent. As compensation, there is little chance of the wood splitting as it bends, provided it is cleft and straight-grained. The bow-back is bent to exactly the shape required, but it is advisable to use a strap to support the outer fibres while carrying out the bending.

Comb Jig

This is used to bend both the comb of the comb-back and the bent rungs of the spindle-back (Fig.

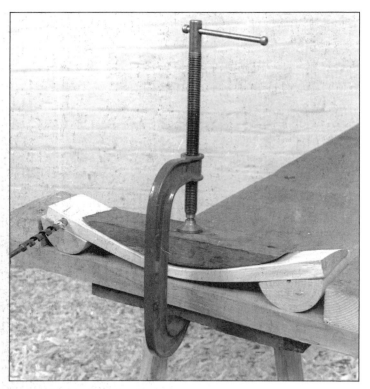

Fig. 12.4   A comb jig.

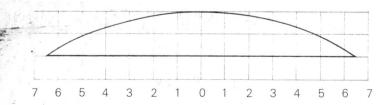

7 6 5 4 3 2 1 0 1 2 3 4 5 6 7

Fig. 12.5   Pattern for the comb former.

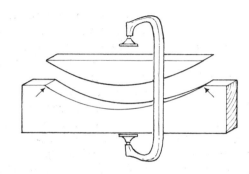

Fig. 12.6   A comb jig sawn from a block.

12.4). It is a fairly gentle bend designed to fit the curve of the sitter's back. The former is shaped as shown in Fig. 12.5. This can be sawn out of a thick block, and the blank can be bent by simply clamping it tightly between the two parts of the block (Fig. 12.6).

One drawback of this method is that the blank tends to be gripped by the jig just where the curve starts. As the blank is forced down, so the fibres on the outside of the curve are stretched and may split apart. The jig illustrated in Fig. 12.4 avoids this problem, as well as giving you yet another chance to use the lathe.

Fix two 3×2" (8×5 cm) blocks (softwood will do) 20" (50 cm) apart, to the low-bench or to a separate block at least 26" (65 cm) long. Find a straight branch about 6" (15 cm) in diameter, more than 4" (10 cm) long. Turn this to a uniform 5" (13 cm) cylinder, cut it to 4" (10 cm) in length, split it down the middle and level the flat surfaces. Shape the moulding block as illustrated in Fig. 12.5. When the comb blank is clamped down, the two half-cylinders can rotate thus relieving the stresses. This jig can also be used for the bent rungs of the spindle-back chair, placing the shorter one between the two longer ones.

Post Jig

This is a beautifully simple jig adapted from one used by Dave Sawyer which requires no straps or G-cramps. It can be bolted to the pole-lathe, or used on its own. The outline is given in Fig. 12.7 and can be made up from a number of pieces of 3×2" (8×5 cm) softwood sawn or axed to shape, planed smooth and then glued, nailed or bolted together. Two slots or holes are cut into the base of the jig about 1¼" (32 mm) wide to grip the base of the chair-posts before bending.

To clamp the top of the posts into place, you can simply lash them with pole-lathe twine. An alternative is to make a simple jig consisting of an 8" (20 cm) length of 3×2" (8×5 cm) softwood with a large tapered mortise drilled out so that it can be fitted over the tops of the posts to hold them in place. The top of the bending jig should also be shaped to fit through this block. A hole should then be drilled into the top of the bending jig to take a peg or large nail to lock the block into place (see Fig. 13.28). Provided it is truly vertical, this jig can also be used as a basis for the drilling

120

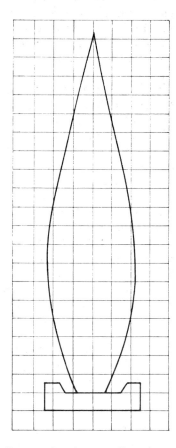

1 sq = 2"

Fig. 12.7   Pattern for the post jig.

Fig. 12.8   The bow jig.

post described earlier. When not in use, it can be unbolted and removed from the lathe until required.

The jig will also be used to grip the posts when drilling the rung mortises. To help locate their positions, mark on the jig a series of horizontal lines the following distances from the bottom of the slots for the chair-posts: 6, 12, 18, 22, 32 and 35" (15, 30, 45, 55, 80 and 88 cm). Taking the bend of the posts into account, the top mortise should be about 3½" (10 cm) below the top of the post.

Bow Jig (Fig. 12.8)

This bend is much more severe than the previous two and will therefore demand more of the wood, the equipment and of course the bender. Start by making a template on thick card from the pattern given (Fig. 12.9). To ensure the symmetry of the jig, cut out half of the pattern and fold this over to give you the outline of the other half.

Making the Jig

Basically, the bending jig is a rigid block the shape of the bow required. This could be sawn out of solid plank; possibly a piece of the plank left over from the seat, or any other plank at least 1½ × 14½ × 20" (4 × 37 × 51 cm). Failing this, you could build up a former from plywood, chipboard or some more 3 × 2" (8 × 5 cm) softwood left over from making the lathe. You will also need a firm backing to the former in order to fix the bow in place with pegs and wedges. If you have a very heavy work-bench, you could either clamp the former flat on the bench-top or fix it

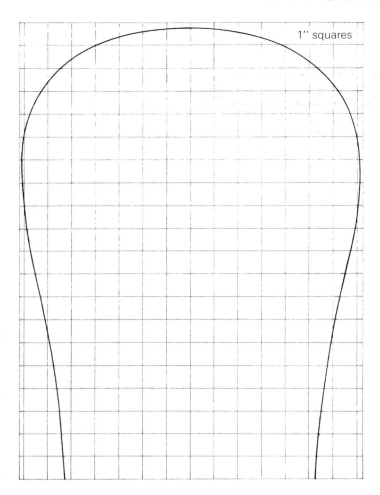

Fig. 12.9   Pattern for the bow jig.

bow blank will have been cut, there is only a slight chance of the wood tearing on the outside of the curve. In this situation, the former is fixed to a heavy iron or wooden bench drilled with a grid-work of holes. One end of the yew pole is held against one end of the former and pulled into shape. As the bend progresses, steel pins are located in the grid behind the bow and wedges driven in. If necessary, the last part can be levered into place and then wedged (Fig. 12.10).

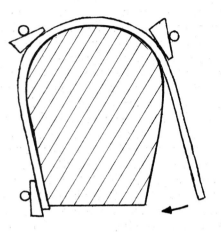

Fig. 12.10   Bending a yew branch.

It is possible to bend cleft ash in this way, but greater leverage is gained by gripping the bow with a flexible strap with a long handle at either end. This also helps to counteract any tendency for the fibres on the outside to break out. If you consider that on the completed bow the outer surface is over 3" (8 cm) longer than the inner, you will realise the stresses that act upon the wood. Obviously, there has to be a compromise between keeping the outside compressed in order to avoid it pulling apart and slackening the inside so as to prevent it from buckling.

An interesting selection of bending techniques is given in the Timber Research Establishment leaflet on the subject. One solution to the problem of splitting out and buckling is to use a spring steel strap with a device at the handles to slacken it slightly as the bend progresses. It is suggested that the outside curve can be allowed to expand up to 3 per cent, which led me to try a material which would expand at about that rate as the bend proceeded. I tried some heavy-duty nylon

vertically on to one end (see Fig. 12.8). If your low-bench is fixed to a tree-stump, you could use that. Should you be bending near the cleaving-break, you could fix the former to the drilling post making sure that the post extends at least 6" (15 cm) above the former. This will enable you to fix a peg into the post to support a wedge which grips the top of the bow. You will also need to use a sash cramp or some similar device to hold the ends of the bow in place when it has been completed. With a little improvisation you could even use one of the A-frames of the pole-lathe to anchor the jig.

If you can obtain suitable yew roundwood this can be bent – as with the previous bends – without any supporting strap. As none of the fibres in the

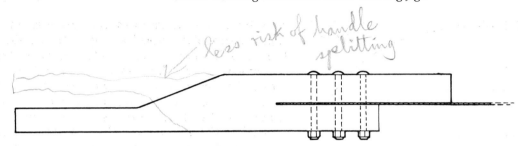

Fig. 12.11   A bending strap.

webbing (normally used as tow-ropes for lorries), but it stretched too much, so now I use two lengths together. It still stretches rather more than I would like, but I have had very few failures with it as yet. I expect this has as much to do with my care in preparing the wood as it has to do with the support from the strap. Its main advantage is the extra leverage from the long handles.

My handles are based on the description in Jack Hill's *Country Crafts* book (see Appendix 1). I used some spare softwood, but straight ash would be better still. Each handle is cut from an 18" (46 cm) length 2½ × 1¼" (6·5 × 3 cm). (Unfortunately, 3 × 2" (8 × 5 cm) is too thick for this job.) Alternatively, you could bolt together two 1¼" (3 cm) square strips of wood to the same shape (Fig. 12.11).

The webbing is clamped tightly into place by three bolts, the second handle being fixed so as to accommodate a bow blank 54" (137 cm) in length. Its operation is described in Chapter 15.

Thirteen

Post-and-rung Stool and Chair

Fig. 13.1   Frame stool with bark seat.

'Mr Gimson told me how quickly Clissett could turn out his work from cleft ash poles on his pole-lathe, steam, bend and all the rest. He seems to have made a chair a day for 6/6d and rushed it in his cottage kitchen singing as he worked. According to old Philip Clissett if you were not singing you were not happy.'

Edward Gardiner 1890
(from *Gimson and the Barnsleys*
by Mary Comino)

Stool

A good introduction to making country chairs is this simple post-and-rung, or frame, stool (Fig. 13.1).

Requirements:

Green wood

1 ash log 13" (33 cm) long, 6" (15 cm) diameter

60 ft (18 m) of inner bark from wych elm or lime *or* 1 hank of sea-grass

Other materials

pot of PVA glue

Danish oil, wax or other finish according to preference

some rags

With your first stool, you would be advised to make one or two extras of each part. Ash is the usual wood for this project because of its strength, easy cleaving properties and attractive grain. If you use sweet chestnut for the rungs, the joints are more likely to stay tight in conditions with fluctuating humidity (see p. 110). If you are having an elm or lime bark seat, you could use the wood left over after stripping the bark to make the frame. Otherwise, you should be able to use any wood as long as it cleaves into straight lengths.

Cut the log (or logs) 13" (33 cm) long and cleave it to produce the following:

5 legs to be turned to 1¾" (44 mm) diameter (when green)

5 bottom rungs to be turned to ⅞" (22 mm) diameter green

5 top rungs to be shaved to ⅞ × 1½" (22 × 38 mm) green

(this allows for one spare of each)

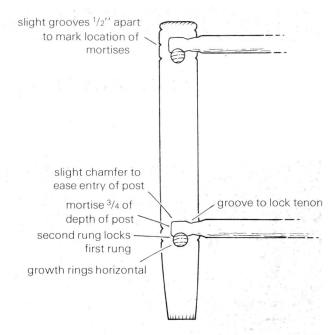

slight grooves ½" apart to mark location of mortises

slight chamfer to ease entry of post

mortise ¾ of depth of post

second rung locks first rung

growth rings horizontal

groove to lock tenon

Fig. 13.2   Joints in the stool post.

1   Posts

Using the bodging processes of cleaving, trimming, shaving and turning (see page 89), produce a set of five cylinders 1¾" (4·5 cm) diameter. The bottom few inches can be tapered slightly and then cut square with the tip of the skew chisel. The tops should be rounded and you can shape each one to produce a flat ball (see Fig. 13.2). It can be helpful at this stage to mark out the points at which you will drill the mortises. Measuring from the top, cut four slight grooves into the leg at the following distances: 1, 1½, 9 and 9½" (2·5, 3·8, 23·0 and 24·3 cm respectively). If the tool rest on the lathe is fixed to one of the poppets, you could mark these distances on to it and use the marks for each of the posts. By placing the ⅝" (16 mm) holes ½" (13 mm) apart, you will achieve the desired locking of the first rail by the second.

Having shaped the posts, you can burnish the surface by picking up a handful of clean shavings and holding them against each post as you revolve it on the lathe. Some woods such as ash, cherry and sweet chestnut respond well and soon develop a shiny surface. On other woods, such as beech and sycamore, burnishing has little effect while they are green.

2 Bottom Rungs

These are simply made by going through the bodging processes, finishing with the flat chisel to produce a set of straight rungs ⅞" (22 mm) diameter. Allow these to shrink so that when dry they will be somewhat larger than ¾" (19 mm) in diameter. You will turn the tenons down to size before assembly.

3 Top Rungs

The top rungs are best shaped with the drawknife and then the spokeshave to the shape illustrated.

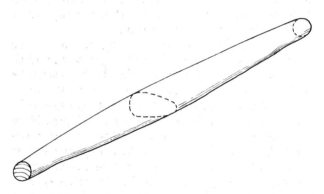

Fig. 13.3   The top rung.

The extra width of wood gives the rung more strength against the inward force created when the seat is sat upon (Fig. 13.4). When cleaving these sections from the log, try to shape them with the growth rings running across the rung horizontally rather than vertically. This follows the technique described on p. 107 to allow any movement in the rail to correspond as much as possible to any movement in the post. The tenons

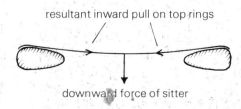

resultant inward pull on top rings

downward force of sitter

Fig. 13.4   Forces acting upon the top rungs.

at the ends can be whittled or turned roughly while green to about ¾" (19 mm) (to allow for shrinkage), so that they can be reshaped when dry to an exact ⅝" (16 mm).

If you are unable to tear yourself away from the pole-lathe it makes little practical difference to the finished stool to turn the top rails identically to the bottom ones.

Seasoning

You now need to allow the rungs to dry completely, while the posts should dry out to around 20 per cent moisture content. If you dry them out in the same conditions for the same time, the tenons will dry before the posts. When that stage is reached, the stool is ready to assemble.

When drilling the holes into the posts, it is worth considering the alignment of the grain. The rungs should be inserted with one of the tangential faces uppermost, so that any subsequent movement vertically will be as slight as possible. When deciding where to drill the mortises, bear in mind that two sets of holes will be drilled at right-angles to each other. It will therefore be impossible to obtain the ideal grain alignment at all the joints; this is where you have to compromise.

One option is to drill the mortises half-way between the radial and tangential faces so that any lateral movement of the post will be the same for both sets of rungs (Fig. 13.5 (a)). I prefer a second option, which relies more on the interlocking joint method. I drill the first set of holes into the radial face where there is the least shrinkage of the mortise around the tenon. However, this will be locked into place by the rungs on the other side of the stool, which will themselves be held by the maximum shrinkage of the mortise (Fig. 13.5 (b)).

In practice, there is probably very little difference between these two options, especially in a small stool. For me the decision is swayed by the fact that when you come to making a chair, there will be greater racking forces forwards and backwards than from side to side. Therefore, it seems best to have the tightest joint where the side rails enter the posts.

Working on this second option for aligning the mortises, place the thinnest of the stool-posts between the pegs on the drilling post and fix it by

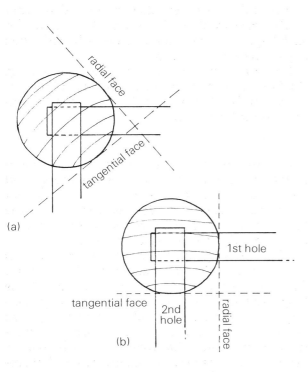

(a)

1st hole

tangential face | 2nd hole | radial face

(b)

Fig. 13.5   Two ways of aligning the grain in the posts.

knocking in the wedge as shown with the radial surface facing you (Fig. 13.6). This can be your practice piece.

To drill the mortises, the ideal device is a large breast drill which incorporates a spirit level. Failing this you can use a standard brace, employing the pins that you fixed into the drilling post to guide your horizontal drilling. Using the brace and ⅝" (16 mm) auger bit, drill a hole while counting the number of turns from when the spurs first start cutting. Check regularly to see when the lead screw first emerges on the far side. Remember how many turns were needed, then subtract about three or more turns (depending on your nerve!) and drill another hole using that lesser number. If the lead screw is in good order, it should drill a consistent depth for a given number of turns. You should now have a second hole which stops short of the far side and is just over 1" (25 mm) deep; if not, keep trying until you get it right. An alternative to this approach is to wrap some adhesive tape around the bit at the desired depth in order to indicate when to stop drilling. Take care, however, that the tape does not slide back along the drill bit.

Now you do it 'for real', wedging one of the other stool-posts on to the drilling post also with its radial surface facing you. Drill a hole with its centre on the 1½" (3·8 cm) mark, using the horizontal pins on the jig to check that you are drilling horizontally. Stop at the correct depth. Now fit a peg into this hole and drill the bottom mortise at the 9½" (24·3 cm) mark, using the top peg to align the drilling (Fig. 13.7). Remove this post and repeat the operation for the other three posts, ensuring that all the mortises reach the same depth.

Now take one of your spare rails and turn a ⅝" (16 mm) tenon at one end with a slight chamfer at the tip and make a groove about ¾" (19 mm) back, as shown in Fig. 13.2. Use the measuring

Fig. 13.6   Drilling a top mortise.

Fig. 13.7   Aligning the bottom mortise.

127

gauge to obtain the correct size. Drive this into a test hole in the first post, using a hammer or a mallet. If it feels tight without splitting the post and the depth is correct, repeat this on all the rails. You will find the shaved top rails very lumpy on the lathe, but it is worth persevering. Otherwise, whittle them to size. If you want to do the job properly, cut a small channel from the tip of the tenons to the shoulder, about 1 mm deep. This will allow any excess glue and air which is trapped in the mortise to escape as the rung is knocked into place.

Assembly

You will need to use the low-bench or some other firm level work-top. Failing this, you can place an old blanket on a level floor to protect the wood and use that as a bench.

Have ready a mallet, club or hammer, as well as some glue and a small stick to wipe it around inside the holes, plus a rag to wipe off any spills. You also need a length of softwood (e.g. roofing batten) to protect the wood when you hit it (Fig. 13.8).

Fig. 13.8   Extras needed before assembly.

1   Take a top and a bottom rung, thoroughly dried and with the tenons shaped as described, together with two of the posts with the holes correctly drilled. It is important to have everything ready and a clear and tidy space in which to work. Even with a slow-setting glue, the dry tenons will soon swell sufficiently to make the joint hard to take apart.

2   Mark the depth of the mortises on to the tenons of the rungs. This will show you when the joints are fully in position (Fig. 13.9).

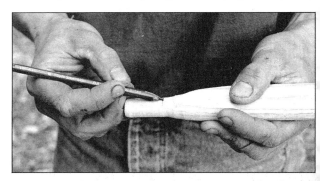

Fig. 13.9   Marking the depths of the joints on to the tenons.

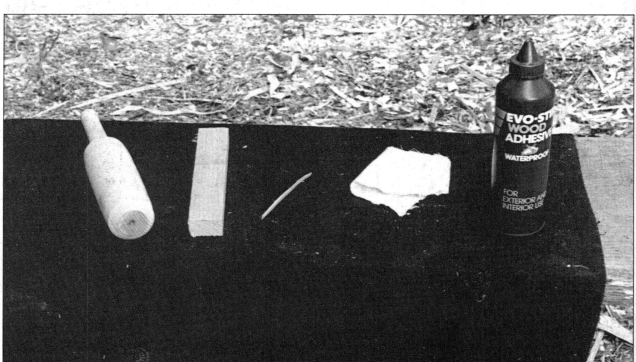

3 Apply some glue to the inside of the mortises of both posts and spread it around to cover most of the surface. Do not put glue on to the tenons, as it will only become removed as they slide tightly into the hole.

4 Place one of the posts flat on the bench with the holes facing upwards and put the bottom rung in its mortise, remembering to align the grain correctly.

5 Drive the tenon fully into place.

6 Repeat this with the top rung.

7 Place the second post on to the two rungs and then, protecting it with a piece of softwood, hit it down until the tenons are fully home (Fig. 13.10).

8 Repeat this process with two other rungs and the two remaining posts. Now it starts to look like a real structure.

Fig. 13.10   Assembling one side of the stool.

9 Return to the drilling post with one of the assembled sides and wedge one of the posts in the same way as when you drilled the first set of holes. The rest of the frame should stick out in the open with the narrower edge of the top rung facing you.

10 Drill the two remaining mortises in the post at 90 degrees to the assembled frame and repeat this for each post (Fig. 13.11).

Fig. 13.11   Drilling the remaining mortises.

Fig. 13.12   Knocking the frame together.

11 Take everything back to the bench and spread more glue into the new holes.

12 Lay one of the frames flat on the bench, insert the last four rungs in place and drive them home.

13 Place the second frame on top and locate each tenon into each mortise.

14 Using the piece of softwood again for protection, knock the two halves of the stool together (Fig. 13.12).

15 Clean off any excess glue and twist the frame around if necessary to make it stand flat.

16 Stand back and admire it!

When the glue has set you can if you like whittle some 4–5 mm oak or ash pegs. Drill the appropriate holes into the bottom joints and glue these pegs in place. However, if everything went well there should be little need for them. When you weave the seat into place, that will help to hold it all together.

Finishes

Before weaving the seat, you should apply a finish to the completed frame. This can be done before assembly if you wish, as long as you take care neither to swell up the tenon nor to allow any finishing material to come into contact with the surface of any joints.

There is a wide range of options to choose from and there are no rights or wrongs. I prefer to avoid any finishes which result in an extra surface on top of the wood. A chair is bound to get knocked about and, sooner or later, any finishing surface will become chipped. That is why I do not use any varnish.

Linseed oil is one of the cheaper options, resulting in a full-bodied finish with a slight lustre. It requires many light applications and therefore calls for patience to achieve a good result. There are several proprietary oils – such as Danish and teak – which combine natural oils with drying agents thus making the job much quicker and easier, if somewhat more expensive (Fig. 13.13). You can make up your own finishes using a mixture such as linseed oil, pure turpentine and methylated spirits; this produces good results quite cheaply.

Beeswax produces a pleasant natural finish, but as with oil is much easier to apply if mixed with some kind of solvent. There are several proprietary brands. However, this is easily spoilt by water unless applied on to a base of either sanding sealer or one of the oils.

Fig. 13.13   Applying a finish.

Weaving the Seat

As mentioned earlier, a variety of materials can be used to weave the seat of a post-and-rung stool or chair. For me the most satisfying is a tradition which was common in America but virtually unheard of in the British Isles. They would weave 'belts' made from the inner bark (or bast) of hickory trees. One obvious reason why this was not used in Britain is that hickory is a rare tree here. However, the technique fascinated me and I have had success with elm bark (particularly wych elm) and also have heard favourable reports from an ex-student who used lime – which in days of old was used to make rope.

Both these native trees are common and their fibrous properties are well known, so why were they not used for such a purpose? I can guess at two possible reasons, both stemming from our comparatively moist British climate. The first is that with plentiful supplies of rush grown throughout the country, this proves to be a more convenient choice than bark. Second, in the damp conditions of the average working man's home, a bark seat would soon fall prey to mould

Fig. 13.14   *Supporting the log.*

and rot. If these suppositions are correct, then central heating could enable the modern green woodworker to introduce a brand-new aspect of country crafts to the British Isles.

The best time to harvest the bark for seat weaving is when the cambium cells are rapidly reproducing, making it easy to peel; that will generally be from March to July. Look for fairly young stems of wych elm or lime, 9" (25 cm) diameter or less, coppice-grown stems being ideal. The stems should have good clean lengths without any side branches or large twigs. Elm has a habit of producing side shoots in a straight line, which makes life easier as the blemishes will all occur in one strip which can then be discarded. Fell the stem and carefully remove the smallest branches (2" (5 cm) diameter and less) so as not to damage the bark. If possible, strip the bark where it is felled so as to avoid having to cut it into short lengths for carrying. It will help if you can support the log a few feet from the ground so that you do not have to bend too much (Fig. 13.14).

Using a sharp drawknife with the bevel upwards, remove the outer (dark section) of

Fig. 13.15   *Removing the outer bark.*

the bark (Fig. 13.15). When you have cleared a small patch, cut a strip with a knife and lift it away from the wood; it should be about 2 mm thick and feel very much like a wet leather belt. When you are happy that you are taking the right thickness, remove the outer bark from a 10 ft (3 metre) length, or as long as you can conveniently manage.

131

Fig. 13.16 Easing off the bark with a knife.

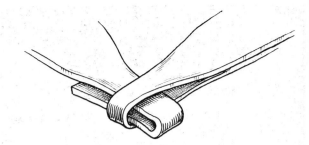

Fig. 13.17 Weaver's knot, stage one.

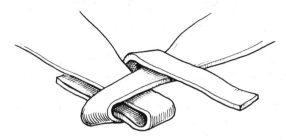

Fig. 13.18 Weaver's knot, stage two.

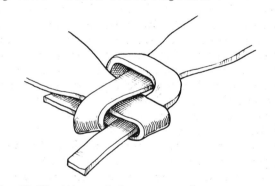

Fig. 13.19 Weaver's knot, stage three.

With your knife, score a straight line along the stem and then a second line parallel to it about 1" (25 mm) to one side. You should easily lift this strip away from the stem, but if it has been felled for a few days or you are working at the wrong time of year, you may need to coax the strip away with the blade of the knife (Fig. 13.16). You may find it a help to roll up the strip as you go. Work your way around the stem, removing the strips as much as possible with the grain.

You can follow the strips along branches or to some extent around them. If there is a row of twigs, try to have them between strips or in the centre of a strip. For this stool, you will need about 60 ft (18 m) of 1" (25 mm) strips. You can either weave it on to the stool straight away or store it in a dry place and re-soak it for a few hours before use. If you choose the latter, do not be put off by the syrupy slime produced.

The only difficult part I found was in learning the weaver's knot. I tried using an interlocking joint to bind the lengths together, but found it rather weak. I suggest you practise the knot several times before using it on the stool.

1   Take two strips and trim the end 4" (10 cm) down to about ⅜" (1 cm) in width. Fold the end 3" (8 cm) of each strip back on itself to form two loops.

2   Holding them at right-angles, feed one loop through the other so that it projects about ½" (13 mm) (Fig. 13.17).

3   Take the loose end of the outer loop and wrap it up around and back over itself, so that it points in the same direction as the other loop (Fig. 13.18).

4   Then tuck it through the other loop and pull the knot tight by pulling the thick ends of the strips in opposite directions (Fig. 13.19).

One good thing about the bark strips is that when they dry out they set into shape, so even if the knot works loose it cannot become undone.

Start weaving the seat by tying one end of a bark strip to one of the top rungs next to a post. On the stool it makes little difference which pair

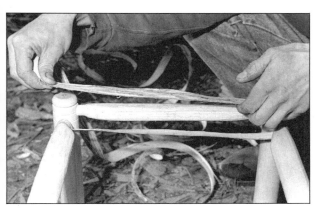

Fig. 13.20   Starting to weave the seat.

Fig. 13.21   Weaving the weft.

of rungs you start with, but when it comes to the chair you will start with the rear rung which will be slightly lower than the side rungs. Pass the strip *under* the opposite rung, then around and over the top and back over the knot you have just tied (Fig. 13.20).

Work the strips so that the bark side is outermost. As it dries, it will cup slightly towards the inner surface which would prove uncomfortable if it were to face upwards. Wrap the bark from one side of the stool to the other, so that the strips move one width sideways on the under-surface and are parallel on top. Tie any knots which may be needed on the underside, so that they are hidden. This is known as the warp.

When the entire top has been covered, bring the last strip over the rung, around the inside of the post and up around the outside of the adjacent rung. Continue now by weaving the weft (Fig. 13.21).

On the under-surface, it is sufficient to weave over and then under two strips of warp at a time. On the top surface, weave over and under each warp strip, alternating over and under as you work across the seat. When you reach the end, simply weave the last weft strip on the under-surface and stop at some point more than halfway across.

As the bark dries, it will shrink considerably in width. When it has stopped shrinking, you can push the strips to one end and feed in some extra lengths to fill up the gaps.

It is likely that the bark will develop a mould as it dries. You may like to play safe and apply a proprietary wood preservative to kill this off and avoid the danger of attack from rot in the future. However, if it is kept in a dry environment, this mould will soon die off by itself without causing any damage to the seat.

The Rush Pattern

Applying rush seating is a craft in itself which can only be learned properly by working alongside an expert. A good alternative is to use sea-grass, which can be bought quite cheaply from craft or rope suppliers. Although this does not match rush seating for charm and comfort, it is cleaner, quicker and can be easily worked by a beginner. For the stool described, you will need about 1 lb of sea-grass (Fig. 13.22).

Start by rolling a ball of sea-grass of a manageable size around an H-shaped piece of plywood (see Fig. 13.42). Sit down, holding the frame of the stool with one of its posts in front of you; then take the ball of sea-grass, holding the loose end against the inside edge of the top rung to your left. Pass the remaining coil over and around the right-hand rung next to the post. Now wrap it up the inside of the first rung, over the top, round the outside and across the frame to the opposite rail up against the next post (Fig. 13.23). Pull it tight as you proceed so that it grips the loose end at the first post. Now turn the stool around a quarter-turn so that the second post is nearest to you and repeat the above procedure. Continue to work round the stool in this manner, keeping the sea-grass tight.

When you need to join lengths of sea-grass you can use the weaver's knot as with the bark

Fig. 13.22   Rush pattern stool top.

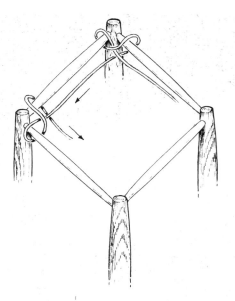

Fig. 13.23   Starting the sea-grass.

seating, tying the knot on the underside near one of the rungs.

Slowly the seat will build towards the middle. On this square stool, the diagonal pattern should meet neatly at the centre. Finish it by separating the strands of the sea-grass and tying them around the grass strands beneath the seat.

Other Seating Alternatives

Once you have mastered one or both of the above techniques, you can explore more elaborate patterns such as herringbone with the bark, or diamond with the sea-grass. There are also other materials such as shaker tape and paper-based stool cord with which you can experiment.

Spindle-back Chair (Fig. 13.24)

After trying out your chair-making skills on the frame stool, you can now turn your hand to the spindle-back chair. This is a close relative of the ladderback chair, but replaces the shaved horizontal slats by turned rungs and spindles. I prefer this version, as all the components are turned and all the mortises are round. However, if you prefer the ladderback you can adapt these plans by substituting three or more slats in place of the turned framework. As with most of the chair projects in this book, I have evolved a design combining the British traditions – as handed down by

Fig. 13.24   Spindle-back chair.

Fred Lambert and Jack Hill – with some of the techniques and designs used by the Americans, in this case Dave Sawyer and John Alexander. As with the Windsor, the result is a chair closely resembling those made in the West of England and Ireland. The tradition has come full circle.

Basically, this chair is an elaborated frame stool with two of the posts extended and the resulting back filled in. Such chairs were often made with all the components being left straight, but it is more comfortable and stable if the legs and backs are steam-bent. To achieve this, you will need to make up the steaming equipment and jigs as described in Chapter 12. This compound bend makes the project more complicated, but I think it is worth the effort.

Requirements:

Green wood

40" (1 m) ash log 8" (20 cm)+ diameter. Possibly an 18" (46 cm) sweet chestnut log for the bottom rungs.

Other materials

as for the stool, but with 20 per cent extra bark or sea-grass. You will also need some thick gloves for the steam-bending.

Start by cleaving all the components. There should be enough left-overs from cleaving the four posts to make the rungs and spindles.

The Rungs

From the cleft sections, cut the following lengths to make the rungs and turn all to ⁷⁄₈" (22 mm) diameter when green:

6 side and back bottom rungs 15" (38 cm) long

2 front bottom rungs 18" (46 cm) long

2 top back rungs 18" (46 cm) long

1 lower back rung 16" (41 cm) long

The tenons on all of these will be shaped to ⁵⁄₈" (16 mm) diameter before assembly. Most of this can be done on the lathe when they are dry, but the three to be used in the back of the chair will be bent and consequently impossible to turn to size. You should therefore turn the end inch (25 mm) to a fraction less than ³⁄₄" (19 mm) diameter, so that they will be almost the right size when you assemble them.

Shave the following seat rungs to an ovoid section as with the stool:

3 side and back rungs 15" (38 cm) long

1 front rung 18" (46 cm) long

(a few spares of each may come in useful).

The Spindles

Now turn three or four spindles (according to choice) 11" (28 cm) long and ⁷⁄₁₆" (11 mm) diameter at the ends (when green). You can pattern them as you like; one suggestion is to shape a ball or a few rings a third of the way from the top (see Fig 13.24). Don't worry about making them identical. It is the one chance on this chair (apart from the finial) to express yourself on the lathe.

Thoroughly dry all these parts except for the back rungs, which will be steam-bent. The best way is to put them in a warm, dry place such as an airing cupboard or under a dark cover in the sunshine; the latter method attracts the warmth without the direct rays of the sun. Because the parts are fairly small in diameter, the process can be speeded up by heating them either in a cool oven or in a warm container placed over a smouldering fire (Fig. 13.25). So long as the

Fig. 13.25 Drying chair parts.

temperature stays below 60° Centigrade you should not encounter any splitting. The wood may warp and it will certainly shrink, but by now you should have come to accept that and be glad that it will not happen later.

The Posts

The rear posts are 39" (1 m) long and the front ones 19½" (50 cm). If later on you find the chair is too high, you can always cut the legs shorter (see Windsor chair, p. 165).

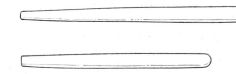

Fig. 13.26   Turned front and rear posts.

At this stage you have to decide whether to
turn the posts or to leave them with a shaved
finish. If the wood is perfectly straight after cleaving and you have a 5 ft (1·5 m) bed on your lathe,
turning is a good challenge; you then have the opportunity to turn a finial on the top of the back
posts (Fig. 13.26). You will need a sturdy tool rest
or a support in the centre, since this is likely to
'whip' as much as the chair-legs. It is of course
essential to ensure that the blank is perfectly
straight and well centred on the lathe. After some
practice, this is a remarkably quick operation.

If the raw materials, the lathe or your confidence are not up to the job, simply shave the
posts with the drawknife and spokeshave. The
thickest section of the posts is from 6" (15 cm) to
18" (45 cm) from the bottom. This should be
1½–1¾" (38–44 mm) diameter, tapering to a
little over 1" (2·5 cm) at each end.

The front posts should be the same as the bottom half of the rear posts, with the tops neatly
rounded over.

Bending the Rear Posts

The next stage is to bend the rear posts and back
rungs. If you are in a hurry, bend the back rungs
before making the posts so that they can dry out
in the meantime. But if steam is harder to come
by than time, steam them both at the same time
and allow a week before continuing. When you
assemble the chair, the posts should be at about
20–25 per cent moisture content. Steaming actually speeds up the drying process, so if the wood
is freshly felled it is best to steam the front legs
along with the rear ones to help dry them.

Before placing the rear posts in the steamer,
check that both ends have a sufficiently small
diameter to fit in the bending jig. They should be
steamed for 1–1½ hours, keeping up sufficient
steam all the time. Before removing them from
the jig, check that everything is ready. You will

need gloves to handle the hot wood, and the jig
should be in place with the clamp or string easily
to hand.

When you and the wood and a helper are
ready, put on your gloves and remove the back
posts from the steamer, *taking care not to scald
your wrists in the steam.* Place the bottom ends
right into their slots in the jig, with the surface
that was outermost on the log facing towards the
outside of the bend. This puts the wood in its
most favourable position for bending, with the
more supple wood to the outside (Fig. 13.27).

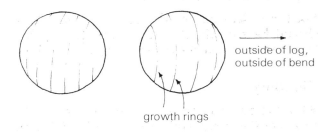

*Fig. 13.27   Aligning the growth rings of the rear
posts for bending.*

You will be surprised how it bends without
needing any levers. When the bend is complete,
clamp the tops tight against the jig (Fig. 13.28).

While the back posts are steaming, you can
also steam the back rungs. These will need 40–60
minutes, being smaller in cross-section than the
posts. Again, make sure that the jig is set up
before bending. Remove the three rungs from the
steamer with care, place them on the round
blocks of the comb jig and clamp down the
former (see Fig. 12.4).

If possible, leave the rear posts in their jigs for a
few days, both to allow them to 'set' properly and
to give them a chance to lose some of their
moisture.

The back rungs should be left in the jig overnight and then put in a warm dry place for a few
days to dry out. This process can be speeded up
by 'kilning' the rungs in the same way as the other
rungs and spindles.

Fig. 13.28   Bending the rear posts.

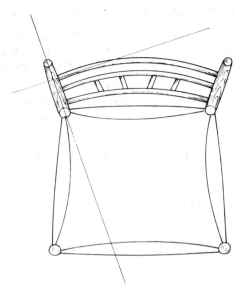

Fig. 13.29   View from above showing the splay of rear posts.

Assembly

The frame should be assembled in two parts, front and back. The method used to assemble the front is basically the same as when assembling one side of the frame stool, the only difference being that there are three rungs instead of two, spaced at 1½, 7½ and 13½" (4, 19 and 34 cm) from the top.

The rear frame is more complicated and should be started with the posts held vertically in the bending jig. Transfer the horizontal lines from the jig (see p. 121) on to the posts to give you the positions of the mortises. You now have to obtain the correct angle to drill the rung sockets in order to splay the rear posts correctly (Fig. 13.29).

Fig. 13.30   Drilling rear mortises.

138

The following method should achieve this:

1 Drill the top three mortises for the bent back rungs into the posts, horizontally and perpendicular to the plane of the jig (Fig. 13.30).

2 Whittle one end of the smaller bent rung so that it fits tightly into the lower of these holes. It should bend outwards from the centre of the jig.

3 The direction for drilling to lower rungs is given by the line joining the two ends of the curved rung. This should be about 70 degrees from the plane of the jig (Fig. 13.31).

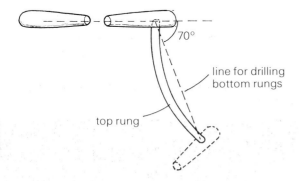

Fig. 13.31 Aligning the rear rungs.

Fig. 13.32 Drilling rear mortises viewed from above.

4 Drill the lower rung holes, using the bent rung to sight the direction of the drilling (Fig. 13.32).

5 Shape the tenons on the top bent rung and one bottom rung.

6 Remove the two rear posts from the jig and assemble them with the top and bottom rungs fully in place.

Fig. 13.33 Measuring the lengths of the rear rungs.

7 Lay this flat and place the other four rungs in their correct positions, then mark the depth of their sockets (Fig. 13.33).

8 By whittling, turning or rounding, shape the tenons on these rungs and cut to length where necessary.

9 Take the two bent back rungs that will hold the spindles and mark the positions for the spindle sockets. Choose these positions to suit the number of spindles and the amount of splay you require. On the chair illustrated they are spaced 1½" (4 cm) at the bottom and 2½" (6·5 cm) at the top.

10 Check the diameter of the ends of the spindles to ensure they have not shrunk below the diameter of the bit you intend to use to drill their sockets.

11 Replace the lower rung in its bending jig and drill the spindle holes, judging by eye the angle of splay. These holes should be about two-thirds of the depth of the rungs (Fig. 13.34).

12 Similarly drill the under-surface of the upper rung, remembering that the spindles will be splayed inwards.

13 Assemble the rear posts and rungs *without gluing* and lay this framework flat on the bench.

Fig. 13.34   Drilling spindle mortises in the bent rungs.

Fig. 13.35   Marking the length of the spindles.

Fig. 13.36   Tapping the spindle assembly together.

14 Place the spindles in their correct positions on top of the two drilled rungs and mark the length they should be (i.e. the distance between the ends of the upper and lower sockets) (Fig. 13.35).

15 Saw a quarter of the way through the spindles on these marks (you will soon see why).

16 Put them on the lathe and turn the tenons to the exact size of the hole. Any pencil marks will have been removed by the gouge, but the saw-marks should still remain.

17 Slightly chamfer the tenons at the saw-mark. This will help them to slide into the holes.

18 Cut the spindles to length.

19 Clear the bench of unnecessary tools and make sure you have hammer, softwood, glue, stick and cloth easily available, as with the stool.

20 Glue the spindles in place between the two rungs, tapping the joints in firmly (Fig. 13.36).

21 Mark the depth of the mortises on to the tenons of the rungs.

22 Smear glue into all of the mortises and tap all the rear rungs into one of the posts (Fig. 13.37).

23 Position the other post over the rungs, fitting each tenon into its mortise.

24 Hit the top post down on to the rungs, protecting it with the softwood until all the joints are fully home and checking that the two posts are not skew when looking from the side (Fig. 13.38).

25 If possible, allow the front and back frames to set before joining them.

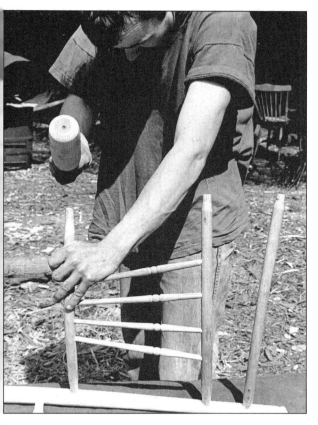

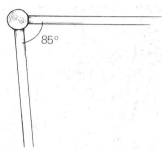

Fig. 13.39 *View of the side rungs fitting into the front post.*

26 Drill the mortises for the side rungs into the front assembly so that they just clip the top of the tenons of the front rungs, as with the stool (Fig. 13.39). This time you must drill at 85 degrees to the front rungs, to allow for the angle of the seat. (Being a degree or so out will not matter.)

27 Now mount the rear assembly with a G-cramp or a similar device on to your drilling post, so that the seat rung and the bottom rung are held against the vertical drilling post. This should give the spindles a backward lean of about 10 degrees (Fig. 13.40).

Fig. 13.37 *Tapping rungs into the rear post.*

Fig. 13.40 *Rear frame fixed to drilling post.*

Fig. 13.38 *Checking the alignment of the posts.*

28 Drill the remaining three holes into each post, just clipping the top of the rear rung and sloping in at 95 degrees. Use a spirit level or a sighting peg to check that these are horizontal.

29 Turn or whittle the tenons for the two top side rungs and the two bottom rungs.

30 Use these rungs to join the front and back assemblies (without glue).

31 Stand the whole thing on a level surface and measure the required length for the centre side rungs.

32 Turn the tenons and cut to length.

33 Mark the mortise depths on the tenons and glue it all together, laying the front assembly with the holes upwards on the bench (Fig. 13.41). Before the final blows, check that the rungs on both sides are parallel to each other. If not, stand the chair upright and pull it into shape.

Fig. 13.41   Assembling the front and back.

34 Wipe off any surplus glue.

35 To strengthen the chair-frame, you could drill a 3 mm hole at each end of the top back rungs where it fits into the posts and glue in a whittled oak pin. Trim this flush when it is dry.

36 Finally, clean up the surfaces and apply your chosen finish.

Filling in the Seat

Bark: if you use a bark seat, the process is the same as with the stool. Start weaving the seat from one of the rear corners from back to front, keeping the strips parallel. Leave the odd triangles for a day or so until the strips have shrunk and you have added the extra ones. Then just weave in sufficient bark to fill in the triangles. Once it is dry, it will happily stay in place.

Sea-grass: Start as with the stool, at a side rung working towards the front. Pass over the front rung, and back up on the inside, over the side rail and under. Now, instead of passing on to the next corner, repeat the previous operation, passing once more over the front rung, back up on the inside, over the side rail and under. Repeat with the second front post (Fig. 13.42). This should start to bring the two sides parallel to each other. Now continue right round the chair (as with the stool), winding once round the rear posts, once round the front posts, then once round the rear again. Now repeat the double wind at the front posts. Continue round and round, including a double wind at the front on each alternate circuit, until the sides are parallel. Then complete the chair as with the stool. If the sides are filled in before the front and back, simply wind to and fro in a figure-of-eight passing over the front rail and under, then pop up half-way, over the back and under, then up and over the front again . . . and so on until it is complete.

The simple side chair is as far as this book goes. However, the post-and-rung design is fairly easily adapted into an arm-chair by adding about 9" (23 cm) to the front legs and shaving two arms which are socketed into the rear posts. The seat should also be made several inches wider in this case. This style of chair is also well suited to having rockers, which avoids the need to bend the

Fig. 13.42 Winding twice around the front post.

rear legs as well as relieving a lot of the stresses on the joints when the sitter leans back. If your stool and side-chair worked satisfactorily, you should be well equipped to experiment. Should you want to try a different approach, move on to the Windsors.

Fourteen

Slab-and-stick Seating

Now at last we come to slab-and-stick seating (which includes Windsor chairs), in whose construction the pole-lathe traditionally played such a prominent part. Unfortunately for the green woodworker, this type of chair differs from the post and rung approach in that it relies heavily on

Fig. 14.1 Windsor stool.

the use of a solid plank for the seat. I say unfortunately, because such a plank cannot be cleft from the log but has to be sawn along the grain.

Traditionally, the planks would be sawn from large elm logs by a team of specialist sawyers. In Britain, at least, elm was considered the only choice for this job due to its twisted grain which gives it an outstanding resistance to splitting – a vital property if it is to withstand having up to 20 tenons driven hard into it.

The log would be supported over a deep pit with the skilled man (the top dog) standing on the log and his assistant (the underdog) providing the power from beneath the log in the pit (Fig. 14.2). Holding a long rip saw between them, they would steadily cut their way along the log to produce the planks.

This is a craft which I must confess I have not attempted, and, although I am sure it would be interesting to try, I would not recommend it as a 'fun way' to produce planks for chair seats. I have in the past used a chain-saw mill which consists of two powerful chain-saws joined by a long bar cutting through the wood with a long sharpened chain. Although not as laborious, it is probably little more fun than the pit saw, being just as dusty and far more noisy. It also results in considerable waste due to the width of the cutting chain. Moreover, the machinery is quite expensive and suffers considerable wear and tear from this type of operation. Nonetheless, if you have a fair amount of good timber in a situation inaccessible to larger machinery, this could be one option.

If you happen to have your own elm trees in good condition, the easiest choice is to apply the traditional approach to the modern situation and hire the services of a professional timber contractor or sawmill to convert the logs into planks for

Fig. 14.2   Sawing elm planks.

you. But if, as is most likely, you do not have your own supply of elm trees, you will need to buy the wood ready planked.

As mentioned earlier, good elm is scarce as a result of the ravages of Dutch Elm disease, and you will have to look around to find a good supply. The planks can be as thin as 1" (2·5 cm) in order to make a chair bottom, but with such planks there is insufficient thickness to carve out a deep hollow. This results in a chair lacking in both comfort and character. I prefer seat planks 1½" (4 cm) in thickness, ensuring that the chair combines lightness in weight with elegance and comfort.

The same property of field elm which makes it best suited for this purpose also makes it the most difficult to work. The grain is constantly changing direction and therefore requires much concentration when hollowing out the seat. Once a good finish has been obtained, however, it has a handsome grain which certainly adds to the character of the finished chair.

Because of elm's scarcity and awkward grain, you may decide to use a different wood. Wych elm, plane, sycamore, beech, cherry and lime are all possible alternatives. Poplar would make a very light seat, easy to hollow and fairly resistant to splitting, but would be very easily marked. In North America, softwoods were used widely and would share most of the properties of poplar.

With any of the other woods, you would be advised to use 2" (5 cm) planks, where the extra thickness will help to compensate for their tendency to split when you drive in the legs. You should also avoid kiln-dried wood, especially if using elm. If the planks have been air-dried, the wood will still retain 15–20 per cent moisture and will not be as hard as kiln-dried timber. This will make it softer to work and, as with the post-and-rung chairs, will allow a little shrinkage at the mortises to tighten up the joints as it dries. Some people would advocate using even wetter wood, but if you do this you will be faced with the problems of warping as it dries. One approach common in earlier days was to cut and hollow the seats before seasoning and then assemble them when they had air-dried. This is of course the same approach as used in most other green woodwork.

I shall proceed with the following chapters on the assumption you are using air-dried field elm for the seat. If this is not the case, you may need to adjust the methods described accordingly by allowing for the extra thickness.

The Wood for Legs and Stretchers

Beech is the traditional wood and it is very pleasing to turn, producing long ribbons of shavings. It has a very bland appearance which some consider an advantage in that the grain patterns do not detract from the patterns produced by the craftsman. Personally, I like to let the wood have a visual say. Due to changes in moisture content, beech is more prone to movement than most other hardwoods, which can be a disadvantage. Beech is at its best in the mainland of central and southern Europe and within the part of the British Isles bounded by the Chiltern and Cotswold Hills. Beyond this range it tends to grow with a wavy grain, making it more difficult to work and less reliable in strength.

Cherry is one of the best alternatives, being attractive, pleasant to turn and generally growing straight. Sycamore and birch are also good on the lathe, although rather lacking in character.

The ring-porous woods such as ash, oak and sweet chestnut usually cleave to produce strong, straight legs, although they are somewhat more awkward on the lathe. With oak and sweet chestnut you will also have problems with the reaction between the tannin in the sap and the iron in the tools. If none of these woods is possible, then experiment with what you are able to obtain.

Before undertaking any slab-and-stick furniture, you will need a means of sawing the wood from the plank. One option is to give your specifications to the timber merchant who may, for a charge, cut the shape you desire. Of course, if you have access to a bandsaw or a good jig-saw, you could use these for the job; otherwise, you will need to make a turning saw as described in Chapter 12.

Windsor Stool

One of the simplest stools is a low, three-legged stool. This requires three short sturdy legs to be socketed into three holes in a plank seat. Rather more sophisticated – and involving more in the way of chair-making methods – is a four-legged stool with stretchers. This can be made without the

need for some of the specialised 'bottoming tools' such as adzes or any steam-bending jigs, and provides a good warm-up for tackling a Windsor chair.

Requirements:

Seasoned wood

1½" (4 cm) thick elm plank cut to 11½" (29 cm) diameter circle

Green wood

19" (48 cm) straight-grained hardwood log

Other materials

length of softwood

Danish oil or other desired finish

heavy cloth

The Legs

One of the major advantages of the techniques used in this book is the extra strength derived from cleaving wood. To make the most of this, I like to make the legs of chairs and stools light and slender. This can be achieved without the danger of short grain; that is, where the fibres run at an angle to the line of the leg instead of along its length. The actual dimensions are not critical just so long as – when they have dried out – the tenons are turned to exactly the same diameter as the drill bits you use to make the mortises.

The joint where the legs are socketed into the plank, I like to make ⅞" (22 mm) diameter, which means turning them to 1" (25 mm) when green to allow for shrinkage. With beech it is safer to make them a fraction larger, as beech shrinks rather more than most other hardwoods. If you prefer to make rather chunkier legs, then just scale up the diameters given accordingly and use a 1" (25 mm) drill for the sockets. The legs I shall describe can be used for the stool or for the comb- and bow-back chairs, so you may choose to make some extra ones at the same time.

Start the stool by making the legs and then the stretchers, so that they can dry out while you think about the seat.

Making the Legs

Cut a length of wood 19" (48 cm) long and cleave,

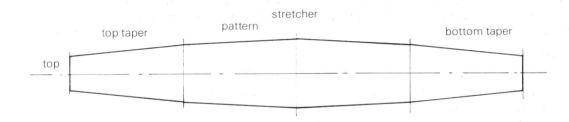

Fig. 14.3   Blank stool leg.

trim and shave it to produce the 'billets'. These are the blanks for the legs and should be rough cylinders of about 2" (5 cm) diameter tapering at each end to 1¼–1½" (32–38 mm). By looking at different chairs, you will see that there are no set rules as to what pattern you should follow when shaping the legs.

There are quite marked differences between the legs of American Windsors and those made in Britain. There are also distinct regional variations, as well as styles belonging to certain periods in history. However, there are certain basic structural constraints to bear in mind and I find the following guidelines useful when deciding the leg pattern.

Rough out the leg on the lathe as illustrated (Fig. 14.3) and, by rotating the leg and holding a pencil against it, mark out four equal lengths. The stretcher will later be fixed into the leg at the centre mark, so this should be the thickest part. The section above this is where you should confine most of your patterning. One purpose of this, apart from decoration, is to allow the leg to flex very slightly, which aids it in absorbing any sharp impact and also permits the completed chair to 'walk' a fraction on an uneven floor – thus helping to prevent it from rocking. The top section should taper gently towards the desired

Fig. 14.4   Wycombe's '3-bead' pattern.

tenon diameter (remembering to allow an extra 12–15 per cent for shrinkage). This also provides a smooth section around which to wrap the lathe cord when shaping the rest of the leg. Only the end inch or so will be touched with the chisels again when the leg has dried out.

From the mid point down, there should be no deep turning, as this part of the leg will not benefit from the support of the stretchers. It is common to leave a bead just below the bottom mark and then turn the rest of this half of the leg to produce a gentle taper which apparently flows through the bead. If your tool rest is attached to the poppet with the fixed centre, you can transfer these three pencil marks on to the tool rest in order to duplicate the positions on the other legs.

The first operation should be to turn the top taper, using the flat chisel. Go gently when you are nearing the desired diameter and check this frequently with the measuring gauge. Then move the cord along to this end or turn the leg the other way round between the centres so that you can work on the remaining sections.

The standard pattern on legs produced around High Wycombe was three simple beads, most of this being carried out with a V-chisel (Fig. 14.4). This chisel has a tendency to pull into the wood and is also rather awkward to sharpen properly, so I prefer to use the small skew even if it takes a little longer.

By now you should have mastered the techniques described in Chapter 6 and be able to form these simple beads by using the tip of the skew

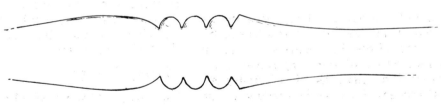

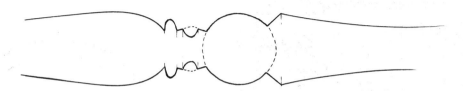

Fig. 14.5   Baluster pattern.

chisel to cut out the initial 'V' and then rounding off the curves with the blade.

Another, rather more elaborate design is the baluster pattern, otherwise known as 'ball, groove and bead' (Fig. 14.5). This name gives a good idea of the shapes to be cut. I suggest you start with the ball and then the bead, leaving a slightly ridged area between them until the rest of the leg has been fashioned.

The final operation is to cut out the groove with the small gouge, leaving a slight rim on either side to crisp up the lines. Once the groove has been cut, the leg will be able to flex at this point – an advantage on the finished chair, but causing it to 'whip' on the lathe.

There are only two measurements you need to make. One is the diameter at the top of the leg, the other is the distance down the leg at which you start the pattern. Otherwise you should try hard to avoid the desire to measure its dimensions. Even if the legs look very different when held alongside each other, this will be far less noticeable once the stool or chair is assembled. You can always put matching pairs together at the front and the back. If you turn several sets at a time, then you can select the ones most similar to be used together.

Stretchers

Unlike the legs, the stool stretchers are quite different from those used on the chair. You can cleave these out of 9½" (24 cm) lengths, which can be obtained by cutting the remainder of the original log in half. The billets should be half-scale versions of the legs, i.e. 1" (25 mm) diameter, tapering slightly at both ends. Mount each one on the lathe, roughing it down to about ¾" (19 mm), and finish it with the flat chisel tapering the ends to ⅝" (16 mm). When they have dried out, the tenons will be turned down to ½" (13 mm). The most useful stretcher pattern for a

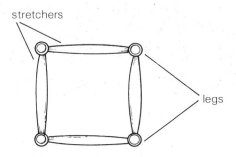

Fig. 14.6   Plan of box pattern for stretchers.

round stool is a box pattern as shown (Fig. 14.6), so you will need four stretchers for each stool, although a few spares may be useful.

Shaping the Seat

Mark a circle of the desired diameter on to the plank. A good size is 11½" (29 cm), enabling it to be cut out in one sweep by the turning-saw (or by an average band saw). If you do not have a convenient circle to use as a pattern, drill a hole in a length of wood the right size for a pencil, and knock a small nail through the other end 5¾" (14·5 cm) away. Tap the nail into the plank and swing the pencil in a circle round it (Fig. 14.7).

Fig. 14.7   Home-made compass.

Clamp the plank on to the low-bench, or some other firm bench, with the marked circle overhanging the edge. Cut out the seat using the turning-saw and holding it as shown (Fig. 14.8). Having cut it out, you have two possible ways

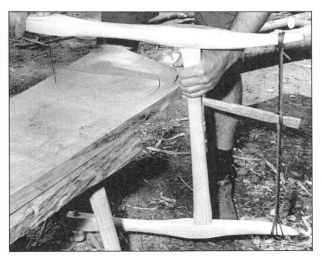

Fig. 14.8   Sawing out the stool top.

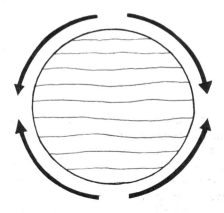

Fig. 14.10   Working with the grain.

of smoothing the seat. One is to turn it using the bowl-turning techniques described in Chapter 16, by driving a wooden mandrel into the underside and setting it on to a pole-lathe. The other option is to smooth the edge with a spokeshave and the top surface with a flat or round-bottomed plane. When smoothing the edge, it is helpful to grip it in a good-sized carpenter's vice, but if you have no such thing you can clamp it to the drilling post (Fig. 14.9) or the low-bench on its side (see Fig. 15.14). Remember to work the spokeshave in the direction of the grain, as shown, in order to avoid tearing the fibres out of the wood (Fig. 14.10). Chamfer the bottom edge and round off the top edge.

To smooth the top surface, you can clamp the remainder of the plank from which you cut the seat to the drilling bench. Inside the circle that

you removed, place a piece of hardboard or thick ply, then put the stool top on to this so that its surface is slightly proud of the plank. Knock a small wedge into the gap between the seat and the plank, which should grip it tightly in place (Fig. 14.11).

If you are using elm for the seat, you will find it safer to plane across the grain so as to avoid it tearing out the fibres. If it is a straight-grained piece of wood, then you should be able to plane in the direction of the grain. You are likely to find that one direction works more smoothly than the other, and you might also find that this reverses as you move across the seat. As pointed out in

Fig. 14.9   Smoothing the edge of the stool.

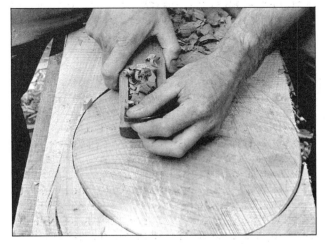

Fig. 14.11   Gripping the stool top (note the small wedge).

Chapter 4, this is due to the natural spiralling of wood fibres along a tree-trunk. You just have to feel the way the tool responds.

One tool I like for this job is the little round-bottomed plane or scooping plane which I use for smoothing the seats of Windsor chairs. It is not cheap, but it cuts even wild-grained elm very sweetly and leaves an interesting ridged texture across the stool top. You can make your own version of this tool by rounding off the bottom of a small wooden block plane and grinding the blade to match.

You can now smooth the surface with a cabinet scraper or with fine sandpaper (see Chapter 15).

Assembly

When the legs and stretchers have dried out thoroughly, you can start to assemble the stool. First you will have to decide if the joints between the legs and the seat will be blind or through. A well-made wedged-through joint certainly adds a decorative feature to the stool and also enables there to be a deeper socket to hold the legs. However, a through joint will require extra work in cleaning up the seat top once it has been assembled. The main drawback of this method is that the exposed end grain of the top of the leg will permit rather more movement in response to changes in humidity; therefore sooner or later the tops of the legs will protrude above the surface of the seat. Because of this, I prefer to make the joints blind, and will use this method in the description that follows. If you choose through joints, then drill the holes from above and remember to drill them with an outward rather than an inward splay. When I describe angles, I prefer to give the number of degrees from a right-angle as for me this has more significance. For example, the angle at which to drill the sockets for the legs I shall describe as 12 degrees to the vertical rather than 102 degrees (Fig. 14.12).

1   Take the four seasoned legs and find the one with the smallest diameter at the top.

2   Set this on the lathe and turn the top 1¼" (32 mm) to the exact diameter of the bit you intend to use to drill into the seat (Fig. 14.13). If the leg has shrunk more than you expected and is smaller than the bit, then you will have to use the next size down. (Better to find out

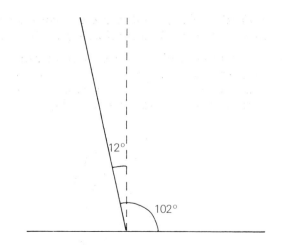

Fig. 14.12   Describing the drilling angle.

Fig. 14.13   Checking the size of the leg tenon.

now than after you have drilled the holes!) Use the roughing-out gouge for this job: it is fine if there are *slight* ridges on the tenon, as these will help to grip the leg in place and provide a space for the glue.

3   Put a small chamfer on the end of the leg to help feed it into the hole.

4   Repeat this with the remaining legs.

5   Mark a circle with 4" (10 cm) radius on the

underside of the stool, using the same centre as when you marked out the shape of the seat.

6 Draw two straight lines through the centre at right-angles to each other. The points at which these lines cross the circle mark the centres of the holes for the legs (Fig. 14.14).

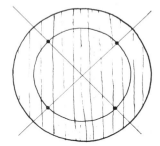

Fig. 14.14 Marking the leg sockets.

7 Grip the seat firmly by wedging it back into the plank from which it was cut while this is fixed to the low-bench. (You may use some other suitable method of holding it horizontally, such as a G-cramp or a bench holdfast.)

8 Set the sliding bevel at 12 degrees to the vertical and stand this on one of the lines that you drew across the seat.

9 Drill the first leg socket holding the drill bit in line with the sliding bevel, and drilling as deep as you dare (Fig. 14.15). If possible, finish off the hole with a round or flat-nosed bit. It is convenient to have a second brace so that you can complete each hole with both bits without having to constantly change the bits in the brace.

10 Repeat this for the other three holes.

11 Drill a similar hole into a piece of waste wood clamped to the bench, having first marked the direction of lean on to the wood.

12 Draw two more lines on this piece at 45 degrees to either side of the original line of lean. This will now be used as a jig to hold each leg while you drill the stretcher holes (Fig. 14.16).

13 To position the holes for the stretchers, take two of the legs and mark on each of them a

Fig. 14.15 Drilling the leg sockets.

Fig. 14.16 Holding the leg to drill the stretcher sockets.

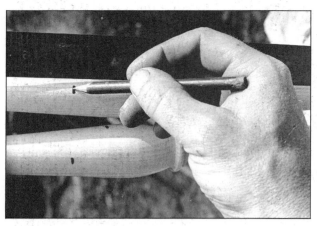

Fig. 14.17 Marking the stretcher sockets.

point 10" (25·5 cm) from the top. It doesn't matter if this is the radial or the tangential face so long as they match.

14 Holding the legs with these points facing you, mark another point on each leg 11" (28 cm) from the top so that these two holes face each other (Fig. 14.17).

15 Repeat this with the other pair. (It may now be advisable to place them in the holes you drilled in the seat, just to check that each of the points has a matching partner at the correct height.)

16 Knock one of the legs into the hole you made in the spare plank, so that each of the marks for the stretcher holes lines up with one of the 45-degree lines on the plank.

17 With the ½" (13 mm) bit, drill these holes, taking care not to tear the grain as the bit enters the wood. (It helps if you start with the bit square to the leg and then lower it as you drill further.) You should now be drilling parallel with the plank in the direction of one of the guidelines (see Fig. 14.16). If you have a good lead screw on the drill bit, you should be able to count how many turns are needed to drill the required depth (about two-thirds of the way through the leg). This can can then be used to drill the other holes. Alternatively you can wrap a tape around the bit at the appropriate depth. If so, make sure it does not move backwards or you will drill with great confidence right through the leg!

18 Drill the hole for the adjacent stretcher a quarter revolution around the leg.

19 Similarly, drill the stretcher holes in the other legs.

20 Mark the depth of the sockets on the tenons of the legs, so that when you assemble them you will know when they are right in.

21 Place the legs in their seat sockets with the stretcher holes correctly aligned, and so that the tenons are only half-way in, i.e. the depth line is about ½" (13 mm) clear of the seat.

22 Hold each stretcher in turn alongside its final position, and mark on it the position of the end of its mortise in the leg. Two of the stretchers should be rather longer than the other two (because they are further down the legs), so remember during assembly to use the right ones in the right places. Once the legs have been knocked firmly into place, the gap between them will be reduced and the stretchers will be doing their job of 'stretching'.

23 Where you made these marks, use the tenon saw to cut a quarter of the way through the stretchers. Later on you will cut right through, but at the moment it is best to retain the original centres at the ends for use on the lathe.

24 Mount each stretcher on the lathe, turning the required tenon for 1" (25 mm) back from the saw-mark. The pencil line will disappear and you are left with the saw-mark to define its length.

25 Make a groove in the tenon and chamfer the end where you made the saw-mark, see Fig. 14.18.

26 Saw the stretchers to the correct length. If you wish, you could try a 'dry run' at this stage to see if it all fits. But I think it adds to the fun to go for it first time. If it works (and there's no reason why it shouldn't), it is a shame to have to take it all to bits again.

27 Before gluing, make sure that the low-bench is clear of debris and that you have a hammer, mallet or club to hand. You should also have a length of softwood to protect the stool parts when you hit them together. Lay a thick cloth

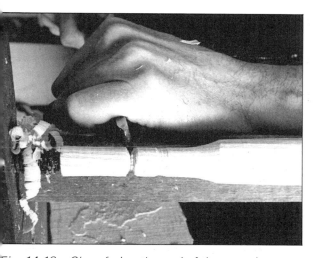

Fig. 14.18   Chamfering the end of the stretcher before cutting to length.

on the bench on which to rest the parts while you hit them.

28 Mark the depth of the mortises on to each of the tenons.

29 Smear glue into each of the holes – just enough to lightly cover all the surfaces.

30 Assemble a stretcher and two legs, making sure that the correct stretcher goes in the correct holes. With both legs in the same plane, lay one of them on the cloth and – protecting the outside of the other with the piece of softwood – knock these two joints tight (Fig. 14.19).

Fig. 14.19   Knocking together two legs and a stretcher.

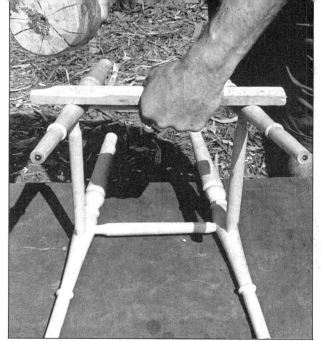

Fig. 14.20   Knocking all the legs together

31 Repeat this with the other two legs and a stretcher.

32 Tap the two remaining stretchers into their holes on one of these assemblies.

33 Place the mortises in the other pair of legs over these stretchers and tap them into place (Fig. 14.20).

34 Pick up this structure, pop the tops of the legs into their holes in the seat and knock them home, each one a bit at a time.

35 Breathe a sigh of relief and clean off any spilt glue.

Your stool may have sustained a few marks during this process. If so, clean them off with a cloth, a scraper or a fine sandpaper. You may want to sandpaper the seat, but avoid the temptation to treat the turned parts in this way. Leave them with a chisel finish as a testament to your first Windsor legs. I discussed finishes in Chapter 13, and much the same applies in this case.

You may well find that the stool wobbles. If the plank seat is not fully seasoned, I suggest you leave it in its new indoor environment to enable it to warp if it so desires. You can then adapt the technique described in the following chapter to level up the legs (see p. 165).

Fifteen

Windsor Chairs

In this chapter I shall describe how to make both a comb-back and a bow-back chair. The two designs used here have an identical undercarriage (seat, legs and stretchers). The holes drilled for the stiles (main back supports) of the comb-back and the bow of the bow-back are also the same. The only difference between them is in the construction of the back. The main structure of the comb-back is in three parts – two stiles and the comb – whereas the main structure of the bow-

back is the single bow. The spindles are longer in the bow-back, but otherwise very similar.

In the history of Windsor chair-making, the next development from the stool was the comb-back and so, I suggest, it should be with you.

The comb-back allows a greater margin for error when drilling the back sockets into the seat. Provided the comb is long enough, the stiles are bound to meet it at some point. The chair may look and feel odd, but you can always put it together; just drill the holes in the comb wherever the tops of the stiles happen to be. With the bow,

Fig. 15.1   Comb-back and bow-back.

once you have bent it and drilled the first of its holes in the seat you are stuck with a given angle for the other end. If it doesn't match the hole you have drilled, there is very little you can do except make a different bow or convert it to a comb-back. You will also find the shorter spindles of the comb-back much easier to turn, and the flat under-surface of the comb makes it much easier to locate and drill the spindle holes. To successfully bend the bow, you will have to find a top quality 5 ft (1·5 m) length of ash (or a good yew pole), whereas the components of the comb-back are not so demanding.

Having given this word of warning, the choice is now yours. You could, alternatively, find a Windsor chair which appeals to you and faithfully copy that, using this chapter merely as a guide. You may then wish to evolve your own variations from the original, as I have done with these designs.

I shall continue by describing how to make the comb-back. To make the bow-back you should follow these instructions where they apply to the undercarriage. I shall then describe how to make the upper half of the bow-back at the end of the chapter.

Requirements:

Seasoned wood

16" (41 cm) square 1½" (38 mm) thick elm plank (or other wood 2" (5 cm) thick) air-dried

Green wood

19" (48 cm) straight-grained log for legs and stretchers

1 × ⅛" (25 × 3 mm) strips of cleft oak heart-wood for wedges

Comb-back

20" (50 cm) ash log 8" (20 cm)+ diameter for comb and spindles

Bow-back

section from 20" (50 cm) ash log for spindles and section from 5 ft (1·5 m) straight-grained, knot-free ash 4–16 growth rings per inch (25 mm) for the bow

Other materials

glue, rags, desired finish

The Legs

The method here is identical to making the legs for the stool. Hopefully, the only difference is that your second set will look better than your first.

The Stretchers

On most chairs the swelling on the side stretchers is slightly to the front of the mid-point. You can do this if you like, but to make life simple start off with all three stretchers the same, with the swelling in the centre. I say three stretchers, because on a common Windsor they are usually in an H-pattern. The stresses are mostly fore and aft, so less sideways support is needed. This therefore enables anyone using the seat to tuck their legs underneath without a front stretcher getting in the way.

Normally, the tenons on the ends of the stretchers are ⅝" (16 mm) in diameter. I have always used ½" (13 mm) tenons, thus making the chair appear more delicate. Because the wood is always cleft, these slender stretchers are still very strong and despite my daughter jumping up and down on them, I have yet to have one break. Here I shall describe the use of ½" (13 mm) tenons, but if you want to use ⅝" (16 mm), remember to adapt the instructions accordingly.

Start with a log 16" (40 cm) long. This should leave you with a spare inch in length on the side stretchers, and even more for the centre one.

Go through the usual bodging stages until you

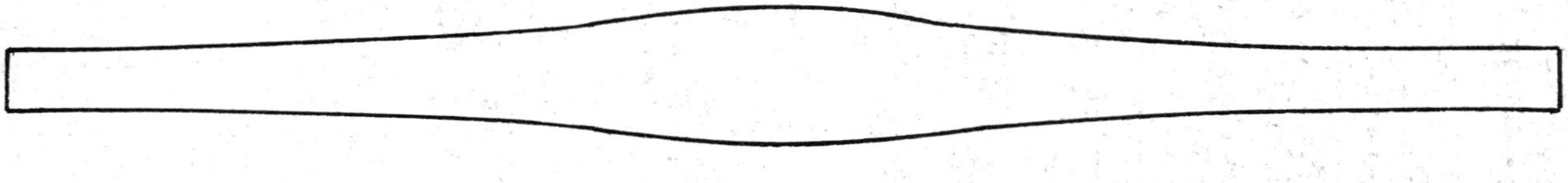

Fig. 15.2 A stretcher.

have a cylinder 1¼–1½" (32–38 mm) diameter in the middle, tapering to a ⅝" (16 mm) tenon at each end (to be turned down to ½" (13 mm) when dry) (Fig. 15.2).

To my mind, a slightly concave taper looks more attractive and will reduce unnecessary weight from the chair.

The Stiles

The stiles are the two turned pieces which support the comb. In effect, these start as legs at the bottom and finish as stretchers at the top. I prefer ash for this job, as they will be subject to considerable bending stress when the chair is in use. If you use a different wood, do not turn such deep patterns on them.

Cleave and turn each one from a section of log 17" (43 cm) long to form a cylinder 1½" (4 cm) at its thickest point, just below half-way. This should taper to 1" (25 mm) at the bottom (⅞" (22 mm) when dry) and ⅝" (16 mm) at the top (½" (13 mm) when dry). A pattern similar to that of the leg can be made below the thickest point (see Fig. 15.1).

The Spindles

On some chairs, the slender uprights are parallel along their length, while on others they taper evenly from bottom to top – in such cases they are known, rather derogatorily, as sticks. A more interesting shape, which also gives a slight degree of support to the back, is for them to swell about a third of the way up; they are then referred to as spindles. They were often turned from beech, but ash will be rather stronger. They should be 16" (40 cm) long and ⅝" (16 mm) at the thickest point, tapering to ½" (13 mm) at the bottom and $^7/_{16}$" (11 mm) at the top (Fig. 15.3). These are all

Fig. 15.3 A spindle.

green dimensions, which should shrink to give $^7/_{16}$" (11 mm) at the bottom and ⅜" (10 mm) at the top. If you want avoid purchasing a special $^7/_{16}$" (11 mm) bit, then add a little to the bottom so that it finishes at ½" (13 mm).

Turning these spindles on the lathe provides

you with another testing challenge as they become very whippy. Here are a few tips:

1 Turn the thicker end down to size first. This will allow the string to run on a sturdier piece while you turn the thin end.

2 Give the cord three turns instead of two to help it grip the thin cylinder.

3 Try to keep the cord as near the end of the spindles as possible. Take care, though, that it does not run off the end and get dirty on the metal centre.

4 Use the flat chisel as soon as all the drawknife marks have been removed with the roughing-out gouge. Place a shaving between your index and middle finger which you wrap around the spindle to steady it as it turns. The shaving acts as protection and helps to stop your fingers from burning. Do not try to work with the chisel facing towards the supporting hand (Fig. 15.4).

Fig. 15.4 Turning a spindle.

If despite this advice it still doesn't work, you can always whittle them with a spokeshave. But if you do succeed, you can look forward to the bow-back with 20" (50 cm) spindles. This is where the Lambert/Hill/Hindle rounders have the advantage (see p. 113).

How many spindles you have is entirely up to you. An odd number has a better visual symmetry, but an even number leaves a space for your spine to fit. This support for the spine was probably one of the reasons for the development of the flat ornamental splat in British bow-back chairs. In the West Country and America, chair-makers never bothered. If you wish to try it using the simple tools on my list, you will find out why! Later, comb-backs used flat strips curved to support the back and were known as lath-backs. Both the splat and the lath are beyond the scope of this book, so I shall stay with spindles. The comfort increases with the number of spindles – normally between five and seven, and sometimes up to nine. In the chair illustrated, I have used six.

The Comb

This is the curved piece that runs above the stiles and spindles. It should be around 20" (50 cm) long, but could be 2–5" (5–13 cm) high. The one I shall illustrate (Fig. 15.5) is 3½" (9 cm). It should taper from nearly an inch (25 mm) at the bottom to about ¼" (6 mm) at the top. This taper should be slightly convex so that it does not narrow too soon, making it difficult to drill the holes for the stiles deep enough. It can be rather narrower in

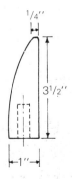

Fig. 15.5   Section through the comb.

the middle, as it will only have to accept the ⅜" (10 mm) holes for the spindles. This will also make it somewhat easier to bend.

Nowadays combs are always sawn out of large blocks, and this is a viable alternative if you enjoy sawing. You might be able to find a piece of wood which has grown with the desired curve, then you could split your comb out of this.

The method I prefer is to split a straight comb out of a straight, well-grown ash log. The easiest way is to cleave a large log 8" (20 cm) or more in diameter until I have a piece of wood nearly the shape I want (Fig. 15.6). If you only have smaller wood, you will have to cleave a section right

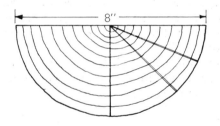

Fig. 15.6   A comb from a large log.

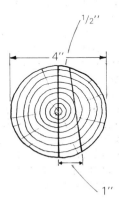

Fig. 15.7   A comb from a small log.

across the log; although this is more difficult, as compensation it creates a more interesting grain pattern (Fig. 15.7).

Having cleft it out of the log, clean up the surfaces with a drawknife. You need not smooth it off completely at this stage. If you have the equipment, you should steam it for an hour or so and bend it using the same jig that was used for the back rungs of the spindle-back. If the ash is fresh and of good quality, you might be able to bend it without steam, but that will require more effort. You could set up the jig in a bench vice to obtain more power than with the G-cramp. Leave it to 'set' overnight or longer, and air-dry it. As this will not be used for tenons, it will not harm if it has not completely shrunk when you assemble the chair.

The Seat

Hopefully, you can obtain a plank of elm 1½" (4 cm) thick and at least 16" (41 cm) wide. If not, then you must use one of the substitutes mentioned in the previous chapter and have it 2" (5 cm) thick. It is best to cut a template out of card

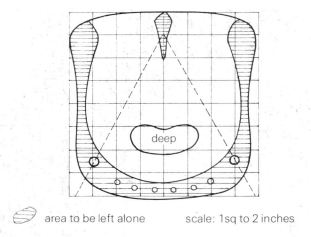

area to be left alone   scale: 1sq to 2 inches

Fig. 15.8   Plan for the seat outline.

based on the plan given (Fig. 15.8). Transfer one half of the outline, cut this out, fold it over and draw the rest of the outline. This will ensure that the seat is symmetrical. Normally the grain runs front to back, which makes it easier to work the grain at the rear of the hollow.

Cramping the plank to the low-bench, saw it out carefully with the turning-saw.

Before starting to shape the seat, I suggest that you drill the holes for the stiles. It will be much easier to judge the angles while the surface is flat. Transfer the centre positions from the plan and draw the line of lean which passes through the centre line 2″ (5 cm) back from the front of the seat. Set the sliding bevel at 20 degrees, placing it on the line marked, and use this to sight the hole. Drill both holes from above, right through the seat, using the ⁷⁄₈″ (22 mm) auger bit. This will enable you to wedge the stiles from beneath when they are in place.

Now you need to hollow the seat and there are several ways to do this. There is a variety of powered tools you could use, some of which are specially made for the job (such as adzing machines) but are expensive to buy and, so I'm told, horrible to use. Equally horrible, but probably very exciting, is to carve it out with a chainsaw. There are also ways of rigging up a router to do the job. Unfortunately it's not much more fun by hand, but at least it is cheaper and quieter.

A tool called an inshave, rather like a draw-

knife somebody has bent into a semi-circle, is one possibility. It only removes shavings and although all right for softer woods, must be very tedious on a good elm plank. A wide 2″ (5 cm) gouge struck with a mallet will remove the wood rather more quickly and quite accurately. Just take care to feel which way the grain runs at any point. Traditionally, this job was done with a curved adze, and that is the way I prefer.

You can still buy flat adzes, but you will have to find a good blacksmith who can not only bend it but put back a good temper into the blade afterwards. Curved adzes (i.e. curved from side to side as well as from front to back) are manufactured in the USA and may soon be available in Britain.

Only rarely does one come across a second-hand curved adze in good condition. I suggest that for your first chair you get by with a gouge; it is cheaper and safer.

Mark out the area to be left alone (see Fig. 15.8) and hollow out the wood *across* the grain; it is then much less likely to tear out. The cheaper,

Fig. 15.9   Adzing the seat.

158

mass-produced chairs often used 1" (2·5 cm) planks and were hollowed out ½" (13 mm) or less. The mark of a good chair is a good deep hollow. With a 1½" (4 cm) plank, you should be able to remove up to 1" (2·5 cm) at the deepest point. Bear in mind the shape it is made for; you do not need to follow every contour, but avoid sloping the sides down to one point in the middle. There should be a wide, fairly flat area which is deepest where you will rest those two bones which ache the day after riding a bike or a horse.

If you are adzing, put the plank on the floor and find some method of holding it firm. As with the stool, one good way is to place it back in the plank form in which it was cut; you can then stand on the plank. Another method is to fix two sloping battens to a sturdy frame and slide the seat in between them (Fig. 15.9). But whatever you do, don't swing the adze with your feet in the line of swing – it can so easily bounce off the plank and cause a very nasty injury. Alternatively you could fix this frame vertically and work on the seat at about waist height allowing the weight of the adze to assist with the work.

Sooner or later you will come to the smoothing stage. If you are using an inshave, just keep going; it may be slow, but it does leave a fairly even finish. The traditional tool was a spokeshave curved from side to side and from back to front, known as a travisher. Old ones are very rare, but you could – together with your blacksmith – convert a spokeshave blade and make a new body. I nowadays prefer to use the scooping plane that I used on the stool (Fig. 15.10). As with most Japanese tools it should be used on the pull stroke, but as long as you do not press on the blade it can just as well be pushed. Before using it on elm, you will have to increase the angle of the bevel on the blade so that the bevel is just skimming the wood. Roger of Tool-mail persuaded me to buy one, and it was already razor-sharp when I bought it. It worked beautifully for two or three chairs but then chipped, and I was furious. But when I had calmed down, I reground it and honed it and it has worked perfectly ever since. As I said, you can as an alternative quite easily convert a small block plane to do the same job. You will just have to sharpen it more often.

At this stage, you can start to work in the same

Fig. 15.10   Using the scooping plane.

direction as the grain where it feels right, but with elm you will have to memorise every twist and turn the fibres take. The best way to control the contours of the seat is to regularly run your hand over the surface. This will show any humps or hollows far more accurately than by vision alone.

When you have gone as far as you can with this stage, you will need to finish off with a scraper (Fig. 15.11). This is a simple, flat piece of steel (often cut from old saw-blades) on the edge of which you have to raise a burr – a thin, sharp ridge of steel. Normally a cabinet scraper has straight edges, but I like to grind mine to a curve.

Fig. 15.11   Using the scraper.

There are different approaches to raising a burr, but I have had most success using the following method (Fig. 15.12).

Grind or file the curved edge of the scraper to about 60 degrees; then sharpen it and hone it, going through the various grades of oilstone until it has a mirror finish. Now smooth the flat face, again producing a very smooth finish. You should now have a razor-edge (albeit at a peculiar angle for a razor).

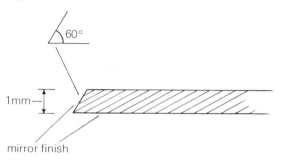

Fig. 15.12   Honing a scraper.

Next you need a gadget called a burnisher or ticketer, which is a smooth length of hardened steel with a handle (you can get one cheaply in a second-hand shop). Hold the scraper firmly and after spitting on the ticketer – that is supposed to help – run it hard along the edge of the scraper about three or four times as shown in Fig. 15.13.

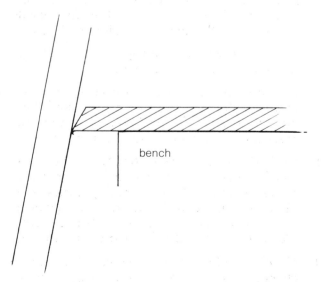

Fig. 15.13   Raising a burr.

This should produce the required burr which, when in use, will remove significant shavings of wood – not sawdust – from even the most awkward elm board. Now you need to work with the grain in either pushing or pulling strokes, sloping the scraper slightly in the direction of the burr.

To clean up the sides, a spokeshave is the best tool. You can grip the seat in a good vice or a 'work-mate', but those of you without such luxuries can clamp it to the low-bench and lay it on its side. This idea is an example of lateral thinking! (Fig. 15.14). Start by bevelling the underside. I like a crisp, straight bevel of about 45 degrees and approximately ½" (13 mm) deep. Then smooth out the saw-marks on the side and finally round off the top edge. At the front you should run this into the surface of the seat.

Now you should finish off the level surfaces of the seat. The sides and the pommel you can blend in with the other curves. At the back, the best tool for the job is a razor-sharp block plane or smoothing plane, but you could manage with a scraper. Traditionally, the underside of the seat was left in the same state as when it left the pit-saw. After all, anyone in a position to look at the

Fig. 15.14   Shaving the seat edge (using the low-bench on its side).

finish on this surface is probably in no fit state to take any notice of its condition! But as I was told when I joined the Somerset Guild of Craftsmen, 'some of our members finish all the surfaces of their furniture'. If you are one of them, then plane that up too.

Wedges

While you are waiting for the turned parts to season, make sure that you have a couple of dry wedges ⅞" (22 mm) wide (see p. 73).

Assembly

When all the turned parts are thoroughly dry, you can start to assemble the chair. First assemble the 'undercarriage': that is the seat, legs and stretchers. The method is similar to that used for the stool so, if you omitted that project, you should read it through now. If you follow the instructions below accurately, the front and rear legs should appear to have the same lateral splay when viewed from the front. I find this plays a large part in the visual effect of the chair. If you have studied American Windsors, you will notice that the position of the legs and the angles at which they protrude are very different from those given here. I suggest you follow the instructions below for your first chair and then vary them according to preference for the next.

Undercarriage Assembly

1   Take the legs and, as with the stool, turn the tenons to ⅞" (22 mm) (or 1" (25 mm) if preferred). If they are undersized, you will have to settle for ¾" (19 mm) which with cleft wood should be strong enough even if it looks spindly. (You will also need a ¾" (19 mm) bit.)

2   Mark a pencil line 1¼"(32 mm) back from the tenon to show when the leg is fully located (obviously, make this less if the hole is shallower).

3   Mark out the centres of the holes for the legs on to the underside of the seat using the plan given (Fig. 15.15).

4   To determine the direction in which to lean when drilling the holes, start by drawing a *dotted* line between the front and rear legs

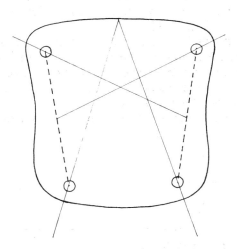

Fig. 15.15   Leg positions and directions of lean.

and mark the mid-points on each. The reason for drawing a dotted line is so that you do not confuse this with the real lines of lean.

5   Now draw a solid line from each of these mid-points to the centre of the opposite front leg.

6   Mark the line of lean for the rear legs from the centre of each hole to the front centre of the seat.

7   Set the sliding bevel at 8 degrees and drill the front holes as near to 1¼" (32 mm) deep as you dare. If you have a round- or flat-nosed bit, finish off the holes with this (Fig. 15.16).

8   Repeat this with the rear legs, this time setting the sliding bevel at 18 degrees.

9   Measure 10" (25 cm) down each leg on the tangential face – the face with the grain forming circles rather than stripes (see p. 106) – to mark the position of the stretcher joints.

10   With the seat cramped firmly to the low-bench, knock the front two legs into their sockets with the stretcher mark pointing in a direction parallel to the dotted line between the front and rear legs. They need not be completely home, but should be firm (Fig. 15.17).

11   Check the diameter of the ends of the stretchers to make sure they have not shrunk more than expected, but do not turn them yet.

Fig. 15.16   Drilling the leg sockets.

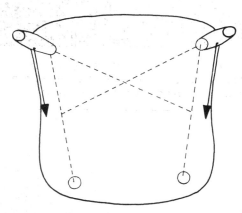

Fig. 15.17   Front legs ready for drilling stretcher sockets.

12 Drill a stretcher hole in each leg parallel with the plane of the seat and in the same direction as the dotted line (see Fig. 15.21). You should aim to drill two-thirds of the thickness of the leg; certainly not less than ¾" (19 mm).

13 Knock in the rear legs, again aligning the stretcher marks.

14 Using rubber bands, hold the two side stretchers at the correct height against the legs. Hold them both to the same side of the legs (Fig. 15.18).

15 Mark on them the point at which they should be sawn off; this is the distance between the ends of the sockets for the stretchers. If the legs have only been knocked half into their holes, the stretchers – as you have measured them – will tighten up nicely when you knock the legs right in (Fig. 15.19). If, when you are measuring up, the legs have already been knocked right in, you should add ¼" (6 mm) to the length of the stretchers to allow them to 'stretch'.

Fig. 15.18   Measuring the stretchers.

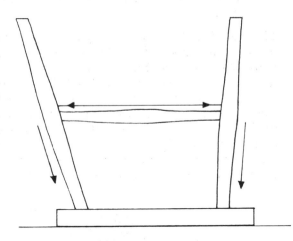

Fig. 15.19   The stretchers stretching as the legs are knocked in.

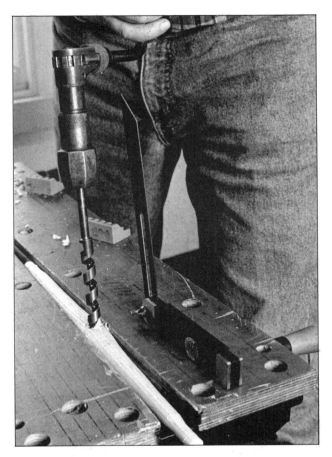

Fig. 15.20   Two methods of drilling into the stretchers (a) (above) vertically in a 'workmate'; (b) (below)   horizontally in the low-bench.

16 Now mark the mid-points of the stretchers and holding the centre stretcher in place and in a similar manner, estimate how long this should be.

17 Set the sliding bevel to reproduce the angle between the side and centre stretchers. If all has gone to plan, this should be about 8 degrees.

18 As you did with the stool, saw part-way through the stretchers on these marks, turn them down to size and cut to length (see Stool instructions 23–25).

19 To drill the holes in the side stretchers, you need to hold them firmly either in a vice, a workmate (Fig. 15.20 (a)), or by driving the stretcher into a suitable hole in a spare block of wood (Fig. 15.20(b)).

20 Using the sliding bevel as a guide, drill a hole into the radial face (the face with the grain forming stripes, not the circles) two-thirds of the way through.

(By orientating the side stretcher this way, you maximise the strength of the joint at the leg if there is any subsequent movement due to changes in moisture content.)

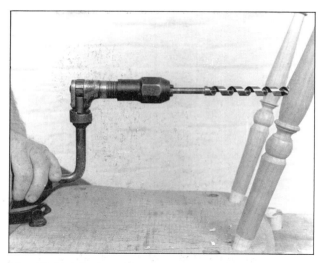

Fig. 15.21   Drilling stretcher sockets in the rear legs.

21 Remove the front legs from the seat and drill the stretcher sockets in the rear legs (Fig. 15.21).

22 Lightly mark the depth of the sockets on each tenon. If you feel the need, you can carry out a dry run (assembling without glue).

Gluing the Undercarriage

23 Clear a space on the low-bench, removing any coffee mugs or other objects likely to bounce on to the floor!

24 Place the seat on top of an old cloth on the bench, with the leg sockets facing upwards.

25 As before, make sure you have a hammer, a piece of softwood, glue and a matchstick.

26 Smear glue into all the holes. You should now work quickly, but not frantically.

27 Fit the centre stretcher into the two side stretchers, making sure that they lie in the same plane (Fig. 15.22). I have seen a centre stretcher torn apart in the attempt to rotate the side stretchers once the joint had been knocked together.

28 Knock them together while protecting them, as on the stool, with cloth and softwood.

29 Fit the front legs on to the front end of the side stretchers (where they splay outwards) and the rear legs on to the other ends. Make sure

Fig. 15.22   Assembling the stretchers.

that none of the legs is the wrong way round (Fig. 15.23).

30 Slip each leg into its appropriate hole and tap them so that they are well located.

31 Lay the assembly with the front legs on the cloth and, using the softwood for protection, knock the legs down on to the stretchers. Make sure the legs do not come out of their sockets (Fig. 15.24).

32 Lay the seat on the cloth and drive the legs fully home (Fig. 15.25).

33 Wipe off any excess glue and take a break.

Unless you are very lucky, you will find that the chair rocks somewhat. You now need to level up the legs, not only so that it stands firmly but also so that it slopes down slightly at the back. This helps to prevent you from sliding off the front when you sit in it.

Fig. 15:23   Fitting the legs (this is where a beard is useful).

Fig. 15.24   Tightening the stretcher joints.

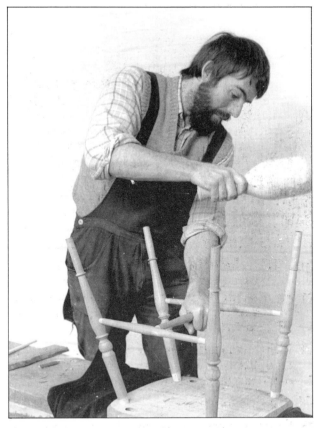

Fig. 15.25   Knocking in the legs.

Levelling Up

1   Stand the chair on a flat, horizontal surface.

2   Slide some shims (thin slivers of wood) under some of the legs, so that the sides are the same height as each other and the front is ¾" (20 mm) higher than the back. You will find a spirit level useful here.

3   Measure down from the pommel, at the front, the desired height: normally 18" (45 cm). (This is where the 18" (45 cm) ruler is so helpful.) Find or cut a block of wood to fit the gap at the bottom (Fig. 15.26).

4   Mark the height of this block against each leg in turn, taking care not to dislodge the shims (Fig. 15.27).

5   Holding the chair steady, saw three-quarters of the way through each leg, parallel to the

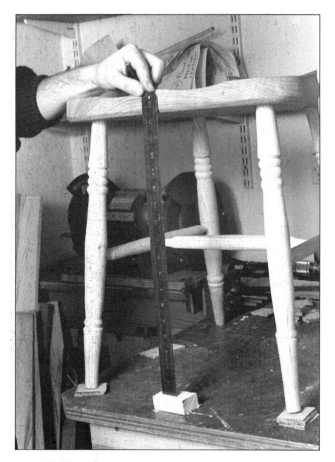

Fig. 15.26   Measuring down from the pommel.

Fig. 15.27   Marking the bottom of each leg.

Fig. 15.28   Sawing the legs to length.

surface on which the chair is standing. If you were to cut right through each time, the chair would wobble (Fig. 15.28).

6   Now you can saw the legs right through. If you did this properly it will stand four-square on the floor. A slight rock of up to ⅛" (3 mm) is permissible as the legs should flex sufficiently to absorb it. If the error is greater, check the flatness of the surface that you used before trying to correct it. Repeat the procedure if need be, but only once more! If it is still not right, trim the offending leg with a knife until you get there.

Now, using a fine sandpaper (400 grit), you can clean up the surface of the seat. It is best to wipe it with a wet rag and then sand it again, repeating this a few times. This process will raise the grain – that is, lift up the fibres which have been flattened by the other tools – which should result in a much smoother finish.

Assembling the Back

1   Put each stile on the lathe and turn the bottom 2" (5 cm) to ⅞" (22 mm) diameter and the top inch (25 mm) to ½" (13 mm) diameter, slightly chamfering both ends.

2   Saw a slot 1½" (4 cm) deep in the bottom end of each stile; this will be for the wedge that fixes the stiles in place. As with the maul head, this wedge should force outwards against the end grain of the seat into which the stile fits (Fig. 15.29).

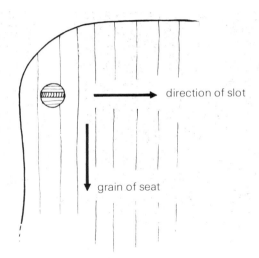

Fig. 15.29   Wedge forcing against the end-grain of the seat.

3 Shape a *dry* oak wedge to fit.

4 Fit the stiles into their sockets *without* glue until the ends project beneath the seat. They should be a tight fit, but not so as to be in danger of splitting the seat. If you are able to use a ratchet brace or twist drill to bore the spindle sockets, you could glue and wedge the stiles into place at this stage. Remember that if you do this, you will not be able to swing a brace full circle when you drill the spindle holes.

5 Hold the comb against the top of the stiles and mark the position and the direction to drill (Fig. 15.30).

6 Gripping the comb by replacing it in the bending jig, drill the stile sockets 1″ (25 mm) deep into the comb, taking care that the drill bit does not burst out of the front or back surfaces (Fig. 15.31).

7 Mark the depth of these sockets on to the top tenons of the stiles.

8 Using a set of dividers, a ruler or a measured stick, mark out the spacing for the spindles on the seat and the comb. For the chair shown, the distances between centres are 1⅝″ (41 mm) at the seat and 2⅜″ (60 mm) at the comb. If you use more or fewer spindles, adjust this accordingly.

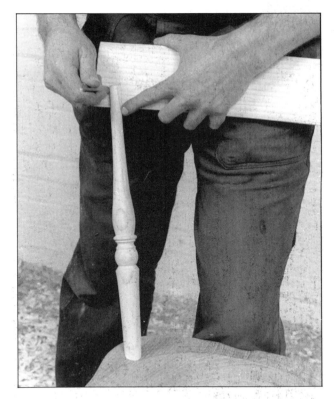

Fig. 15.30   Marking the stile sockets.

Fig. 15.31   Drilling the stile sockets.

9 Fit the comb on to the tops of the stiles, leaving them ½" (13 mm) above the mark on the tenons.

10 Measure the distance between each spindle mark on the seat and its corresponding position on the bottom of the comb. They should all be much the same. Add 1" (2·5 cm) which, when added to the extra ½" (13 mm) you will have to lower the comb, will give a tenon of ¾" (19 mm) at each end.

11 Mark this length on to the spindles and turn the end ¾" (19 mm) down to the desired diameter, putting quite a large chamfer on the tips. These will be under compression when the chair is in use, so there is no need to make them quite as tight as the other joints, although you want to avoid them rattling. If you have made or bought a rounder (p. 113), this is very good for reducing the tenons on the spindles to size.

12 Having turned them to size, cut the spindles to length.

13 With the comb still in place, drill the spindle holes 1" (2·5 cm) into the seat, using the spindle marks on the comb to judge the angle. You can angle the holes slightly to the front of the comb which will tend to curve the spindles, giving better back support (Fig. 15.32).

14 Place the spindles into these holes and mark their angles of lean on to the front of the comb.

15 This is also a good time to decide the exact shape of the comb.

16 Remove the comb and replace it in its bending jig.

17 Using the pencil lines as guides, drill the spindle holes ¾" (2 cm) into the comb. Remember that the spindles will slope in from behind the stiles.

18 Shape the comb with the turning-saw, draw-knife and spokeshave, and smooth it off with a scraper and sandpaper.

19 Remove the stiles, then glue and wedge them into place (if you have not already done so).

Fig. 15.32 Drilling the spindle sockets into the seat.

20 Clear the bench and get together the same accessories as when assembling the under-carriage (p. 128).

21 Smear glue into all the holes.

22 Tap the spindles gently into the comb.

23 Place the comb (containing the spindles) into place on the stiles.

24 Pull the spindles, one at a time, into their holes in the seat. All tenons should now be located in all mortises.

25 Support the back of the seat on the edge of the bench and, protecting the top of the comb with the softwood, knock the comb right down to the mark on both stiles. Take care during this process that none of the spindles come out of their sockets. A second pair of hands is useful here.

26 Stand back, check that the comb is level and

remove any excess glue. If you have a twist drill with ⅛″ (3 mm) bit, the following operation makes a nice finishing touch and adds to the strength of the chair.

27 At ½″ (13 mm) above the bottom of the comb, drill a small hole, about ⅛″ (3 mm) diameter, to pass through the top of each stile.

28 Whittle two slightly tapered pegs (preferably oak) to fit these holes (see Fig. 11.11).

29 Dab some glue into the holes and, carefully, tap in the pegs. When the glue has set, trim them flush and sandpaper the comb, repeating the wetting process used on the seat (see p. 166).

30 Saw the bottom ends of the stiles flush with the bottom of the seat.

31 Apply your choice of finish.

Bow-back Chair

If the comb-back went together satisfactorily, you should be able to tackle the bow-back. You will of course need to make the bending jig described in Chapter 12. Having given you a warning about this project, I must now confess that for me bending bow-backs is the most exciting of all the projects in this book. It demands not only speed and confidence, but also a delicate feel for the wood. However, it is much easier to carry out with two people and preferably a third to help.

Traditionally, the best bows were made from small diameter (1½–3″ (4–8 cm)) yew poles, bent in the round and shaped later. This material is not easy to obtain as it should be straight and have no large knots (over ¼″ (6 mm) diameter). If you find such wood, it will bend easily after steaming and if you cut it a foot or two over length, you should not need a strap. Other woods such as oak, beech, cherry and wych elm can all be bent, but are rarely found straight enough to be cleft. You would probably have to rip-saw them out of straight-grained planks and hope for the best.

In the absence of yew poles, I always use cleft ash. As mentioned many times already (and for steam-bending it is especially important), you should look for a straight knot-free log with rings

4–16 to the inch (2·5 cm). It also makes life easier if it has very little spiral.

You will need a 54″ (137 cm) length for the bow in question and the log it comes from should be at least 4″ (10 cm) in diameter, but preferably nearer 8″ (20 cm). The younger the tree, the less chance it has had to cover over any small knots and to straighten itself out. For this reason – and also because it is rather more pliable – you should aim to use the outermost section, utilising the inner wood for less demanding purposes such as spindles.

I like the finished bow to be about ⅞″ (22 mm) square in section, so you should aim to cleave it as near as possible to 1¼″ (32 mm) square. You may need to trim it with the axe and then the drawknife, gripping it in the shaving-horse and tucking the excess length under one arm (Fig. 15.33).

You will have maximum success in bending the

Fig. 15.33 Shaving the bow (and checking for straightness).

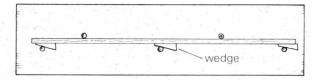

Fig. 15.34   *Gripping the bow to plane it.*

bow if it is as uniform in thickness along its length as possible. Having shaved it, you should now grip it on the low-bench and square it up accurately with a smoothing plane. A simple jig to grip the wood is to drill five holes into the bench and locate a 1" (2·5 cm) diameter peg in each (Fig. 15.34). Place the length of ash as shown and fix it in place with wedges. It helps if the pegs and wedges are just lower than the bow blank (i.e. about ¾" (19 mm)). A sixth peg can be used to prevent it from sliding forward.

You should aim to remove any marks left by the axe or the drawknife, otherwise these will create points of weakness at which the bow can start to crumple or split. It is more important to

follow the flow of the fibres than to make it dead straight. If the outside surface of the log, just beneath the bark, can be left intact, that will also be beneficial; you then know that no fibres have been severed on that surface and it can thus be positioned to the outside of the bend with a much reduced chance of the fibres tearing out. After planing, the bow blank should be as near as possible to 1" (25 mm) square in section, but not less. Do not forget to allow for shrinkage.

When the bow blank has been planed, check that it is a tight fit in the bending strap. If it is too long, cut it exactly to length. If it is too short, cut some chocks to fit between the ends of the bow and the strap. Decide which is the best face for the outside (usually that furthest from the centre of the log). On one of the adjacent faces, mark the mid-point along the bow with an arrow pointing towards the inside face of the bend. When you take it out of the steamer, you should spend as little time as possible in having to think these

Fig. 15.35   *Bending the bow.*

things out. Once you have steam up in your steamer, put in the bow for 1–1½ hours, making sure that the steam does not subside.

Before bending make sure that the jig is in place: either on the end of the pole-lathe, the drilling post or a well-anchored bench. You also need pegs and wedges or a clamp to hold the bow in place in the centre and at the ends. A hammer and some thick gloves will be useful, as well as the bending strap. Try also to have one or two helpers at this stage. Most people will be only too glad to share the experience.

When the bow is ready, put on the gloves and remove it from the steamer. Be careful of the steam; you can easily scald your wrists as you reach for the bow. Place it correctly in the strap, which you then put in the jig with the mid-point of the bow on the centre point of the jig. Hold it there firmly with a wedge. Pull on the handles of the strap, moving steadily without jerks and with both sides moving at the same rate (Fig. 15.35). When the bend is complete, quickly clamp or wedge the ends into place. Ideally, this should all happen within a minute of removing the bow from the steamer.

After an hour or so, the bow should have cooled and be well on the way to setting. To hold it in place, saw the very ends off the bow, in line with each other, and nail a thin strip of wood between them. The bow can now, if necessary, be removed from the jig and allowed to dry (Fig. 15.36). Obviously the longer the bow is left on the jig the better, to allow it to set without disturbance.

The steaming process actually speeds up the seasoning of the wood, but it is best to dry it for a month or more in warm, dry conditions before assembly.

Spindles

The spindles should start at 20" (50 cm) in length, although some will be cut shorter during assembly. The diameters are the same as for the comb-back (see p. 156). You could try to turn these on the lathe, but they will be very whippy. Or you could make a device called a steady to support them half-way, but the simplest solution is to whittle them. Of course, if you have rounders, they are very useful for this operation.

Bow-back chairs often have an extra support

Fig. 15.36 Bow held by a strip of wood.

provided by two extra spindles socketed into a projection at the rear of the seat, called a bob-tail. If the ends of the bow are fixed a few inches in front of the spindles, sufficient 'triangulation' is obtained to support the back without the need for bob-tail and struts. This is both easier to construct and results in a simpler, more elegant outline. I have therefore chosen the latter approach in this chair.

Assembly

First, assemble and smooth the legs' stretchers and seat as described earlier. Then proceed with the following steps:

1   Shape the bow, using firstly a drawknife and then a spokeshave until its cross-section is roughly as shown (Fig. 15.37). The ends should be shaped into the ⅞" (22 mm) cylinders required to fit the sockets in the seat. You will find that using a spokeshave on ash tends to tear at the grain, so finish off the smoothing with a rasp or coarse sandpaper.

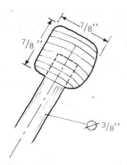

Fig. 15.37 Cross-section through the bow.

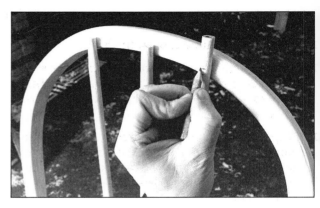

Fig. 15.38 Marking the spindles.

2 Saw a slot in each end of the bow 1¼" (3 cm) deep, in such a direction that when the wedges are driven in they will force against the end grain of the seat and not split it (see Fig. 15.29).

3 Locate the bow into its sockets *without* glue.

4 Mark the position of the spindle sockets on the seat (1⅝" (41 mm) centres for six spindles). They should be roughly parallel with the back edge of the hollow in the seat.

5 Check the diameter of the spindles and drill their sockets 1" (25 mm) deep, judging the angle and direction of lean by eye. You can use the bow *in situ* to drill the first hole, and then remove it. Insert a sighting peg in the first hole to help guide the others. Replace the bow to its full depth.

6 Using the lathe, a rounder or a spokeshave, turn the end ¾" (2 cm) at the bottom of the spindles to fit these holes.

7 Fit these tightly into the sockets and space them evenly against the bow. Stand well back and check that they look right.

8 Mark their centres on the front face of the bow and draw a line on this face to give you the angle to drill their sockets (Fig. 15.38).

9 Mark the length of the spindles at these points. They should penetrate just over half the depth of the bow.

10 You could try turning the tops of the spindles on the lathe, using the same technique as with the stretchers. However, it is probably easier to saw them to length and then whittle them.

Alternatively, you could use a rounder if you have one.

11 Remove the bow and, gripping it firmly upside-down, drill the spindle holes to between half and two-thirds of the depth of the bow. The holes for the outermost spindles are awkward. You can start the hole by drilling at right-angles to the bow and swing the drill around to the correct angle (Fig. 15.39). A twist drill or ideally a spoon-bit is best for this.

Fig. 15.39 Starting the spindle sockets.

12 This is one situation where I do recommend a dry-run assembly before gluing.

13 Make suitable wedges for the bows.

14 Clean up and sandpaper all the surfaces.

15 Prepare for gluing as usual.

16 Smear glue into all the holes.

17 Locate the spindle tops in the bow.

18 Lower the bow into its sockets and lower the spindles gradually, one at a time, into their seat sockets without their coming out of the bow.

19 Supporting the back of the seat on a bench or horse, protect the bow with the softwood strip and knock it down hard until both ends emerge from the under-surface of the seat (Fig. 15.40).

20 Turn the chair upside-down with the bow resting on a cloth on a firm surface, and glue and drive in the wedges.

21 When the glue has set, saw the bottoms of the bows flush with the seat bottom.

22 Sand and finish as usual.

Fig. 15.40   Knocking the bow into place.

Sixteen

Bowls and Platters

'I'd rather make bowls than make money.'
George Lailey – the last of the professional pole-lathe bowl turners.

Long before the bodgers were plying their craft of making chair-legs, the pole-lathe was being used for making domestic ware. I have described how it can be employed to make spoons, but its most

chuck for the lathe cord to run on. The outside is shaped as with any other spindle turning; the inside is then hollowed out with a small gouge, leaving a cone of wood in the middle to rotate on the metal centre (Fig. 16.2).

Sooner or later the base of this cone will become weak. The goblet is then removed from the lathe, the core is cut away with a spoon gouge

Fig. 16.1   Bowl made from cherry wood.

significant application was in the making of wooden bowls. Small bowls can be turned using spindle-turning techniques with the grain of the wood running between the lathe centres. In this way, egg-cups and goblets can be produced. An extra section can be left at one end to act as a

and the goblet is sawn away from the chuck. If this is made from a round-wood section, there will be a core of pith in the centre and there is a danger of its cracking radially. If it is turned from a cleft section, it is less likely to crack but will dry out to an oval. For some purposes this shape does not matter, but for an egg-cup it will mean that the egg will rock.

To turn anything larger than 3–4" (8–10 cm) in

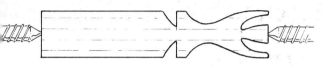

Fig. 16.2   Turning an egg-cup.

diameter, more reliable results are obtained with the grain of the wood running perpendicular to the axis of the lathe. This calls for a different method of rotating the wood. It is much more difficult to obtain a smooth finish on the work, because the wood fibres are constantly hitting the chisels at different angles as the wood rotates (Fig. 16.3).

The larger the diameter of the workpiece, the greater becomes its momentum, so much more force is required to rotate it and the rhythm

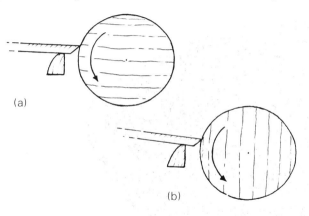

(a)

(b)

Fig. 16.3   'Faceplate' turning (a) rough finish (b) smooth finish.

becomes slower. This extra momentum also creates a greater force on the chisel, making it essential to use much heavier tools.

These reasons have been sufficient to keep me at arm's length from bowl turning. However, several friends have felt inclined to pursue this form of turning and, when you have the right lathe and appropriate tools, it provides a very rewarding pastime.

Again, we need to turn to tradition to find out how to proceed. Despite the development of treadle and then powered lathes, there were at least three families in the British Isles who were still making their living by turning bowls on a

pole-lathe until the mid-twentieth century: the Hughes in Armagh, Northern Ireland; the Davies in Abercych, Wales; and the Laileys in Buckleberry, England. I cannot resist this opportunity to reinforce my point that you do not require a large workshop in the country to work on a pole-lathe. An account by Megan MacManus (see Appendix 1) describes the last pole-lathe turners in Ireland, the Hughes family:

> Felix, who lived from 1848–1933, moved to the City of Armagh sometime in the 1890s and there he continued to operate the pole-lathe. Felix had eight sons. He showed all of them how to use the lathe, but a number of them found work in a local spinning mill. However, the sons kept the lathe or 'loom' in a house in an entry behind an urban terrace and they kept the craft alive. One son called Joseph, a twin, was still engaged in pole-lathe turning when he demonstrated his skills at the Royal Dublin Society Show in 1936.

So, despite all the drawbacks mentioned above, there must be some good reasons for using the pole-lathe for bowls. Small bowls obviously do not face the problems caused by the greater momentum of the spinning wood. The secret of large bowls is to turn them as a nest; that is, to turn one inside another (Fig. 16.4). Thus, several bowls are produced from one block of wood which reduces greatly the waste of timber. Even more significantly, it reduces the waste of effort involved in turning over 80 per cent of the wood into shavings as with powered lathe turning.

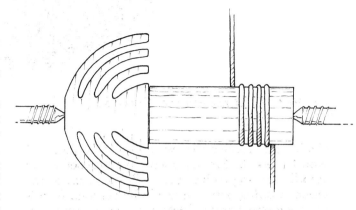

Fig. 16.4   A nest of bowls.

Fig. 16.5 Turning a sycamore bowl with a hooked tool.

Only during the past few years have turners attempted to reproduce these methods on powered lathes. If the bowl revolves continuously in one direction, there is a danger that the shavings will build up in the gap between the bowls, thereby wrenching the tool out of the turner's hands. On a pole-lathe, the shavings are thrown out each time the bowl spins backwards.

To successfully turn a nest of bowls is probably the pinnacle of achievement to anyone who has fallen in love with pole-lathes.

As far as bowl turning goes, I must confess that my knowledge is mostly theoretical, based on the half-dozen or so articles that I have been able to find on the subject. My only practical experience – apart from turning a few stool tops – was when I met Stephen de Brett who had spent 20 years studying bowl turning on the pole-lathe. He came to a weekend event in the Forest of Dean, and brought along his special chisels and showed us how to use them. He did not turn a nest, but made a single sycamore bowl (Fig. 16.5). I also made a small one then, but had not tried again since. In the meantime, we both swotted up on the subject and after a recent discussion, I made another attempt. Here is how it went.

First I had to adapt the lathe. I replaced the left-hand tool-rest support by a longer piece of 5×1″ (13×2·5cm), 18″ (45cm) in length (Fig. 16.6). I removed the standard treadle and rigged up a 3 ft (90cm) length of 4×½″ (10×1·5cm) pallet wood, hinging it with the lathe cord to the cross-pieces on the right-hand A-frame. I took the only suitable wood I had to hand: a cherry log which had been felled two years ago. It was still quite fresh inside, but the sapwood had started to

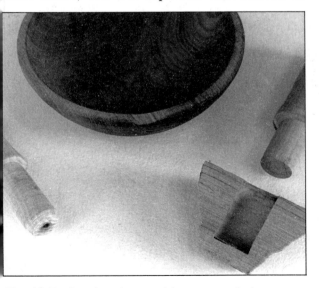

Fig. 16.7 Bowl and core with two mandrels.

decay. Having decided on a 9″ (23cm) diameter bowl, I took a section of the log already cleft in half and cut a 9″ (23cm) length. With an axe, I cut away some wood from the outside to produce as accurately as possible a 9″ (23cm) diameter

hemisphere (half a sphere). Then I cleaned up the flat face to remove the central pith. Unfortunately, during its two years of storage the exposed end had cracked. If I had had a straight section further from the end of the log, this crack could have been avoided. Using a freshly-felled log would also have avoided the cracking problem, but would have resulted in a more oval bowl – no big problem unless I had used it as a giant egg-cup!

The next job was to make a mandrel (or mamper) – a cylinder attached to the bowl for the lathe cord to grip. This was 7″ (18cm) long and turned to 2″ (5cm) diameter. I then turned the end 2½″ (6cm) down to 1¼″ (32mm) diameter, giving it a square shoulder (Fig. 16.7).

Fig. 16.6 Adapted tool rest.

I also turned a slight hollow in the centre of the thicker section to stop the cord running off the ends. Then I drilled a 1¼″ (32mm) diameter hole 2½″ (6cm) into the bowl blank and tapped in the mandrel. It should be a snug enough fit to grip tightly, but not so tight as to crack the bowl. I must admit this did not help the crack that was already there; it now resembled a mushroom!

I located the mandrel end of the mushroom on to the left-hand centre, and carefully centred the other end so that the mandrel rotated evenly. With the gimlet, I deepened the hole at this centre and lubricated it with linseed oil.

I knew that turning the bowl would need more

effort than spindle-turning, which is why I had changed the treadle. The end of the section of pallet wood was hinged so as to pivot vertically beneath the lathe bed. I took the cord between the beams of the bed, wrapped it five times around the mandrel and then fixed it to my ¼" (6 mm) shock-cord which was stretched 8 feet (2·5 m) above the lathe between two vertical poles. I pressed down on the treadle, which went down all right, but the spring was far too weak to spin the heavy block backwards. Fortunately I had kept a length of ⅜" (10 mm) shock-cord from my original bungy cord trials (never throw anything away). I fixed this in place and was able to turn the bowl to and fro at about 40 beats a minute. By pressing on the treadle much nearer the string, and vertically as opposed to the arc of the other treadle, I was able to stretch the 10 mm cord, which I had previously thought impossible.

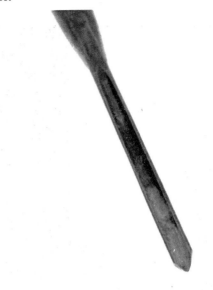

Fig. 16.9   Gouge adapted for bowl turning.

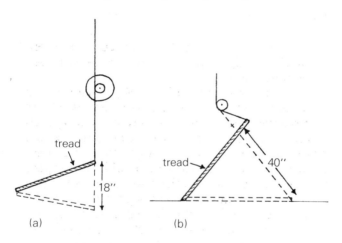

Fig. 16.8   Treadle movement (a) bowl turning (b) spindle turning.

You can see from the diagram that using this method gives less than half the deflection of the shock-cord – 18" (45 cm) as compared with 40" (1 m) – but provides the extra power required (Fig. 16.8).

The first stage was to shape the outside of the bowl. I used a long spindle gouge which I had once ground unevenly for smoothing stool tops. The tip is also quite pointed (Fig. 16.9).

I turned the tool rest round and drilled a ½" (13 mm) hole through the right-hand end and into the tool-rest support.

After locating a ½" (13 mm) pin through the hole to pivot the tool rest at that point, I then drilled a ½" (13 mm) hole into the new left-hand tool-rest support and located a pin to hold the tool rest in place as near as possible to the bowl without touching it (see Fig. 16.6).

With a little practice I was able to work towards the open end of the bowl, first cutting with the pointed tip of the gouge and then scraping with the long edge. This is where I had to break all the rules I outlined for spindle-turning. The finish was by no means perfect, but it was starting to look like a bowl.

At this stage I felt I should be higher in relation to the work, so I stood on a 10" (25 cm) high box for the rest of the job. I also modified the lathe by hinging a second length of pallet wood, 18" (45 cm) long, to a 2×2" (5×5 cm) beam located between the two A-frames of the lathe. Because the two parts of the treadle operate in different planes, I used two 'universal joints'. The short treadle has a 1¼" (32 mm) hole at one end, which sits over a ½" (13 mm) peg fixed into the crossbar. The other end is suspended below the long treadle with a piece of lathe cord (Fig. 16.10).

By pressing on the short treadle, I was able to avoid banging my knee on the bed of the lathe.

I then turned the bowl and mandrel around in the lathe and cleaned up the outer rim. Now came

Fig. 16.10   Adapted treadle.

gouge. There is no doubt that a special hooked tool would make the final stages easier when hollowing out the bottom of the bowl. It would then be possible to undercut the core further without having to remove so much wood. The turners of old used a whole range of such tools to cut out this curved shape rather than having to scrape. A tool of this kind would need to be curved to fit the outline of the bowl, with a tiny cutting hook at the end (Fig. 16.11). With such a long tool I would also have much more leverage, making it less important for the tool rest to be

Fig. 16.11   Special bowl-turning hook.

the tedious part: boring out the inside. This was a matter of cutting out a section of wood to leave a ½" (13 mm) thick wall to the bowl and a 4" (10 cm) diameter 'core' in the middle. The more wood I removed, the lighter became the work, but the more awkward it was to control the gouge. When the bowl was about 3" (8 cm) deep and the core had tapered from 4" to 2" (10 cm to 5 cm), I removed the bowl from the lathe. Then came one of those moments like steam-bending or knocking together a chair, when all these relaxing, rhythmical activities reach a nerve-tingling climax. I sat down on the horse holding the bowl, still connected to the mandrel, snugly in my lap. With a sharp strike from the hammer on to the mandrel where it enters the bowl, I snapped the core away from the rest of the bowl. It worked! All that then remained was to use a spoon gouge to clean up the scar at the bottom of the hollow which had been left by the core.

I have written this as a description rather than in instructions because there is much room for improvement. (Not that this doesn't apply to the rest of the book!)

The mandrel could be rather shorter, with 3" (8 cm) for the cord and 3" (8 cm) into the bowl (see Fig 16.7). This would put the poppets closer to each other, which would put the tool rest nearer to the work and provide more support for the

close to the work. It would need regular sharpening and would, therefore, have to be reshaped every now and then.

With this type of tool (or tools) it would then be quite possible to make a nest of bowls. I have seen descriptions of two methods of making such a nest. One method is to turn the shapes of all the bowls in one operation, only removing them from the lathe when they have all been shaped. With the other method the outer bowl is turned, removed from the lathe and separated from the remaining core. The core is then re-mounted on to the lathe and the next bowl turned to shape. This process is repeated until the final core is too small to turn into a bowl. Rather more time-consuming, but it seems to be easier and probably results in a better outer surface on the bowls. Apparently the Laileys of Buckleberry would clean up the outside with a spokeshave, but the Irish ones I have seen appear to be straight from the chisel.

There is now a ringed turning tool on the market which looks as if it would work well on the outside of the bowls, but I have not yet tried it.

There are a number of alternatives to the type of mandrel I described. In fact, most references describe a mandrel fitted with a number of iron spikes which drive into the face of the bowl before mounting it on the lathe (see Fig. 16.15). This is obviously quicker than drilling a hole and gives a firmer hold than one might expect. A tapered mandrel could of course be fitted into a tapered hole in the bowl; this method has nowadays been adapted for use in powered lathes.

I was surprised how well my lathe coped with this comparatively heavy work. Most of the old pictures show enormous lathes being used – sometimes hewn out of large tree-trunks or telegraph poles. Often one of the poppets is incorporated into one of the uprights. Such lathes nearly always had an extra horizontal beam behind the turner to give him more support as he pushed down on the treadle. However, the reconstruction of a medieval lathe used by Carole Morris is a much more lightweight affair. This range of sizes is accounted for by the fact that the turners in recent centuries turned enormous bowls – up to 24" (60 cm) in diameter, mainly for the dairy industry – compared with the much smaller bowls turned by the medieval craftsmen and myself.

This brings me to the best type of wood to use. Sycamore was certainly the favourite in Wales and Ireland because of its clean appearance, lack of smell and, not least, the ease with which it can be worked. On the other hand, the Laileys worked mostly in elm – difficult enough when green, but apparently they seasoned it for five years first. It is resistant to splitting, has a handsome grain and was once very common, but they must have earned every penny they received for their bowls. Apparently the reason for their seasoning the wood first was to make it lighter. Because green elm is so wet this process would reduce the weight by more than half, making the bowl much easier to rotate. This must have offset the extra work needed to cut it.

Back in medieval days, alder and ash were the most popular woods, presumably before sycamore was so widespread. I dare say that birch would make a good bowl, as should beech if turned while it is still green. My piece of cherry looks quite handsome (despite the crack) and it smelled delightful while I worked on it.

Certainly the easiest way to obtain the blank for the bowl is to use the natural shape of half a log as your starting point (Fig. 16.12 (a) & (b)). Cut it to the same length as the width of the log

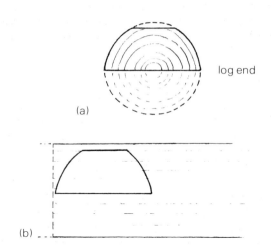

Fig. 16.12 Cutting a bowl from a half log (a) section across log (b) section along log.

and remove the corners with an axe. This does not take too long if the wood is green. A popular project among the power-lathe fraternity is the 'natural-edge' bowl, which involves cutting the bowl out of the log in the opposite way to the above method (Fig. 16.13 (a) & (b)). When using a band-saw to cut out the blanks, it makes little difference which way they are cut from the log. If you have to trim the blank with an axe, your wrist will ache after shaping a 'natural edge' blank. However, you may consider it worthwhile.

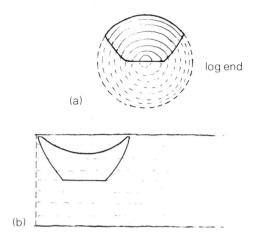

Fig. 16.13 Cutting out a natural-edge bowl (a) section across log (b) section along log.

Should you intend to use the bowls for food, then oil them several times with a normal cooking oil. This should be repeated every few months to keep them in good shape.

Carved Bowls

A rather less strenuous way to make bowls, even if just as time-consuming, is to carve them. All you need to do is to find a suitable log, split it down the middle and carve it inside and out. One of the biggest problems is to hold it steady as you hollow out the middle, but this can be overcome by leaving the bowl attached to the rest of the log until the hollowing is complete. You then saw it from the log and shape the outside. I normally use a large gouge and a mallet for the inside, but you could try using a small one-handed adze. In Wales these adzes are even used for hollowing ladles. The outside of the bowl can be shaped with the gouge again, or with a heavy chisel (or a chain-saw if you have one). You can clean it up with a spokeshave, but you may decide that the tool-marks add to its character.

Whether turning or carving bowls, it is best to remove the bulk of the wood in one session. Do not leave it partially hollowed, or the varying thicknesses in different parts may cause it to crack. Some people would disagree and advocate partially turning a bowl, then letting it season before finishing it off. If you are intent on a perfectly spherical, shiny bowl, then provided that the walls are fairly even in thickness after the first stage you could adopt this approach. Otherwise, turn it green and let it warp.

Platters

Wooden plates or platters are really just very shallow bowls. Cleave a flat section out of a log

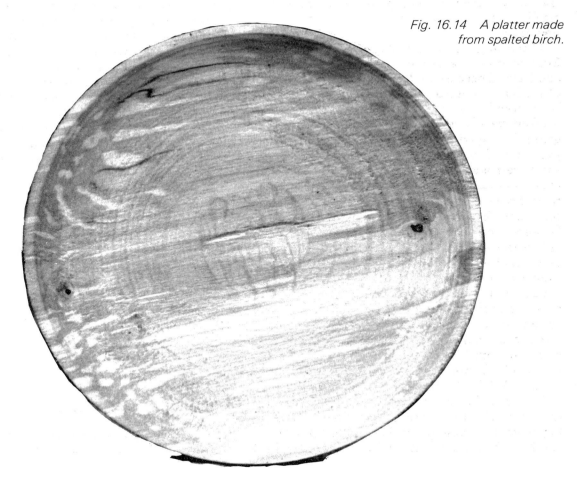

Fig. 16.14   A platter made from spalted birch.

181

Fig. 16.15   Fitting the spiked mandrel.

and saw a circular outline with a turning-saw (see Chapter 12). You will be unable to use the drilled mandrel method, so you should make a mandrel with iron spikes (Fig. 16.15). This – unlike on the bowls – should be driven into the bottom of the platter. You will then be able to smooth 99 per cent of the face of the platter, just leaving a small stub which can be cut off after removing the finished work from the lathe.

There will be a danger of the wood cracking if it is too green, since a flat platter cannot contract in on itself in the same way as a bowl. I would advise you to avoid woods that split easily, such as ash or sweet chestnut. London plane, however, is a wood that turns well, is resistant to

splitting and has no taste, so that would be my first choice.

Stool Tops

The same methods apply to turned stool tops as those described for platters. The only difference is that ideally they should be sawn out of elm planks.

Seventeen

Fences, Rakes and Other Projects

So far I have concentrated mainly on the green wood crafts in which the pole-lathe plays an important part. There are of course numerous other crafts which make use of green wood. Some of these were carried out as quite separate trades producing items such as swill baskets, trugs, cricket bats, coracles, barrels and much more. Many of these crafts are still practised and involve quite intricate operations, most of which I haven't even started to discover. However, there are a number of other crafts which require a great deal of skill and practice to achieve a professional result, but nonetheless can quite easily be undertaken by the beginner. I have selected a few such projects for this chapter, where the end product may well have an application in the home or garden.

Tent-pegs

The wood to make these should come from 8–15"

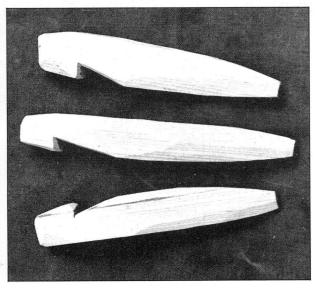

Fig. 17.1   Tent-pegs.

(20–38 cm) diameter ash or sweet-chestnut logs, cut to the length of the pegs desired (8–24" (20–60 cm) depending on their purpose). Using the cleaving axe or the froe, cleave the log radially down into narrow segments and, depending on the size of the log and the pegs, cleave them down tangentially. The blank for a 9" (23 cm) tent-peg should be about $1\frac{1}{2} \times \frac{3}{4}$" (4 × 2 cm) with sloping sides caused by cleaving radially from the log (Fig. 17.2).

Fig. 17.2   Cleaving a tent-peg from the log.

At 3" (8 cm) from the top you should saw a slot into the narrow edge about ½" (13 mm) deep, running slightly upwards to help retain the rope when in use.

I shall now digress to tell you about my first experience of tent-peg making in the Forest of Dean while I was running one of my courses. The craftsman, known as 'Happy', turned up with a device called a stock knife (Fig. 17.3). This is basically a large blade with a long handle at one end and a hook at the other which hinges into an eye on a heavy wooden block. Best known in the making of clogs, it can also be used in shaping spoons. It combines the power of leverage with great control, operating very much like a guillotine. He had learned the craft 40 years beforehand when a lad, but had left the trade (like most others) for better money elsewhere.

He used a very heavy froe, swinging it down on to the log like an axe, holding the wood with his left hand to stop it falling over (which would

Fig. 17.3   A stock knife.

If you are unable to lay your hands on a stock knife, then you can use either the turner's side axe on a chopping-block, or a drawknife and shaving-horse. To the best of my recollection, this is the shape to aim for (Fig. 17.4).

Roofing Shingles

These are in effect wooden tiles, and were widely used as a roofing material when good wood was more abundant. They were usually made from oak, but sweet chestnut can be employed. In mainland Europe and North America, they are still widely used although normally made from various conifers, Western red cedar being one of the best. When fixed into place each shingle

waste time). After making the saw-cut, he took the blank to the stock knife and, with a series of lightning flashes of the blade, shaped the peg. A bystander casually asked how many cuts he needed. 'Happy' replied that he had never counted, so we all counted the strokes as he made another peg. '15, 16, 17' we chanted. 'Should be 18,' grunted a deep voice from the back of the crowd and up stepped one of 'Happy's' contemporaries who had made pegs for the same firm many years earlier. Now he shaped a peg and, as anticipated, took one stroke more. After a little discussion, they found that Happy had left out one last delicate cut just under the groove for the rope; probably enough to make a few years difference to the life of a tent-rope.

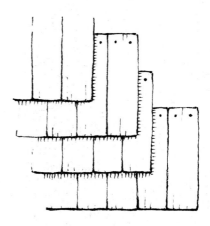

Fig. 17.5   Shingles fixed to a roof.

should overlap about two-thirds of the one before. They should start at the eaves of the roof and work up towards the ridge (Fig. 17.5).

To make shingles you will need large, straight knot-free logs. In oak, these are hard to come by in Britain nowadays, except after hurricanes. Sweet chestnut is also resistant to decay outdoors, but when it grows too large it is prone to ring shakes and a strong spiral.

The logs should be cut to length and the bark removed; traditionally this would have been left to dry and sold to a tannery where it would have been used for tanning leather. Then cleave the log in half and radially split each half into half again until down to the correct thickness, about ½"

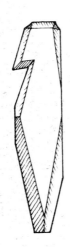

Fig. 17.4   Side view of a tent-peg.

(13 mm). Obviously it will be thicker towards the outside of the log. The only tool suitable for the job is the froe, which in Germany – where it is still manufactured for this purpose – it is referred to as a shingle iron. You now need to remove any sapwood as well as the very inner section near the pith. The surfaces should then be cleaned up with a drawknife.

To obtain shingles 5" (13 cm) wide, you will need a log of at least 12" (30 cm) diameter so as to allow for the shingles to be split from the radius with a little waste on both edges. Nowadays shingles are usually sawn from the log, but this is bound to sever some of the fibres which would otherwise be left intact by cleaving. Sawn shingles, therefore, need a thorough preserving treatment which is unnecessary on cleft oak.

Laths

These are long thin strips of wood employed traditionally in building work. The smaller type –

Fig. 17.6 Geoff and Ian with their laths.

about 1 × ¼" (25 × 6 mm) in cross-section – were used very widely, being nailed to walls and ceilings as a foundation for plaster-work. Larger ones up to 3 × 1" (8 × 2·5 cm) were used as battens for stone or tile roofs, and others were woven into a very strong framework for walls. They were usually cleft from oak, sweet chestnut, or sometimes willow. Again good quality wood is required but, unlike the shingles, it can come from smaller-dimension coppice wood. To make laths, you need to start with a froe and a cleaving break in order to guide the split. The last few splits can be made with a large knife, as with wattle hurdles. Cleaving several thousand metres of ceiling lath will sharpen up your skills in using the froe (see my article in *Woodworker* magazine).

Fencing

There are many ways in which green wood skills can be used in making fences. To make the stakes for simple *post and wire* fencing, logs can be cleft down into halves, quarters or eighths, using a pair of wedges and a maul. A few deft blows with a 4 lb (2 kg) axe will put a point on the end. Again, oak and sweet chestnut are the woods for this, but it is best to remove the sapwood. The remaining heartwood post should outlast virtually any alternatives.

One very attractive fence I have seen a lot in Kent and Sussex is a type of *post and rail* (Fig. 17.7). The posts are nowadays sawn and mortised by machinery, but the rails are cleft – usually from large coppice-grown sweet chestnut or oak. Each post has two pairs of mortises and the rails are tapered to slot through them. Each set of rails has to be slotted into place as the posts are erected, and no nails or other fixings are required to hold them in place.

How one replaces a broken rail I do not know, but I imagine such an operation is seldom called for.

Fig. 17.7 'Sussex' post and rail fence.

Fig. 17.8   Chestnut palings.

Cleft chestnut is still widely used to make *paling* fences, and this is one of the few coppice crafts that is still thriving. A paling fence consists of a row of vertical sections of cleft wood bound in place by two horizontal rows of wire (Fig. 17.8). This can then be rolled up and easily transported. Such fences are frequently used around building work, show grounds and anywhere else where entry by humans is to be discouraged. They look ineffective, but can be extremely painful to climb over. It is interesting to note that this is a fairly recent craft only developed over the last century. Chestnut coppice was previously grown on a large scale to provide poles to support the hops grown for beer making. When wire became widely available,

this was used for the job and fewer poles were needed – which, of course, reduced the demand for coppice-grown chestnut. Then some bright person invented paling fences, enabling the wire which had threatened the livelihood of the coppice workers to give the craft a new lease of life.

Hurdles

These were the forerunner of the electric fence, being used as a movable barrier to control farm stock, usually sheep. There are two distinct types: gate (or gait) hurdles and wattle hurdles.

Gate Hurdles

These take the form of a standard farm gate, but are much lighter. There are various local patterns, but all include three main components: upright posts, cross-bars and braces.

Fig. 17.9   Mick with his Sussex hurdle.

The best materials for making gate hurdles are coppice-grown logs of sweet chestnut, ash or willow from 2–4" (5–10 cm) diameter. These should be cleft using a froe and a cleaving-break to produce a number of half-round sections. The uprights should be made from two halves of the same log so that any curves are the same at both ends. This should be 4 ft (1·2 m) long and 3–4" (8–10 cm) diameter. The cross-bars are 2–3" (5–8 cm) diameter, traditionally being 8 ft (2·4 m) long but you may choose to make them shorter. Three shorter lengths of a similar diameter are used for a central upright and two diagonals.

Start by cleaving the cross-bars and shaving the tenons to about 2⅝" (50×16 mm) with a slight taper towards the ends. It is crucial, in order to avoid a crooked hurdle, that these tenons are in the same plane and do not 'wind'

with the wood. A good way of gripping them for this job is to fix a vertical post in the ground at the 'back' of the cleaving-break (that is, opposite the lower end of the horizontal beam) about 30" (75 cm) away from the nearer beam. It should be cut to about the height of the lower beam and a double-ended nail driven into the top with its point projecting about ¼" (6 mm). Each rail can now be wedged over the lower beam of the break and under the upper beam, which will then spring it down on to the spike on the new post.

Now shave the cleft surfaces of the uprights to produce a fairly flat face and, using an axe, point one end of each. Lay these, flat side upwards, on the ground and place the cross-bars on to them with about 8" (10 cm) between centres (slightly closer at the bottom to keep in the lambs). Now mark the positions and widths of the tenons on to the posts, also marking which cross-bar goes where. With the posts held horizontally, using the cleaving-break and spiked post, drill the top

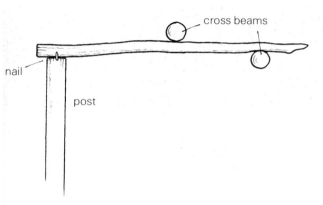

Fig. 17.10   Holding a hurdle post in the cleaving break.

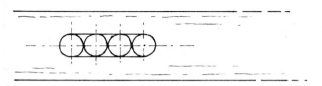

Fig. 17.12   Drilling the mortise.

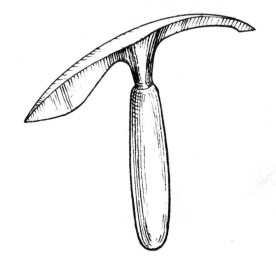

Fig. 17.11   A twybil.

and bottom of each mortise with a brace and ⅝" (16 mm) bit.

Ideally you should clean out the remainder of the mortise with a tool called a twybil (or twyvil) (Fig. 17.11). At one end is a blade which you slice

along the sides of the mortise to loosen the chunk of wood between the two holes. You then lever out this chunk with the other end of the twybil which resembles a curved mortise chisel. If you are unable to obtain a twybil, you can achieve the same result by drilling an extra hole or two in the centre of the mortise and cleaning it up with a chisel or a knife (Fig. 17.12).

You can now assemble the post and cross-bars but take care not to force them together so hard as to split the posts. You can fix these joints with wooden pegs or by nailing.

Traditionally, cut nails were used for this purpose, as they are less likely to split the wood. If you cannot obtain these, use ordinary nails, blunting the points with a hammer before driving them into the wood to help prevent them from splitting it. The nails used on the cross-bars should be long enough to project from the far side; they can then be bent over with the hammer to prevent them from falling out. This is a technique quite accepted by country craftsmen and is called clench-nailing.

Finally shape the remaining three pieces as shown (see Fig. 17.9) and nail these to the cross-bars. If you now wish to make more hurdles, this one can be laid on the ground and used as a pattern.

If you are unable to obtain suitable coppice poles, then you will have to cleave sections out of larger logs. This will be more laborious but could well result in a more sophisticated hurdle – if such a thing exists.

There is, of course, no reason why you could not adapt this design to a more urban use such as a garden gate, fence or trestle for climbing plants.

Wattle Hurdles (Fig. 17.13)

These are best made from hazel, although willow can be used. You need a large number of straight rods ½–1" (13–25 mm) thick, preferably grown from coppiced plants. These hurdles are rarely used on farms today but make a very attractive and effective garden fence, and I am told that the demand now exceeds supply.

Yet again, it takes a few minutes to learn the theory and a lifetime to get it right.

To make a successful wattle hurdle, you have to get the knack of two particular operations. The first is cleaving the long thin rods, up to 10 ft

Fig. 17.13   Mr Davis trimming up a Dorset hurdle.

(3 m) in length, down the middle. For this a small bill-hook is usually best, although a large knife, a small axe or even a small adze can be used. The cleaving-break could be employed, although another method is to push the split rod against a vertical post to open up the split while levering it open at the same time. Yet another technique is to stand with one foot supported about 9" (23 cm) off the ground. You then pass the rod under the lower leg and rest it on the thigh of the other leg. By pressing down or pulling up the rod, you can

guide the split as you open it with the hooked tip of a bill-hook or a large knife (Fig. 17.14).

The second tricky operation is bending and twisting the rods when they make a U-turn at the ends of the hurdle. Without this twisting motion, which separates the fibres, the rod would simply snap when it is bent.

To start with, you need to make a base about 6 or 7 ft (1·8 or 2·1 m) long. This should be made from a heavy log with a gentle curve which will give the hurdle the same shape. When they are stacked, convex side up, the weight of the pile flattens them to tighten the weave.

Into this base at about 9" (23 cm) intervals you

should drill ten 1" or 1¼" (25 mm or 32 mm) vertical holes. Then into each of these you place a stout rod, the end one being 4 ft (1·2 m) long and the others about 6" (15 cm) shorter. The hurdle is normally made upside down, so the two outer uprights should be pointed at the top in order that they can be driven into the ground when the hurdle is put to use.

Next you should take a number of slender rods which you do not cleave. There are several ways of weaving these rods, one of the simplest being to intertwine them in pairs, not only between the uprights but between each other so that they bind tightly on to what will be the top of the hurdle (Fig. 17.15). At the ends of the hurdle you apply the bend and twist technique, then weave them back again. After several pairs of these, you weave in the cleft rods. It is a help to keep the cleft halves together so that they can be woven into the hurdle one above the other. If they have been cleft evenly, this will ensure an even pressure on either side of the uprights. You should see what I mean when you try it. Just before the top, you plait in several pairs of slender rods as before.

The hurdle can then be lifted out of its base, the ends of the uprights being trimmed to 1" (25 mm) from the woven section – except, of course, the two pointed ends – and all loose ends trimmed back. The hurdle should now be placed on a stack with the others! Ten a day was the going rate.

Fig. 17.14   One way of cleaving hazel.

Fig. 17.15   The initial weave.

Fig. 17.17   Binding the besom twigs.

Besom

Besom making continues to this day, producing simple 'witches' brooms' for sweeping up dead leaves and other such uses. A besom consists of a bundle of twigs, usually birch or heather, into which is driven a shaved stick 3–4 ft (90–120 cm) long for a handle. The best results are achieved by using the twigs from coppice-grown birch which are still straight and vigorous. The dangling twigs of older trees are a poor substitute.

The twigs should be cut and then left in bundles for several months to dry out somewhere sheltered, but well ventilated. The poles should also be cut, barked and seasoned. The important things is that the bundle of twigs is very tight and to achieve this, various devices have been utilised. The simplest of these consists of two strong sticks and a loop of cord. The bundle of twigs is placed with the thick ends on top of the loop. This loop is then crossed over above the bundle and a stick passed through each end. These then cross over the bundle and are levered around the twigs, pulling them tightly together (Fig. 17.17).

While they are gripped in this way, you can bind the bundle with two permanent ties. These can be made of wire, which you will have to twist tight with pliers. Alternatively you can try some more natural binding, which can be made from thin strands of ash wood, inner bark from lime or wych elm, thin twigs of willow or lengths of bramble (with its thorns removed). Of course,

Fig. 17.16   A besom.

you could use some kind of twine or string just as well.

The tight end of the bundle should now be cut cleanly with an axe or bill-hook and any straggling twigs removed. Put a point on one end of the handle and support it on a solid surface with the point facing upwards. Position the bundle of twigs over the point and knock the handle downwards. The bundle will be forced down into the point, which will tighten the binding still further. To finish it off properly, drill a ¼" or ⅜" (6 mm or 10 mm) hole through the bundle and the handle between the two bindings, then drive in a wooden peg to make sure that the besom does not lose its head.

Hay Rake

I have saved my favourite non-pole-lathe project until last. To enjoy it to the full you will have to acquire or make a wonderful gadget called a tine cutter. This is a tube with a ½" (13 mm) internal diameter (or a fraction larger), fixed to a metal base at one end and tapered to a sharp rim at the other (see Fig. 17.21).

It is used to produce tines – that is, the wooden teeth for a hay rake – by driving a short length of wood through the tube so that it comes out as a ½" (13 mm) cylinder at the other end. It works best if the diameter of the inside of the tube increases further down, so as to reduce the friction on the wood sliding through. An alternative is a simple steel plate with a ½" (13 mm) hole drilled through, but this will only work properly if the wood is nearly the right size before knocking it through. Apart from its use in making hay rakes, the tine cutter can produce pins for a multitude of odd jobs.

I propose to give the dimensions for a smallish hay rake which you could use in the garden for raking up grass and leaves, or in your workshop to clear up all your shavings. In fact, you can use it to filter your wood-shavings. The larger ones suitable for burning will be collected by the rake, while the smaller shavings from the lathe will stay behind to be collected for a garden mulch or for animal bedding when they have dried out.

To do the job properly you should work, as with chairs, by preparing some of the components when green and then leaving them to season before completing the work. However as

Fig. 17.18 A hay rake.

a fun project, especially with children, you can do most of it in one session and make adjustments later if necessary.

You will need a straight pole, preferably ash or hazel, for the handle. It should be approximately as long as its user is tall, and should taper to about 1" (2·5 cm) at its smaller end. There are several ways of strengthening the handle; my favourite being a bent hoop made from 40" (1 m) long hazel, ash, willow or elm rod somewhat

Fig. 17.19   Bending the hoop.

Fig. 17.20   Splitting the tines.

greater than ½" (13 mm) in diameter. The handle should ideally be seasoned – as always, out of the weather, but well ventilated – for a year or so. It is a good idea to lay in a stock of these whenever they become available. The hoop can be bent while green, or steamed if it has dried out to make it supple again. Bending this hoop is similar to the bending carried out for the bow-back chair. Find or cut a semi-circular shape and wedge the middle of the hoop tightly against the mid-point of the curve (Fig. 17.19). This should prevent it from kinking. Steadily bend it to shape, tie the ends and leave it to season. This is a good way to experience bending wood. If you have the steamer going, you could also use it to soften the handle so that you can straighten out any bends it might have along its length.

Next, make the tines. For this you need a 6" (15 cm) length of ash, oak or willow, preferably from a 4–8" (10–20 cm) diameter log still in the round. A lovely method of splitting the tines has been handed down via Fred Lambert and Jack Hill to me and now to you:

Tie one or two lengths of string around the log

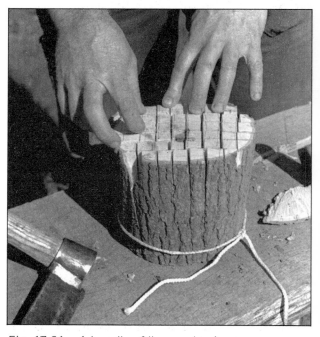

Fig. 17.21   A bundle of 'long cubes'.

Fig. 17.22   Cutting the tines.

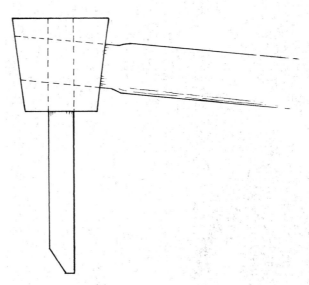

Fig. 17.23   Cross-section through a rake head.

and place it on a firm chopping-block. Mark out on the log a grid of ⅝" (16 mm) squares on the end-grain. Using the froe and club, split the log down the centre line, and then into smaller strips until you have split all the lines in one direction (Fig. 17.20). The string should still hold them all together. Now split along the lines at right-angles, again starting with the centre line, until you have a bundle of elongated ⅝" (16 mm) cubes (Fig. 17.21). You should really let these dry out, but you can hurry the process by mildly cooking them in a container over a low fire, by laying them in the hot sun or using any other suitable method at your disposal.

While you are doing this, whittle a small wedge ⅞" (22 mm) wide, preferably oak, and dry it at the same time. This will hold the handle in place later.

When the tines are dry enough, you can drive them through the tine cutter with a *wooden* club or mallet (Fig. 17.22). If you use metal, you will soon destroy the sharp edge. Just before the tine disappears, place the next one over the top and knock it through; this will push the first one out of the bottom and should avoid the club blunting the cutter. If you want a guaranteed way of keeping a bunch of primary school children occupied, get them making hay-rake tines – they just cannot bear to stop while there is still a tine in the tube!

Now you need to make the rake head, which should be cleft from a length of ash or willow 24–30" (60–75 cm) long (shorter for children or for use in confined spaces). Shave it to the cross-section shown, using a drawknife (Fig. 17.23). This shape may appear by itself if you cleave a wedge from a suitable log.

On the smaller side, draw a straight line and mark on it the positions for the tines. These should normally be 2" (5 cm) apart. Make the middle holes either side of the centre of the head, so that the hole for the handle does not go through a tine. Clamp the head firmly to a bench or drilling-post and carefully drill the two end

195

Fig. 17.24   Drilling the tine holes.

Fig. 17.25   Fitting the bow.

holes. You can stop before they emerge from the other side, but I prefer them to go straight through – it is then easier to replace any tine which happens to break. Do not worry about the splinters as the drill emerges; these will be cleaned off at the end.

To align the other holes, tie a loop of string around the two end tines and drill out the remaining holes, keeping the drill bit centred within the loop (Fig. 17.24). Crooked teeth will not only spoil its looks, but make the rake less effective. Now knock in the tines until they emerge on the far side of the head. You may find that some of the tines are circular at one end, but ran off line as they went through the cutter; if so, put the round ends in the holes to make a tight fit. If the head was made from green wood, it should tighten up on the tines in time as it shrinks.

Now return your attention to the handle. Traditionally, this was smoothed off by a gadget called a stail-engine – an adjustable form of rounding plane which was steadily screwed smaller as it travelled down the handle. If you feel

like making one, it provides yet another fascinating aspect to this project. Otherwise, smooth the handle as well as you can with a spokeshave.

Next shape the small end of the handle to 7/8" (22 mm) (plus or minus 1/8" (3 mm) if you have a suitable auger bit). Drill the correct-sized hole perpendicular to one of the sloping faces in the centre of the head and out the far side. It should be at about 80 degrees to the tines; this will cause the tines to slope back towards the handle, giving rise to the term 'raked back'. Saw a slot in the end of the handle 1" (2·5 cm) deep and drive it into the hole in the head (not as gruesome as it sounds) with the slot at right-angles to the grain of the head (as with previous wedged joints). Shape the wedge to fit and knock it into the slot.

Hold the hoop in position above the rake so that its ends are about 3" (8 cm) from the ends of the head. Mark the angle at which they meet and drill a 1/2" (13 mm) hole at each joint, stopping before the drill emerges. Shape the ends of the hoop to fit the holes and spring the hoop into

Fig. 17.26   Lashing the bow to the handle.

Fig. 17.28   Angling the ends of the tines.

place so that it passes just *above* the handle (Fig. 17.25). When the rake is in operation, this will be forced against the handle. Now lash the two together where they cross (Fig. 17.26).

Tie the loop of string again between the end tines 3–4" (8–10 cm) from the head, making sure that no tines are shorter than this gap.

Fig. 17.27   Marking the length of the tines.

Mark the position of the string on to each tine (Fig. 17.27), and saw them square so that they are now all level. Rest the rake with the tines on a none too precious piece of wood, and using a chisel and mallet cut an angle on the ends of the tines opposite the handle as shown (Fig. 17.28). This is so that the leading edge of each tine is not lifted off the ground by the trailing edge.

Finally, run a spokeshave along the top of the

Fig. 17.29   *The fruits of a week among the trees.*

rake head to level off any protruding tines and remove any scars caused by the drill. Similarly, trim the protruding wedge and handle. The patterns of the end grain should contrast pleasantly with the long grain of the head. When you have finished admiring it, rub it with linseed oil.

Apart from the pole-lathe, this has proved to be one of my most popular projects with children. If you have prepared some of the materials beforehand (e.g. seasoned and smoothed the handle and shaped the head), it makes a wonderful project for a summer's afternoon.

I hope that after reading this you will want to dash out and try everything. I have worked through most of the projects myself, and have attempted to iron out the majority of problems before writing down the method. Nevertheless you will undoubtedly encounter difficulty at some stages, but I hope that you will steadily adopt the attitude that an answer can usually be found with the exercise of just a little ingenuity. If ever we meet, I would be keen to hear about any problems you encountered in carrying out these projects and even keener to hear how you solved them! By working with your hands, your head and hopefully your heart, you should have many happy days of green woodwork ahead of you.

Fig. 17.30   *A budding bodger testing a wych elm stool.*

Appendix 1 Bibliography

Abbott, Mike.
'The last lath', *Woodworker*, November 1987.
'How to make a pole-lathe', *Woodworking International*, February 1989.

Alexander, John D.
Make a Chair from a Tree, Taunton Press, 1978.

Barratt, Mary.
Oak Swill Basket Making in the Lake District, Mary Barratt, 1983.

Berry, Wendell.
Landscape of Harmony, Five Seasons Press, 1987.

Blandford, P. W.
Tools for Country Crafts, David & Charles, 1974.

Building Research Establishment – Technical Notes
No. 10 The strength of timber
No. 38 The movement of timbers
No. 52 The bending of solid timber
No. 54 Selecting ash by inspection

Comino, Mary.
Gimson and the Barnsleys, Evans Bros., 1980.

Dunbar, Michael.
Make a Windsor Chair, Taunton Press, 1984.

Dunwell, J. and Kingdon, M.
Stool Seating Methods, J. Dunwell, 1970.

Edlin, Herbert L.
Broadleaves. Forestry Commission booklet No. 20, HMSO, 1st edn 1968, 2nd edn 1985.

Collins Guide to Tree Planting and Cultivation, Collins, 1st edn 1970, 3rd edn 1975.

Trees, Woods and Man, Collins, 1st edn 1956, 3rd edn 1970.

Woodland Crafts of Britain, Batsford, 1947.

Fine Woodworking on Chairs and Beds, Taunton Press, 1986.

Fine Woodworking on Bending Wood, Taunton Press, 1985.

Fine Woodworking on Wood and How to Dry it, Taunton Press, 1986.

Fitzrandolf, H.E. and Hay, M. D.
The Rural Industries of England and Wales, vol. iv, E.P. 1977.

Hartley, D.
Made in England, Eyre Methuen, 1939.

Hill, Jack.
The Complete Practical Guide to Country Crafts, David & Charles, 1979.

Making Family Heirlooms, David & Charles, 1985.

Holtzapffel, J. J.
Hand or Simple Turning, Dover Publications, 1976.

Jenkins, J. G.
Traditional Country Craftsmen, RKP, 1965.

Jenkins, J. G. and Davies, T. Alun.
The Wood Turner's Craft, Welsh Folk Museum.

Joyce, Ernest.
Furniture Making, Batsford, 1st edn 1970, revised Alan Peters, 1987.

Kealy, Tom.
'The Somerset Chairs of Tom Kealy', *Woodworking International*, February 1988.

Lambert, F.
Tools and Devices for Coppice Crafts, Centre for Alternative Technology, 1977.

Langsner, Drew.
Country Woodcraft, Rodale Press, 1978.

Macmanus, Megan.
Joseph Hughes: an Armagh Woodturner, Tools and Trades History Society Journal Vol. I, 1983.

Manners, J. E.
Country Crafts Today, David & Charles, 1983.

Mayes, J. L.
The History of Chairmaking in High Wycombe, RKP, 1960.

Morris, Dr Carole A.
  'Pole-Lathe Turning', *Woodworking Crafts*,
  August 1985

Nutting, Wallace.
  A Windsor Handbook, 1st edn 1917, Charles E.
  Tuttle 1973.

Peters, Alan.
  Cabinetmaking, the Professional Approach,
  Stobart & Son, 1984.

Rose, Walter.
  The Village Carpenter, 1st edn 1937, A. & C.
  Black, reissued 1987.

Sainsbury, John.
  *Sharpening and Care of Woodworking Tools and
  Equipment*, Guild of Master Craftsman
  Publications, 1984.

Sparkes, Ivan.
  The English Country Chair, Spurbooks, 1973.

  English Windsor Chairs, Shire Publications, 1981.

  Woodland Craftsmen, Shire Publications, 1977.

Underhill, Roy.
  The Woodwright's Shop, University of North
  Carolina Press, 1981.

  The Woodwright's Workbook, University of
  North Carolina Press, 1981.

Walker, Philip.
  Woodworking Tools, Shire Publications, 1980.

Wales, Rod.
  'A look at the work of David Colwell',
  Woodworking International, February 1988.

Appendix 2 Useful Addresses

1　Tool manufacturers

Ashem Crafts,
2 Oakleigh Avenue, Hallow, Worcester WR2 6NG.
Telephone: Worcester (01905) 640070.
　　Rounding planes and accessories.

Ashley Iles (Edge Tools) Ltd,
East Kirkby, Spilsby, Lincolnshire PE23 4DD.
Telephone: (01790) 763327.
　　Chisels and gouges.

Bristol Design,
14 Perry Road, (Park Row), Bristol BS1 5BG.
Telephone: (0117) 9291740.
　　Tools for chair-making, green woodwork and
　　carving, also old woodworking tools.

Clico Tooling,
Unit 7, Fell Road Industrial Estate, Sheffield S9 2AL.
Telephone: (0114) 2433007.
　　Drill bits, spokeshaves and other specialist tools.

Henry Taylor Tools Ltd,
Peacock Road, Livesey Estate, Sheffield S6 2BL.
Telephone: (0114) 2340282.
　　Carving and turning tools.

Matt Sears,
Y Stabl, Bancau, Brynberian, Crymych, Pembrokeshire
SA41 3TS.
Telephone: (01239) 891644.
　　Hand-forged green woodworking tools.

Robert Sorby,
Athol Road, Woodseats Road, Sheffield S8 0PA.
Telephone: (0114) 2554231.
　　Chisels, gouges and other woodworking tools.

Visa Hand Tools Ltd,
Unit 3, Tweed Road Industrial Estate, Clevedon, Bristol BS21
6RR.
Telephone: (01275) 876047
　　Axes, wedges and other woodcraft tools.

2　Tool suppliers

Axminster Power Tool Centre,
Chard Street, Axminster, Devon.
Telephone: (01297) 33656.
　　Wide range of woodworking tools.

The Relics Collection,
35 Bridge Street, Witney, Oxfordshire OX8 6DA.
Telephone: (01993) 704611.
　　Restoration and finishing products,
　　sealing materials etc.

Michael Richmond,
5-15 Weyhill, Haslemere, Surrey GU27 1BY.
Telephone: (01428) 643328.
　　Forestry and tree surgery equipment.

Alec Tiranti,
70 High Street, Theale, Reading RG7 5AR.
Telephone: (01734) 302775.
　　Woodcarving tools and accessories.

Mike Abbott,
Ragged Stone Cottage, Hollybush, Ledbury, Herefordshire
HR8 1ET.
Telephone: (01531) 635300.
　　Also sells pole-lathe cranks.

3　Organisations running green woodwork courses

Anglesey Chair Bodgers,
Carreg Rhys, Paradwys, Bororgan, Anglesey LL62 5PB.
Telephone: (01407) 840249.

Brotus Craft Centre,
Ladybank, Fife.
Telephone: (01337) 830882.

Commonwork Trust,
Bore Place, Chiddingstone, Edenbridge, Kent TN8 7AR.
Telephone: (01732) 463255.

Country Workshops,
90 Mill Creek Road, Marshall NC 28753
USA.

Victor Crutchley,
North Eggardon Farmhouse, Powerstock, Nr Bridport,
Dorset DT5 3ST.
Telephone: (01308) 485332.

The Green Wood Trust,
Station Road, Coalbrookdale, Shropshire TF8 7DR.
Telephone: (01905) 432769.

Handcraft Woodworks,
PO Box 1322, Mendocino, Ca 95460 USA.

Hay Bridge Nature Reserve,
Bouth, Ulverston, Cumbria LA12 8JG.
Telephone: (01229) 861412.

Jack Hill Workshops,
PO Box 20, Midhurst, West Sussex GU29 0DJ.
Telephone: (01730) 813368.

West Dean College,
West Dean, Chichester, West Sussex PO18 0QZ.
Telephone: (01243) 811301.

The Woodland Skills Centre,
The Church Hall, Llanafan, Builth Wells, Powys LD2 3PN.
Telephone: (01597) 860469.

4   Places to visit

The Ancient Technology Centre,
Cranbourne Middle School, Cranbourne, Wimbourne, Dorset
BH21 5RP.
Telephone: (01725) 517618.

The Centre for Alternative Technology,
Machynlleth, Powys SY20 9AZ.
Telephone: (01654) 702400.

The Chiltern Open Air Museum,
Newland Park, Gorlands Lane, Chalfont St Giles,
Buckinghamshire HP8 4AD.
Telephone: (01494) 872163.

Museum of English Rural Life, Whiteknights, Reading,
Berkshire.
Telephone: (01734) 318660.

Ulster Folk Museum,
153 Bangor Road, Holywood, Belfast.
Telephone: (01232) 428428.

Weald and Downland Open Air Museum,
Singleton, near Chichester, West Sussex.
Telephone: (01243) 811348.

Museum of Welsh Life,
St Fagans, Cardiff CF5 6XB.
Telephone: (01222) 569441.

Wilderness Wood,
Hadlow Down, near Uckfield, East Sussex TN22 4HJ.
Telephone: (01825) 830509.

The Woodland Park,
Brokerswood, near Westbury, Wilts BA13 4EH.
Telephone: Woodland Park (01373) 822238;
Heritage Museum (01373) 823880.

Wycombe Local History and Chair Museum,
Castle Hill House, Priory Avenue, High Wycombe, Bucks
HP13 6PX.
Telephone: (01494) 421895.

5   Other relevant organisations

Arboricultural Association,
Ampfield House, Ampfield, Romsey, Hants SO51 9PA.
Telephone: (01794) 368717.

The Association of Pole Lathe Turners,
11 Bridge Street, Brigstock, Northants NN14 3ET.
Telephone: (01536) 373738.

The Coppice Association,
Penrhiw House, Llanddeusant, Llangadog SA19 9YW.
Telephone: (01550) 740641.

Forestry Commission,
231 Corstorphine Road, Edinburgh EH12 7AT.
Telephone: (031334) 0303.

The National Small Woods Association,
Hall Farm House, Preston Capes, Northants NN11 6TA.
Telephone: (01327) 361387.

Royal Forestry Society of England, Wales and Northern
Ireland,
102 High Street, Tring, Herts HP23 4AF.
Telephone: (01442) 822028.

The Woodland Trust,
Autumn Park, Grantham, Lincs NG31 6LL.
Telephone: (01476) 74297

6   Some other useful addresses

The Guild of Master Craftsmen,
166 High Street, Lewes, East Sussex BN7 1XU.
Telephone: (01273) 477374.

The Regional Furniture Society,
Trouthouse, Warrens Cross, Lechlade, Gloucestershire
GL7 3DR.
Telephone: (01367) 252880.

Index

TITLES AVAILABLE FROM
GMC Publications

BOOKS

WOODWORKING

40 More Woodworking Plans & Projects	*GMC Publications*	Making Chairs and Tables	*GMC Publications*
Bird Boxes and Feeders for the Garden	*Dave Mackenzie*	Making Fine Furniture	*Tom Darby*
Complete Woodfinishing	*Ian Hosker*	Making Little Boxes from Wood	*John Bennett*
Electric Woodwork	*Jeremy Broun*	Making Shaker Furniture	*Barry Jackson*
Furniture & Cabinetmaking Projects	*GMC Publications*	Pine Furniture Projects for the Home	*Dave Mackenzie*
Furniture Projects	*Rod Wales*	Sharpening Pocket Reference Book	*Jim Kingshott*
Furniture Restoration (Practical Crafts)	*Kevin Jan Bonner*	Sharpening: The Complete Guide	*Jim Kingshott*
Furniture Restoration and Repair for Beginners	*Kevin Jan Bonner*	Stickmaking: A Complete Course	*Andrew Jones & Clive George*
Green Woodwork	*Mike Abbott*	Woodfinishing Handbook (Practical Crafts)	*Ian Hosker*
The Incredible Router	*Jeremy Broun*	Woodworking Plans and Projects	*GMC Publications*
Making & Modifying Woodworking Tools	*Jim Kingshott*	The Workshop	*Jim Kingshott*

WOODTURNING

Adventures in Woodturning	*David Springett*	Practical Tips for Turners & Carvers	*GMC Publications*
Bert Marsh: Woodturner	*Bert Marsh*	Practical Tips for Woodturners	*GMC Publications*
Bill Jones' Notes from the Turning Shop	*Bill Jones*	Spindle Turning	*GMC Publications*
Bill Jones' Further Notes from the Turning Shop	*Bill Jones*	Turning Miniatures in Wood	*John Sainsbury*
Colouring Techniques for Woodturners	*Jan Sanders*	Turning Wooden Toys	*Terry Lawrence*
Decorative Techniques for Woodturners	*Hilary Bowen*	Understanding Woodturning	*Ann & Bob Phillips*
Essential Tips for Woodturners	*GMC Publications*	Useful Techniques for Woodturners	*GMC Publications*
Faceplate Turning	*GMC Publications*	Useful Woodturning Projects	*GMC Publications*
Fun at the Lathe	*R.C. Bell*	Woodturning: A Foundation Course	*Keith Rowley*
Illustrated Woodturning Techniques	*John Hunnex*	Woodturning: A Source Book of Shapes	*John Hunnex*
Intermediate Woodturning Projects	*GMC Publications*	Woodturning Jewellery	*Hilary Bowen*
Keith Rowley's Woodturning Projects	*Keith Rowley*	Woodturning Masterclass	*Tony Boase*
Make Money from Woodturning	*Ann & Bob Phillips*	Woodturning Techniques	*GMC Publications*
Multi-Centre Woodturning	*Ray Hopper*	Woodturning Test Reports	*GMC Publications*
Pleasure and Profit from Woodturning	*Reg Sherwin*	Woodturning Wizardry	*David Springett*

WOODCARVING

The Art of the Woodcarver	*GMC Publications*	Useful Techniques for Woodcarvers	*GMC Publications*
Carving Birds & Beasts	*GMC Publications*	Wildfowl Carving - Volume 1	*Jim Pearce*
Carving on Turning	*Chris Pye*	Wildfowl Carving - Volume 2	*Jim Pearce*
Carving Realistic Birds	*David Tippey*	The Woodcarvers	*GMC Publications*
Decorative Woodcarving	*Jeremy Williams*	Woodcarving: A Complete Course	*Ron Butterfield*
Essential Tips for Woodcarvers	*GMC Publications*	Woodcarving: A Foundation Course	*Zoë Gertner*
Essential Woodcarving Techniques	*Dick Onians*	Woodcarving for Beginners	*GMC Publications*
Lettercarving in Wood: A Practical Course	*Chris Pye*	Woodcarving Test Reports	*GMC Publications*
Practical Tips for Turners & Carvers	*GMC Publications*	Woodcarving Tools, Materials & Equipment	*Chris Pye*
Understanding Woodcarving	*GMC Publications*		

UPHOLSTERY

Seat Weaving (Practical Crafts)	*Ricky Holdstock*	Upholstery Restoration	*David James*
Upholsterer's Pocket Reference Book	*David James*	Upholstery Techniques & Projects	*David James*
Upholstery: A Complete Course	*David James*		